Helping kids answer questions about their faith

D1591511

Answers for Kids

BIBLE CURRICULUM

1:1

answersingenesis
Petersburg, Kentucky, USA

by Stacia McKeever & illustrated by Dan Lietha

Second printing: January 2011

For more information write: Answers in Genesis, PO Box 510, Hebron, KY 41048.

ISBN: 978-1-60092309-8

Cover design: Dan Lietha & Diane King
Text layout: Diane King
CD content: Daniel Lewis
Editors: Lori Jaworski, Becky Stelzer, Gary Vaterlaus

Scientific content editors: Bodie Hodge, Dr. Jason Lisle, Dr. David Menton, Dr. Terry Mortenson, Dr. Georgia Purdom, Michael Oard, Roger Patterson

Printed in China

Contents

About the Authors

Stacia McKeever graduated from Clearwater Christian College and worked full-time for Answers in Genesis–USA for more than ten years. She coauthored the "Answers for Kids" section in *Creation* magazine for several years and has written articles for *Answers* magazine, *Teach Kids!*, and the AiG website. She is currently the project manager for AiG's VBS programs and lives with her husband and children in the Greater Cincinnati Area.

Dan Lietha has been drawing since he was a child. He graduated in 1987 from the Joe Kubert School of Cartoon and Graphic Art and has been a full-time professional cartoonist since 1991. Since joining the Answers in Genesis staff in 1997, he has illustrated several books (including *A is for Adam, When Dragons' Hearts Were Good,* and *The Great Dinosaur Mystery Solved!*), created comic strips for the AiG newsletter and website, and produced countless illustrations which the AiG speakers use to effectively communicate the message that God's Word can be trusted from the beginning. Dan, his wife Marcia, and their daughter Hannah currently reside in the Greater Cincinnati Area.

Introduction

The *Answers For Kids Bible Curriculum* is a 30-lesson apologetics program for upper elementary students. It may be used as a Sunday school curriculum, a Christian school or homeschool course, or for family devotions. Our goal is to help children develop a truly biblical worldview, and provide answers to the questions that children have about the Bible, history, and science.

The Seven C s of History

Answers For Kids begins by teaching children about the Seven C's of History—seven foundational events from the beginning to the end of time. We help children develop a biblical worldview and see how these events have affected (or will affect) the world in which we live.

We recommend posting the *Seven C's of History Timeline* in your classroom so that you can refer to it while teaching. This will reinforce the Seven C's, and show students that the events and topics they are learning about connect with real history, and are not just "Bible stories."

Following these first eleven foundational lessons, students will begin to explore questions about the Bible, the earth, creation, evolution, dinosaurs, etc. We want to help young students see how the Bible relates to all of life, and how biblical history (as taught in the Seven C's) helps explain the world in which we live today.

Lesson Components

1. Teacher Preparation: The first page of each lesson lists the Scriptures that will be used, the memory verse for that week, any visuals or materials needed to teach the lesson, the main lesson truths, and suggestions for teacher preparation.

2. Lesson Overview: This section gives a brief overview of the lesson for the teacher, stating the main points of the lesson.

3. Lesson Time: This section is what you will teach. **Bolded** sentences are to be read to students. Non-bolded sentences are notes to the teacher. <u>**Illustrations**</u> are marked as such. It is best if you can familiarize yourself with the lesson content so you don't have to read it to the students verbatim. In various places throughout the lessons, we suggest having children read a verse or paragraph out loud. Please feel free to modify this idea according to the abilities of your students or your constraints as a teacher.

4. Activity Ideas: This section provides suggested ideas for activities for you to incorporate into the lessons, as you have time.

5. Extension Activities: For those interested in using *Answers for Kids* as a springboard to discussing other topics, or as part of a homeschool unit study, we have provided additional study ideas.

6. Recommended Resources: This section provides a list of materials that supplement the topic being discussed.

Additional Resources

1. The online Teacher's Resource Page has Internet links to all the online articles that are mentioned throughout the lessons so that you can find more information on the topics discussed. These articles are organized by lesson and can be found at www.AnswersInGenesis.org/go/AnswersForKids.

2 The *Song CD* contains all of the songs that are used in the lessons.

3. The *Teacher Resource DVD-ROM* contains the illustrations and handouts that will be used throughout this curriculum. It includes lesson illustrations in Microsoft PowerPoint™ format, and as printable JPEG images or PDF files. There is also a folder with JPEG images of the memory verses that you can print out and use in your classroom.

4. Student Handouts: You will need one set of student handouts per child in your class (there is one student handout per lesson, and several information charts—these are not included on the DVD-ROM). We have included one complete set in the back of this book—additional sets for you classroom may be purchased from www.AnswersBookstore.com.

Verse Review Ideas

Each lesson contains a suggested memory verse for each week. We have listed just a few of the many ways to help the students learn the Scripture passages.

- Write the verse on a chalk or white board. Have students repeat it together. Erase a word and repeat it again. Continue to do this until you've erased the entire verse.

- Make a song out of the verse—make up your own tune, or use the tune of a familiar song.

- Write each word of the verse on an index card and have children put the cards in order (if you have a large class, you may want to make several sets of the verse).

- Ask for volunteers to say the verse without looking at it—have the other students follow along and help the volunteer when he needs it.

Scripture Reading Ideas

This curriculum is based heavily around reading passages from the Bible. There are several ways you might do this (depending on your constraints as a teacher, the class time you have, etc.):

- Choose one student to read the entire verse assignment.

- Choose one student to begin reading, and have each student read a verse or two in turn.

- Assign parts to students, e.g., narrator, Adam, Eve.

- Read the passage while students follow along.

- Have students read the passage silently.

Evaluation Form

At Answers in Genesis we are committed to producing high-quality resources that help believers proclaim and defend their faith. But we rely on your input for continued success. Please take a few minutes to give us your feedback on the *Answers for Kids Bible Curriculum*. There is an evaluation form on the DVD-ROM. Please print this out, fill it out as completely as possible, and send it back to us. As a thank you for returning this evaluation, you will receive 10% off of a future purchase at our online bookstore (see bottom of evaluation form for details).

We trust this curriculum will be a blessing and encouragement to you and those in your class. If you have any questions or comments, please email us at education@ answersingenesis.org.

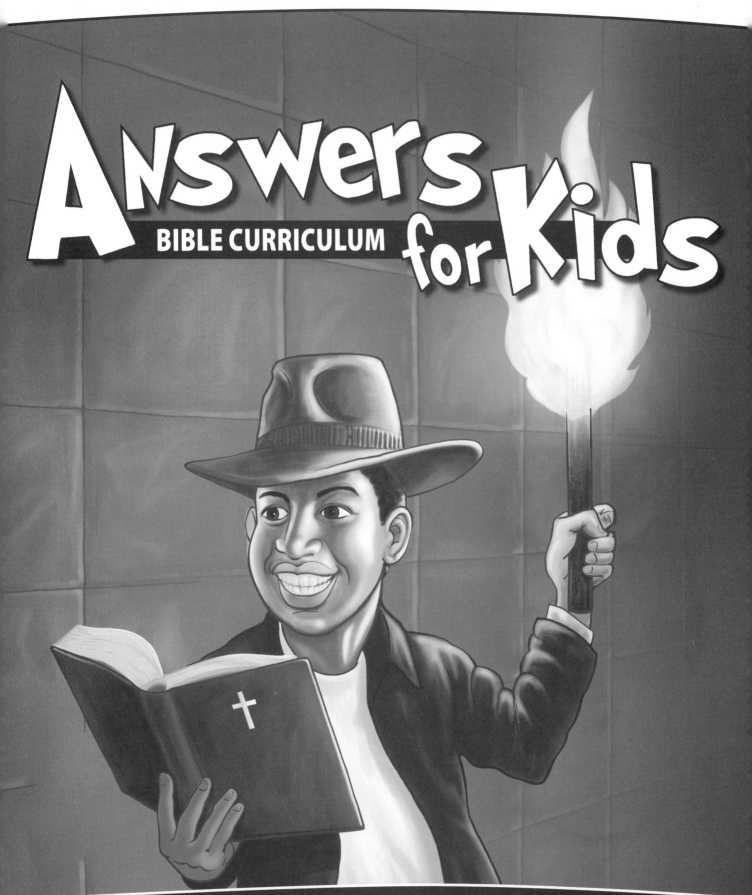

Helping kids answer questions about their faith

Answers for Kids

BIBLE CURRICULUM

Teacher Manual

by Stacia McKeever & illustrated by Dan Lietha

Creation part 1

In Six Days . . . c. 4004 BC

Scripture

Genesis 1:1–2:3

Memory Verse

Genesis 1:1

Visuals & Materials

Flashlight, small ball; from CDs: Illustrations 1-00–1-10, L1a, L1b, Memory Verse graphic, *The Seven C's of History* (song)

Lesson Truths

- God is the Creator of everything
- God is good; everything He made was "very good"
- God created in six normal-length days, about 6,000 years ago

Preparation

1. Read "Could God Really Have Created Everything in Six Days?" at the online Teacher's Resource Page (www.AnswersInGenesis.org/go/AnswersForKids)
2. Study the Scripture passage for this week
3. Review the lesson before class so that you are familiar with the content
4. Pray that God will open the eyes and hearts of your students to glorify Him as Creator and understand the importance of taking His Word as written

Lesson 1

Lesson Overview

Some people believe the universe is billions of years old. It is often pictured as coming from the result of a giant explosion—the big bang. These people believe that all living things (and we ourselves!) came from a series of accidents (mutations) happening gradually over millions of years. Others believe that God used evolution to "create" over millions of years. Still others believe that God created progressively over millions of years.

But these views do not agree with the biblical record. These are the views that we need to "tear down" in the minds of our children. In their place, we need to "build up" the truth that the Bible, God's Word to us, records the true history of the universe. It gives a completely different account of how everything came to be and what has happened since then. The Bible reveals that God didn't use evolution to create and that the earth isn't millions of years old. In this lesson, children will learn that God created all things in six actual days and that the original creation was "very good."

Lesson Time

Welcome

Welcome students to class, open in prayer, etc.

How We Know about Events that Happened in the Past

How many of you know your birth date? Wait for answers. **Of course you do—but how do you know which day it is? Can you remember back that far?** Wait for answers—parents told me, etc. **Of course, you can't remember the event, but at least one of your parents was there, and probably a doctor and nurses, and one of them recorded the date for you. They were eyewitnesses to the event of your birth—they saw it happen, didn't they? So they know when you were born, and hopefully you can trust them to tell you the truth about that day.**

What about other events that have happened in the past? For example, the Civil War. How do you know the Civil War actually happened? Wait for answers: learned about it at school, watched a TV program/movie, read about it in history books, etc. **Where did the information in those television shows or history books come from?** Wait for answers. **It mainly came from eyewitnesses to the events—either they wrote down what they experienced, or told other people what happened, and those people repeated it to others who repeated it, and so on. Sometimes, however, the original accounts have been changed over time, or the person who witnessed the event wanted to tell the story in a particular way to make himself look better, or the witness saw only part of the event.**

What about events that have happened even farther back in history—events that happened thousands of years ago? What we need is an eyewitness who always tells the truth, who can never lie, and who has been around at least since the beginning. Can you think of anyone like that? God. **Right—God has been orchestrating events since before the beginning. What do we call the collection of 66 books in which He has recorded what He wants us to know?** The Bible. **Right—the Bible. Since God never lies, we can trust the Bible to tell us the truth concerning the events God tells us about.**

<u>Illustration 1-01</u>. In fact, we could call the Bible "The History Book of the Universe."

The Seven C's of History and the First C: Creation

Over the next few months, we're going to be learning about seven major events that the Bible tells us about that have affected—and one that _will_ affect—the history of the world

<u>Illustration 1-02</u>. **These events are Creation, Corruption, Catastrophe, Confusion, Christ, Cross, and Consummation.** Have students review the words with you a few times. **You may not understand what each word means right now, but we'll learn about them as we go along. Today we're going to begin with the first C, Creation.**

Pass out the student handouts for this week, and have students turn to the back side of the page, _The First Six Days Are History!_ Read through this page with the students as an introduction to this topic.

Like we read in the cartoon, some people say we're not to believe that the first couple chapters of Genesis record actual history. However, God knows what He did, and we can trust Him to tell us the truth. Today and next week, we're going to learn a bit more about what the Bible says happened on the first six days of history.

Day One of Creation

Have students open their Bibles to Genesis 1. Read Genesis 1:1–5 together.

<u>Illustration 1-03</u>. **What did God create on the first day?** Light, earth, day-and-night cycle. **God created light, and a day-and-night cycle, but does this set of verses mention anything about the sun?** Wait for answer: no. **Right—God created only light on this day— not the sun. He created the sun three days later. Today, the sun gives us light during the day, and the moon gives light during the night. So, in the beginning, how could there be day and night without the sun? Let's find out.**

Actually, we have figured out that all it takes to have a day and night is a rotating earth that is spinning and light coming from one direction. The Bible tells us clearly that God created light on the first day, as well as the earth. Use a flashlight and small ball to

illustrate. Turn the flashlight on, direct it at the ball, and then begin rotating the ball—where the light hits the ball is "day" and where it doesn't is "night." **We can figure out that the earth was already rotating in space on the first day and that light was shining on it—so in the beginning, there was still day and night, even though there wasn't any sun yet.**

There are some people who believe that the sun is the source of all life. However, does the Bible teach this? Wait for answers. **No; in fact, God seems to be making a very big point that *He* is the Creator of everything—including the sun, which He didn't create until later. God doesn't "need" the sun in order to create life. In fact, He warns against worshipping it.** Have the students turn to Deuteronomy 4:15–19 and choose a student to read it.

Day Two of Creation

Okay, let's find out what God created on the second day. Have students turn back to Genesis 1:6–8, and choose a student to read the passage.

<u>Illustration 1-04</u>. **The first thing He did on this day was to create an expanse that separated the waters above the earth from the waters that were on the earth. This is when He formed the atmosphere that would be needed to support the life that He would soon create. Can anyone tell me what the atmosphere is?** Wait for answers. **It's the stuff that we breathe in. Everyone take a deep breath. Okay, now let it out. That "stuff" that we just breathed in is called the atmosphere. God knew we would need to breathe, so He created stuff for us to breathe on the second day.** [See Note 1 on page 20.]

Day Three of Creation

Let's move on to the third day. Read Genesis 1:9–13 together.

<u>Illustration 1-05</u>. **What happened during the third day?** Wait for answers. **Right; dry land appeared with all the dirt that plants need to grow in, and God then created the various kinds of plants. Why?** Wait for answers. **God knew that the animals and humans He would create later in the week would need something to eat, so He created plants for them to eat and enjoy. God was taking care of His creation, wasn't He? He made the atmosphere so we could breathe, and plants so we could eat!** [See Note 2 on page 20.]

Day Four of Creation

Read Genesis 1:14–19 together.

<u>Illustration 1-06</u>. **Why did God create the sun, moon, and stars on the fourth day?** Wait for answers. **Again, He did it for us—the sun gives us light and warmth during the day, and the moon gives us light during the night. The stars mark off signs and seasons, although the seasons we have today are probably more extreme than they were in the**

beginning. **In fact, God not only created the stars, but He also gave them names! Let's turn to Isaiah 40:26.** Choose a student to read this verse. **The Bible also talks about God's power over the stars in Job 38.** Have students turn to Job 38:31–32. **And it tells us that the heavens declare His glory.** Read Psalm 19:1–4.

Illustration 1-07. **He also created the rest of the planets and other stellar bodies on this day.** [See Note 3 on page 20.]

Day Five of Creation

Illustration 1-08. **Okay, let's move on to the fifth day.** Read Genesis 1:20–23 together. **What kinds of creatures live in the seas?** Wait for answers: whales, octopi, starfish, sea cucumbers, fish, coral, etc.

Illustration 1-09. Use this illustration to encourage students to also list plesiosaurs. **What type of creature is this?** Many will know it's a plesiosaur—be sure they understand that this type of creature was created on the same day as all the other sea creatures (*not* millions of years ago) and lived along with fish, whales, etc. in the beginning.

What types of creatures fly in the air? Birds, bats, etc.

Illustration 1-10. Use this illustration to encourage students to realize that this type of creature was also created on this day, along with all other flying things. **What type of creature is this?** Pteranodon.

There are some people who believe that land animals eventually turned into birds and whales, but is that what the Bible teaches? Encourage students to see that land animals were created *after* flying and sea creatures.

What should we do when we hear this type of thing—maybe from our teachers, or textbooks, or TV, or a movie? Encourage the students to see that we can know that such stories aren't true, because the only eyewitness has told us that birds and whales were created a day before the land animals were created.

Review and Prayer

Review the memory verse for this week: Genesis 1:1. Pray with your students, praising God as Creator and thanking Him for His amazing creation.

Next week we are going to look at the sixth day of creation, what kinds of animals were created, and how man was specially created.

Discussion Questions

1. In this first series of lessons, we're discussing the Seven C's of History—seven major events that have affected (or will affect) the world. How did the first C, Creation, affect the world?

    Answer: Creation was the beginning of everything!

2. What is our month based on?

    Answer: The movement of the moon around the earth.

3. What is our year based on?

    Answer: The movement of the earth around the sun.

4. The way the earth is tilted in space determines our seasons, but what determines that a week is seven days long?

    Answer: The account in Genesis (have them recite Exodus 20:11).

5. When did plesiosaurs and pteranadons first appear on earth?

    Answer: On Day Five of creation, about 6,000 years ago—not millions of years before humans. (We are going to learn a lot more about dinosaurs in one of our later lessons.)

Activity Ideas

1. Start a "Days of Creation" booklet. Have the students draw pictures of the major events of each day. Use handout L1a. Or use L1b and have students color in the days.

2. Start a timeline on a large sheet of paper (e.g., the kind used to cover tables). Mark off six millennia, perhaps to the scale of 1,000 years=1 foot or 1,000 years=2 feet (whatever you decide based on the space available). During this lesson, label "Creation, 4004 BC" and "Today, AD 2000." (See lesson 16 for help in determining the age of the earth.) Have students choose a creation day to illustrate, or makes copies of L1b, cut each day apart, and pass out the different days to students (depending on your class size, there will be duplication of days). Have them color a day. Tape or glue the various days to the timeline under "Creation." We'll be adding to the timeline each week during the Seven C's lessons.

Extension Activities

These are ideas you can use to supplement your discussion of the various days of creation.

Physics (Day 1)

Spend some time studying the nature of light. See "What is Light?" on the online Teacher's Resource Page for a simple explanation on the nature of light. Volume 2 (experiment 5) of *Science and the Bible* provides a neat experiment on light.

Use a concordance to find out what else the Bible has to say about light.

Find out more about gravity—the attractive force between all objects. Who is the One who truly holds all things together? See "Gravity: The Mystery Force" at the online Teacher's Resource Page. Volume 1 (experiment 22) of *Science and the Bible* offers a simple experiment that illustrates the effects of gravity.

Angels (Day 1)

When did God create the angels? When did Satan fall? See "Demons on a Leash" at the online Teacher's Resource Page for some insights.

Chemistry (Day 2)

Spend some time studying the properties of water. See chapter 10 of *Exploring the World of Chemistry* for help. Volumes 1 (experiment 30), 2 (experiment 26), and 3 (experiment 30) of *Science and the Bible* offer great simple experiments that will help in discussing this topic.

Botany (Day 3)

Learn about some of the amazing design features found in the plant world from the "Get Answers: Botany" section of the Answers in Genesis Website (use the link on the online Teacher's Resource Page at www.AnswersInGenesis.org/go/AnswersForKids). What is photosynthesis? (See chapter 7 of *Exploring the World Around You*.) Take a walk outside and collect different plant specimens, then press and dry them. Once dry, glue them onto different sheets of paper and write a brief description beneath or beside each plant. Start a garden (outside if you have the space, or inside in pots).

Astronomy (Day 4)

How do the heavens "declare the glory of God" (Psalm 19:1)? Visit the "Get Answers: Astronomy" section of the AiG website for some ideas. Put together a booklet with brief summaries and pictures of your findings. What is wrong with the big bang idea? See "What Are Some of the Problems With the Big Bang Hypothesis?" at the online Teacher's Resource Page.

Recommended Resources

The Answers Book for Kids, volume 1 (book for children)

Exploring Planet Earth (textbook for children)

Exploring the World Around You (textbook for children)

Exploring the World of Chemistry (textbook for children)

Science and the Bible, volumes 1–3

Six Short Days! (DVD for children)

Available from www.AnswersBookstore.com or by calling 1-800-778-3390.

Notes

1. If you are familiar with the "vapor canopy" model, please note that many creation scientists have abandoned the vapor canopy model or no longer see any need for such a concept. For more information, read "Noah's Flood: Where Did the Water Come From?" at the online Teacher's Resource Page.

2. The creation of plants on Day 3—before the sun and animals—is contrary to the beliefs of evolutionists and other "long-agers" who teach that plants arose long after the sun came into existence.

   Are plants "alive"? The Bible makes a clear distinction between the status of plants and animals. Plants are not alive in the biblical sense. People and animals are described in Genesis as having, or being, *nephesh* (Hebrew)—see Genesis 1:20–21, 24, where *nephesh chayyah* is translated "living creatures," and Genesis 2:7, where Adam became a "living soul" (*nephesh chayyah*). *Nephesh* conveys the basic idea of a "breathing creature." It is also used widely in the Old Testament, in combination with other words, to convey emotions, feelings, etc. Perhaps *nephesh* refers to life with a certain level of consciousness. Plants do not have such *nephesh*, so Adam eating a carrot did not involve "death" in the biblical sense.

3. Some people ask, "If the universe is only a few thousand years old, then how can we see light from stars that are over one billion light-years away?" There are several possible answers to this question, and creation scientists are actively researching this topic. See "Does Distant Starlight Prove the Universe Is Old?" at the online Teacher's Resource Page for more information.

Lesson 2

Creation part 2

IN SIX DAYS . . . c. 4004 BC

Scripture

Genesis 1:1–2:3

Memory verse

Revelation 4:11

Visuals & Materials

From CDs: Illustrations 2-00–2-13, L2a, Memory Verse graphic, *The Seven C's of History* (song)

Lesson Truths

- God is the Creator of everything
- God is good; everything He made was "very good"
- God created in six normal-length days, about 6,000 years ago

Preparation

1. Read "A Young Earth—It's Not the Issue!" at the online Teacher's Resource Page (www. AnswersInGenesis.org/go/AnswersFor Kids)
2. Study the Scripture passage for this week
3. Review the lesson before class so that you are familiar with the content
4. Pray that God will open the eyes and hearts of your students to glorify Him as Creator and understand the importance of taking His Word as written

Lesson 2

Lesson Overview

Some people believe the universe is billions of years old. It is often pictured as coming from the result of a giant explosion—the big bang. These people believe that all living things (and we ourselves!) came from a series of accidents (mutations) happening gradually over millions of years. Others believe that God used evolution to "create" over millions of years. Still others believe that God created progressively over millions of years.

But these views do not agree with the biblical record. These are the views that we need to "tear down" in the minds of our children. In their place, we need to "build up" the truth that the Bible, God's Word to us, records the true history of the universe. It gives a completely different account of how everything came to be and what has happened since then. The Bible reveals that God didn't use evolution to create and that the earth isn't millions of years old. In this lesson, children will learn that God created all things in six actual days and that the original creation was "very good."

Lesson Time

Welcome and Review

Welcome students to class, open in prayer, etc. Review the memory verse from last week.

Last week we started learning about the first of the Seven C's of History. Who can tell me each of the Seven C's? Wait for them to answer—**That's right! Let's say them together: Creation, Corruption, Catastrophe, Confusion, Christ, Cross, Consummation.**

Illustration 2-00. **This week we're continuing to look at the first C—Creation. Did you know that creation isn't only in Genesis, but it is mentioned throughout the Bible? Turn to the last book of the Bible—Revelation.** Have a student read Revelation 4:11. **This is our memory verse for this week. Let's all read it together.**

Last week we went over the first five days of creation. Do you remember what was created on each day? Day One: light, earth, day-and-night cycle; Day Two: the atmosphere; Day Three: dry land; Day Four: sun, moon, stars; Day Five: sea creatures, flying creatures.

Day Six of Creation: Land Animals

Today we are going to focus on the sixth day of creation. Turn in your Bibles to Genesis 1. Choose a student to read Genesis 1:24–26.

Illustration 2-01. **What types of animals did God create on the sixth day?** Cows, dogs, cats, deer, crocodiles, kangaroos, elephants, koalas, etc. **These are all land animals.**

<u>Illustration 2-02</u>. **God also created the various dinosaur kinds on this day, like this one—who knows the name of this one?** Wait for them to answer—triceratops.

<u>Illustration 2-03.</u> **Who knows the name of this one?** (tyrannosaur or *T. rex*).

Day Six of Creation: Man and Woman

God also created the very first person on the sixth day, which means that humans and dinosaurs lived together in the very beginning! What was the name of the first person? Adam.

Genesis 2 gives us some more details about the first man and the events of the sixth day. Choose a student to read Genesis 2:7–9. **Some people believe that humans came from ape-like creatures many years ago, but how many of you have a grandfather who looks like this?**

<u>Illustration 2-04</u>. **What does the Bible say about how Adam was formed?** From the dust—not from an ape-like creature.

Read Genesis 2:15–20 together.

Other people believe that the first people didn't have many abilities, but what do verses 16–20 indicate about Adam? Encourage students to see that he was able to speak right away, understand when God spoke to him, and give names to the animals.

<u>Illustration 2-05</u>. **And what types of animals did Adam name?** He named cattle ("domestic" animals), birds, and beasts of the field. Note that he didn't need to name creeping things or sea creatures. [See "How Could Adam have Named All the Animals in a Single Day?" at the online Teacher's Resource Page (www.AnswersInGenesis.org/go/AnswersForKids) for more information.]

After Adam finished naming the animals, he probably realized there was no other creature like him on earth.

<u>Illustration 2-06</u>. Read Genesis 2:21–25 together.

God formed Adam from the dust of the ground, but how did He create Eve? From Adam's rib. **Did you know that your ribs** (show students where your ribs are located) **are able to grow back when they're removed? So Adam didn't have to live his life with a missing rib!** [For more information, read "The Amazing Regenerating Rib" at the online Teacher's Resource Page.]

Genesis tells us about the beginning of everything—the earth, the universe, the plants, animals, and people. It also teaches us about the beginning of marriage and that marriage is to be between one man and one woman.

<u>Illustration 2-07</u>. **Adam and Eve were the first married couple! And because all humans are descended from Adam (including Eve, who was made from his rib), we are all related!**

Read Genesis 1:27–28 together.

<u>Illustration 2-08</u>. **What do you think it means to be made in the image of God? What makes us different from the rest of God's creation?** Possible responses might include our greater intelligence, creativity, communication ability, ability to have a relationship with God, etc.

<u>Illustration 2-09.</u> Use this illustration as a starting point to encourage students to think of other ways we're different from animals.

Original Diet of Man and Animals

Read Genesis 1:29–30 together.

<u>Illustration 2-10</u>. **What does the Bible says that God gave animals and humans to eat?** Plants, fruit, vegetables.

<u>Illustration 2-11</u>. **So, what do you think *T. rex* was eating in the beginning?** Some may still say meat.

<u>Illustration 2-12</u>. **The Bible says that every animal (and man) was eating only fruits and vegetables—that includes all of the dinosaurs, too! There was no death or disease in God's original creation.**

God's Very Good Creation

Read Genesis 1:31. **How does God describe His completed creation?** It was "very good."

<u>Illustration 2-13</u>. **Throughout Genesis 1, God says different things are good after He creates them. Can you tell me what they are?** Genesis 1:4: light; Genesis 1:10: seas and dry land; Genesis 1:12: plants; Genesis 1:18: sun, moon, stars, etc.; Genesis 1:21: sea and flying creatures; Genesis 1:25: land animals. **In Genesis 1:31, He says everything is very good—His creation was finally complete. He created everything for a reason, and everything was performing its duty perfectly.**

Adam and Eve had complete fellowship with God and lived in harmony with the rest of the creation. It's hard for us to imagine what such a perfect place would be like, isn't it? We certainly don't live in a perfect place, do we? In the next lesson, we'll learn more about what happened to that perfect place.

Day Seven of Creation

Read Genesis 2:2–4 together. **At the end of the seventh day, God finished creating and rested from His work. Why do you think He rested?** Some may say because He was tired, but remind them that God never gets tired and never sleeps. **Let's look at what Psalm 121**

says about God. Read verses 1–4. **He rested from His work because He was finished—He's still very active in His creation, though. God knew that we would need to rest, so He created in six days and rested for one to set a pattern for us to follow. We are to work for six days and rest for one, as He did.**

Review and Prayer

From the Bible, we learn that God created everything in six days, around 6,000 years ago. Isn't God amazing?

Review the memory verse for this week: Revelation 4:11. Pray with your students, thanking God that He gave us His Word, and that we can believe what He has written.

Discussion Questions

1. When did dinosaurs first appear on earth?

    Answer: On Day Six of Creation Week, about 6,000 years ago—not millions of years before humans. (We are going to learn a lot more about dinosaurs in one of our later lessons.)

2. In what ways are we similar to animals? How do our similarities show that we were made by the same Creator? In what ways are we different?

    Answer: Responses may vary but could include: We have similar bodies—arms, legs, hair, noses, eyes, ears, etc. We breathe the same air, eat the same types of food, drink water. These show that we were designed by the same Creator to live in the same world. Differences may include the ability to use tools to make other tools; the ability to draw what we see—beautiful sunsets, people, animals; the ability to use complete sentences to communicate.

Activity Ideas

1. Read "What is the difference?" on the first page of the student handout, and go over the "games" on the back page of the handout.

2. Finish the "Days of Creation" booklet started last week.

3. Print out L2a and make copies for students to color.

4. Continue work on the timeline started last week.

Lesson 2

Extension Activities

These are ideas you can use to supplement your discussion of the various days of creation.

Zoology (Days 5 and 6)

Explore the "design features" of various sea, flying, and land animals. Keep in mind that the animals we see today are descendants of the original "kinds" (see "Zonkeys, Ligers, and Wolphins, Oh My!" at the online Teacher's Resource Page) and are living under a curse (see "How Did Defense/Attack Structures Come About?" at the online Teacher's Resource Page). While we expect to see marvelously designed features throughout the world, we also realize that these things are merely remnants of a once-perfect creation (due to the corruption that entered the world—see next lesson and lesson 26, "Why Are Snakes So Scary?"). See the "Get Answers: Zoology" section of the AiG website for ideas (use the link from the online Teacher's Resource Page at www.AnswersInGenesis.org/go/AnswersForKids). Have students choose some of their favorites and write a short paper on the animals they've chosen. Have them draw a picture of each animal to go with their paper.

Creation compromises

The gap theory, progressive creation, theistic evolution, the day-age theory, and the framework hypothesis are all ideas that deny the plain teaching of Scripture in Genesis. The general topic of compromise is addressed in later lessons, but if you would like to learn more about each position, visit the "Get Answers: Creation Compromises" section of the AiG website (use the link from the online Teacher's Resource Page).

Recommended Resources

The Answers Book for Kids, volume 1 (book for children)

Exploring Planet Earth (textbook for children)

Exploring the World Around You (textbook for children)

Exploring the World of Chemistry (textbook for children)

Science and the Bible, volumes 1–3

Six Short Days! (DVD for children)

Skeletons in Your Closet (book for children)

Available from www.AnswersBookstore.com or by calling 1-800-778-3390.

Lesson 3

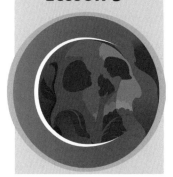

Corruption part 1

Scripture

Genesis 2:15–17
Genesis 3–4

Memory verses

Genesis 2:17

Visuals & Materials

From CDs: Illustrations 3-00–3-09, L3a, Memory Verse graphic, *The Seven C's of History* (song)

Lesson Truths

- Adam and Eve disobeyed God and brought corruption into the world
- The results of the Curse include death and suffering
- God provided a "covering" for our sin in the Lord Jesus Christ

Preparation

1. Read "Lessons From the Fall" at the online Teacher's Resource Page (www.AnswersInGenesis.org/go/AnswersForKids)
2. Study the Scripture passages for this week
3. Review the lesson before class so that you are familiar with the content
4. Pray that God will use this lesson to show your students their need for a Savior

Lesson 3

Lesson Overview

We learned in the last lesson that God created all things in six days and declared all things "very good." But we don't see a "very good" world today—rather, we live in a world filled with suffering and pain. Today's lesson reveals what happened to change the original paradise into the world we experience today. Children will learn that Adam's disobedience to God's command (and our sin) brought corruption to God's once-perfect world. They will discover the changes that sin introduced and will see the reason we need a Savior from sin.

Lesson Time

Welcome and Review

Welcome students to class, open in prayer, etc. Review the memory verse from last week.

In this series of lessons, we're learning about the seven major events that the Bible tells us have affected, or will affect, the world.

<u>Illustration 3-00</u>. **Who remembers which one we talked about the last two weeks?** Creation

Who remembers all seven events? Creation, Corruption, Catastrophe, Confusion, Christ, Cross, Consummation.

<u>Illustration 3-01</u>. **When God finished creating, what did He say about His creation?**

<u>Illustration 3-02</u>. **It was very good, Genesis 1:31. For a few seconds, think about what a very good place might look like.**

<u>Illustration 3-03</u>. **Does this look like what you thought a very good world would look like?** Wait for answers.

The First Law

Today we're going to learn about the event that caused things to be this way—the next C—Corruption. Does anyone know what *corruption* **means?** Wait for answers. **Well, it means that something has changed from good to bad. Something that is corrupted is spoiled or ruined—it's no longer very good.** Read Genesis 2:15–17.

<u>Illustration 3-04</u>. **Who is God speaking to in these verses?** Adam. **Was Eve around when God said this?** No, she wasn't created until later in the day. **God put before Adam a choice. What was it?** To obey God's command not to eat from the tree, or to disobey.

We mentioned in the last lesson that Genesis is a book about "beginnings"—in fact, that's what the word *Genesis* means! In these verses, we learn about the first "law." Who made that law? God. **As the Creator, He has the right to make laws.**

After God created Adam and Eve, He finished His creation and rested on the seventh day. We don't know how long it was between that time and the event we're going to read about, but it probably wasn't very long at all—maybe just a few days. [See Note 1 on page 31.]

Twisting God's Word

Let's turn to Genesis 3. Read Genesis 3:1–3 together.

Illustration 3-05. **Let's stop here and compare what Eve said to the serpent with what God actually said in Genesis 2:17.** Wait for them to read both verses again. **What is different about the two?** Eve said that God said they couldn't eat it and they couldn't touch it, but God only said they couldn't eat from it. God said they could freely eat from any tree but one, yet Eve omitted the word "freely." **What did Eve do to the words God had told Adam?** She changed them. **And how did the serpent change God's commands?** The serpent denied that they would die, and he asked Eve if they couldn't eat from every tree.

Illustration 3-06. **Let's read what the Bible says in another place about how we are to treat God's Word.** Have students turn to and read the following verses: Deuteronomy 4:2, 12:32; Proverbs 30:6. **We need to be very careful about how we read and study the Bible—we must not twist the words to make them say what we want them to say.**

The Disobedience of Adam

Read Genesis 3:4–7. **We talked before about the choice God gave Adam. What did Adam choose to do?** Adam chose not to obey. Disobeying God's commands is called *sin*.

Illustration 3-07. **What do you think you would have done if you were Adam? Would you have obeyed God?** Wait for discussion. **Actually, we've all disobeyed at least once in our lives, haven't we? Let's read Romans 5:12.** Have students turn to Romans 5:12. **This verse tells us that Adam is responsible, but it also tells us that each of us, a descendant of Adam, is also responsible—we've all sinned, haven't we?** Have students read Romans 3:10–12, 23.

What did Adam and Eve do after they disobeyed? Genesis 3:7–8—they made clothes of fig leaves and hid themselves.

<u>Illustration 3-08</u>. **But was their attempt at covering their sin good enough to please a holy God?** Read Genesis 3:21. **God had to kill at least one animal, shedding its blood, to provide clothing for them.**

<u>Illustration 3-09</u>. **In fact, this is why we wear clothing today—because of sin. This was also the first time anything had died in God's beautiful creation. That's very sad, isn't it? This was the saddest day in the history of the universe.**

Sometimes, when we sin, we might try to cover up what we've done. Have you ever done that? Wait for answers. **But our attempts at covering sin aren't good enough for God—any sin is an offense to our holy and righteous God. The good news, which we'll talk more about next week, is that God did provide a covering that completely takes away the sin of His children. Jesus!**

Read *Good Enough Isn't Good Enough!* (page 2 of the student handout). Emphasize the point that we are all sinners in need of a Savior and that nobody can be "good enough" to get into heaven on their own merit.

Review and Prayer

Review the memory verse for this week: Genesis 2:17. Pray with your students, thanking God for His Word, and asking Him to help us obey Him.

Discussion Questions

1. What does "corruption" mean?

   Answer: Changed from good to bad.

2. How did Adam and Eve try to cover up what they had done? How did God cover their sin?

   Answer: Adam and Eve made clothes of leaves and hid. God provided a covering of animal skins, shedding the blood of the animal in the process.

Activity Ideas

1. Read the book *When Dragons' Hearts Were Good* to introduce the idea that "dragons" could actually have been dinosaurs.

2. If you started a time line with "Creation," now add "Corruption" right next to Creation. Print L3a and makes copies for students (one fruit per child). Have students color fruit and then write their name across the middle. Glue or tape each fruit to the time line to remind students that all of us are sinners and disobey God, just as Adam did.

Extension Activities

Biology

Study the food chain and population controls as they operate in today's fallen world. See *Exploring the World Around You*, chapters 8–11.

Recommended Resources

The Answers Book for Kids, volume 1 (book for children)

Science and the Bible, volume 3

The Day the World Went Wacky (book for children)

When Dragons' Hearts Were Good (book for children)

Why Is Keiko Sick? (book for children)

Available from www.AnswersBookstore.com or by calling 1-800-778-3390.

Notes

1. Adam and Eve were told to "be fruitful and multiply," so they would not have waited to carry out this command, yet all of Eve's children were born sinners (Romans 5:12, 18–19), so she had not conceived in her sinless state.

Notes

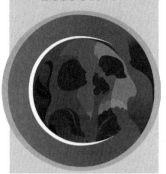

Corruption part 2

TO OBEY OR NOT TO OBEY

Scripture

Genesis 2:15–17
Genesis 3–4

Memory verse

Romans 8:22

Visuals & Materials

A variety of knives, carrots (or a variety of fruits and vegetables); from CDs: Illustrations 4-00–4-09, L4a, Memory Verse graphic, *The Seven C's of History* (song)

Lesson Truths

- Adam and Eve disobeyed God and brought corruption into the world
- The results of the Curse include death and suffering
- God provided a "covering" for our sin in the Lord Jesus Christ

Preparation

1. Read "The First Sin" at the online Teacher's Resource Page (www.AnswersInGenesis.org/go/AnswersForKids)
2. Study the Scripture passages for this week
3. Review the lesson before class so that you are familiar with the content
4. Pray that God will use this lesson to show your students their need for a Savior

Lesson 4

Lesson Overview

We learned in the last lesson that God created all things in six days and declared all things "very good." But we don't see a "very good" world today—rather, we live in a world filled with suffering and pain. Today's lesson reveals what happened to change the original paradise into the world we experience today. Children will learn that Adam's disobedience to God's command (and our sin) brought corruption to God's once-perfect world. They will discover the changes that sin introduced and will see the reason we need a Savior from sin.

Lesson Time

Welcome and Review

Welcome students to class, open in prayer, etc. Review the memory verse from last week.

Last week we began looking at the second C of the Seven C's of History. Which one was it? Corruption.

<u>Illustration 4-00</u>. **What command did God give Adam?** To not eat from the Tree of the Knowledge of Good and Evil. **Did Adam and Eve obey God?** No. **What was the first thing Adam & Eve did after they disobeyed God?** They made clothes of fig leaves and hid themselves from God. **What did God do for them?** He killed at least one animal, shedding its blood, to provide clothing for them.

Results of the Fall: The Curse

Let's continue our lesson today by reading about what else happened as a result of Adam's disobedience. Remember, Genesis is the book of beginnings. As we read through these next verses, let's look for things that began here.

Read through Genesis 3:8–24 together. **What "beginnings" does this passage teach us about?** Snakes would now crawl on their bellies, women would endure pain in childbirth/child-rearing, man would now work hard for food, plants would grow thorns and thistles (this is why we get pricked with thorns if we're not careful when we pick or smell a rose), and the first clothing was worn.

<u>Illustration 4-01</u>. **What does verse 19 say is part of the punishment for Adam's disobedience?** Death: from dust you were taken and to dust you will return.

There are lots of things that changed when Adam disobeyed, aren't there? In fact, let's look at what Romans 8 says about it. This is our memory verse for this week. Have a student read Romans 8:22.

Illustration 4-02. Adam's one act of rebellion toward God's Word was so serious that it caused the whole creation to change from "very good" to bad.

Results of the Fall: Changes in Animals

Remember earlier when we talked about what was on the *T. rex* menu in the very beginning?

Illustration 4-03. **Right—fruits and vegetables. But Adam's sin also changed the animals. So now *T. rex* had other things on his mind.**

Illustration 4-04. **This is why we often see animals eating each other on nature programs or in other places, instead of munching on fruit as they did in the beginning.**

Illustration 4-05. **Only after the Fall of man did *T. rex* start using his teeth to eat other creatures. Did you know that actually there are quite a few animals that have sharp teeth today that eat fruits and vegetables?**

Illustration 4-06. **What do you think this guy eats?** Wait for answers. **He likes to munch on fruits. Just because animals have sharp teeth doesn't mean they eat meat—it just means they have sharp teeth.** If you'd like to demonstrate this point, bring in a variety of knives (steak, butter, etc.) and some carrots. Which knives are better for cutting up the carrots? The sharper ones.

Sometimes, we see many animals that seem to be "designed" to kill other animals. Can you think of any examples? Allow students to answer: snakes are effective at killing with their fangs, etc.

Illustration 4-07. **Before Adam disobeyed, he and Eve might have been able to play with the dinosaurs, like we see here. But after Adam sinned, something happened to change the animals, so that today they no longer get along with each other.**

Results of the Fall: Suffering and Death

How many of you have had someone that you love very much get sick and maybe even die? Wait for answers. **It's very sad when that happens, isn't it? But we need to remember that sickness and death weren't a part of God's original creation—that came because of Adam's sin (and ours).** [See Note 1 on page 39.]

Our sin makes the world a pretty bad place, doesn't it? But let's read verse 15 again. Turn to Genesis 3:15. **This is another "first." God promised Adam and Eve that He would one day send a Savior to conquer sin—One Who would provide a covering for sin. Who is that?** Jesus Christ. **This is the first mention of the gospel! God loves His children so**

much that He promised to save His people from their sin. We're going to learn more about that in a later lesson. Read Genesis 4:1–8.

<u>Illustration 4-08</u>. **This was the world's first murder. Adam and Eve disobeyed, and their sin was passed on to their children, who also disobeyed and sinned, like we see Cain doing here. It's very sad to see what sin has done to God's once-perfect creation, isn't it?**

Who Was Cain's Wife?

Read Genesis 4:9–17. **If Adam and Eve were the first two people on earth, and Cain and Abel were the first two recorded children of Adam and Eve, then who was Cain's wife?** Wait for answers. Then have students turn to and read Genesis 5:4.

<u>Illustration 4-09</u>. Some people suggest Adam and Eve may have had over 50 children! **Does this verse give you any clues as to who Cain's wife was?** Wait for answers. **Well, Cain's wife was either his sister or another close female relative. In the beginning, brothers and sisters married and had children. Does that sound strange to you?** Wait for discussion. **Let's think about this for a minute. Adam and Eve were perfect in the beginning, so their children would have been as close to perfect as you can get—they wouldn't have had the problems we have when brothers and sisters marry today.** [See Note 2 on page 39.]

Read Genesis 4:18–22. **Some people believe the first people weren't that smart—they say that they were "primitive." However, we already talked in the last lesson about how Adam could name the animals, and he even gave Eve her name. What do these verses teach us about our early ancestors?** Some knew how to build and play musical instruments, work with metals, etc.

But each of these people, because they were children, grandchildren, and great grandchildren of Adam and Eve, were born sinners and disobeyed the Lord.

Review and Prayer

Let's review the effects of Adam's sin. Read page 1 of the student handout and review the effects of Adam's sin on the world today.

Review the memory verse for this week: Romans 8:22. Close in prayer, acknowledging that we are sinners in need of salvation, and thanking God for providing Jesus as our Savior.

Discussion Questions

1. What was the original diet of man and animals?

   Answer: They ate plants and vegetables (Genesis 1:29–30).

2. How did this event (Corruption) affect the world?

   Answer: It changed the world from "very good" to bad. The world is now under a curse.

3. How would you explain to someone where Cain got his wife?

   Answer: He married a close relative—probably a sister (see Genesis 5:4).

Activity Ideas

1. With younger students, create a "dinosaur plate" to remind them that in the beginning, dinosaurs (and all creatures) were vegetarian. Hand each student a paper plate and allow them to draw (or trace, if you have dinosaur toys available) a dinosaur in the center. Then, give them each a paper bag and go on a scavenger hunt: head outside or into your kitchen to collect some dinosaur "food." Remind them that they're looking for things that dinosaurs would have eaten in the beginning: fruit, vegetables, grass, berries, leaves, flowers (show them what they're allowed to collect and what they're not allowed to collect). Then, bring the "food" back inside and help them glue it onto their plates. Or make a "dinosaur salad" from items in your refrigerator (lettuce, carrots, celery, berries, melons, nuts, raisins, tomatoes, etc.) and then allow children to eat the salad.

2. Make a collage that illustrates the effects of Adam's sin. Write Romans 8:22 at the top and Romans 6:23 at the bottom, and find pictures (from old magazines, etc.) that show the effects of sin: thorns, clothing, hard work, meat-eating, natural disasters, etc. Next to the picture, write a verse from Genesis 3 that applies.

3. Go over the *Did you know . . . ?* page of the student handout.

4. Print L4a and make copies for students to color.

Lesson 4

Extension Activities

Physics

Although some people believe that the second law of thermodynamics began at the Fall, this isn't so. Not all processes that involve the second law are "decay" processes, although all involve an increase in entropy. For example, breathing involves air moving from high pressure to low pressure, producing a more disordered concentration of molecules, and digestion breaks down large complex food molecules into their building blocks, but both processes were present before the Fall. Learn about the laws of thermodynamics. Who discovered them? How do these laws run counter to evolutionary ideas? Volume 3 (experiment 25) of *Science and the Bible* offers a simple experiment to illustrate the second law (although it also suggests the second law began at the Fall). See the "Get Answers: Thermodynamics" section of the AiG website (use the link at the online Teacher's Resource Page).

Recommended Resources

The Answers Book for Kids, volume 1 (book for children)

Exploring the World Around You (textbook for children)

Science and the Bible, volume 3

The Day the World Went Wacky (book for children)

Why Is Keiko Sick? (book for children)

Available from www.AnswersBookstore.com or by calling 1-800-778-3390.

Notes

1. We don't know exactly how things changed into what we see today, though we know that being "subjected to frustration . . . by the will of the one who subjected it" has left the whole creation in "bondage to decay," suffering the downhill effects (e.g., genetic copying mistakes) of the Curse (Romans 8:20–22). Though the Lord holds all things together (Colossians 1:17), perhaps God partially withdrew His all-sustaining power after the Fall (for example, Israelite clothes and sandals in Deuteronomy 8:4; 29:5; Nehemiah 9:21—possibly an insight into pre-Fall conditions in Eden and in the future "new heavens and new earth"). See the "Get Answers: Death & Suffering" section of the AiG website for more information (use the link at the online Teacher's Resource Page at www.AnswersInGenesis.org/go/AnswersForKids). This topic will be dealt with further in a later lesson.

2. Two things to consider on this point:

    A. Adam and Eve were perfect, with no genetic mistakes. The first generation of children would have inherited relatively few mutations from their parents and would have been able to marry freely (provided it was one man for one woman for life) with their close relatives without worrying that their children would inherit serious defects. Today, 6,000 years after the Curse, genetic mistakes have accumulated generation after generation, so that each of us now carries many mutations in our genes. If close relatives were permitted to marry today, there would be many more offspring with serious defects.

    B. "Incest" is a modern word describing a variety of actions, some of which have always been sinful, although not brother-sister marriage originally. The biblical laws against brother-sister marriage were instituted around 2,000 years after Adam—during the time of Moses (Leviticus 18). These laws also forbade marrying one's half-sibling, but about 400 years earlier, Abraham was still able to marry his half-sister, Sarah, without breaking any law of God. See "Cain's Wife—Who Was She?" at the online Teacher's Resource Page for more information.

Notes

Lesson 5

Catastrophe part 1

Scripture

Genesis 6–9:19

Memory Verse

Genesis 7:23

Visuals & Materials

From CDs: Illustrations 5-00–5-11, L5a and L5b (one of each per child), Memory Verse graphic, *Billions of Dead Things* (song)

Lesson Truths

- God is holy and must judge sin and disobedience
- The Ark was a huge ship, adequate to house Noah's family and the animals, with plenty of space for food and supplies
- The Genesis Flood was an earth-covering event, forming most of the rock layers and fossils around the world
- Jesus is our "Ark" of salvation

Preparation

1. Read "Was There Really a Noah's Ark & Flood?" at the online Teacher's Resource Page (www.AnswersInGenesis.org/go/AnswersForKids)
2. Study the Scripture passage for this week
3. Review the lesson before class so that you are familiar with the content
4. Pray that God will help your students understand God's judgment of sin and our need for Jesus—our "Ark" of salvation

Lesson 5

Lesson Overview

Many people believe that the vast number of sedimentary rock layers containing fossils found around the world formed over more than 500 million years. They believe that dinosaurs died out many millions of years before humans appeared on earth. However, the biblical record of history makes it clear that the earth has only existed for a few thousand years. Therefore, these rock layers must have formed within this time frame, i.e., within the past few thousand years. The earth-covering Catastrophe discussed in this lesson provides a basis for reconnecting the Bible to the real world of fossils and rock layers. The global Flood of Noah's day showcases God's righteous judgment on the sin of mankind and spotlights His merciful provision for salvation in the Ark.

Lesson Time

Welcome and Review

Welcome students to class, open in prayer, etc. Review the memory verse from last week.

Illustration 5-00. We're learning that the Bible is the history book of the universe.

Illustration 5-01. The Bible tells us about some major events in history that have changed the world in some way. Who remembers what all seven events are? Creation, Corruption, Catastrophe, Confusion, Christ, Cross, Consummation.

Illustration 5-02. **We've talked about the first two C's—Creation and Corruption— already. Who remembers how the creation event affected the world?** Wait for answers: God brought everything into existence in six days. **It was a perfect place to begin with. And what was the corruption event and how did it affect the world?** Adam disobeyed God's command, and his disobedience changed everything from "very good" to very bad.

Illustration 5-03. Use this illustration to review the effects of the Curse: death is a part of life, thorns and thistles are part of the plant world, we wear clothing, we work hard for our food, we no longer live in the Garden of Eden.

So, now we're living in a world that was originally created by God as very good but is now filled with sin.

Illustration 5-04. **Today we're going to talk about the next C—Catastrophe. Who knows what a catastrophe is?** Wait for answers. **A catastrophe, as we're using it here, is a sudden, violent change in the earth's surface. The Bible tells us about a catastrophe that changed the whole earth. Do you know what that event was?** The Flood of Noah's day.

Before the Flood

Have students turn in their Bibles to Genesis 6. Read Genesis 6:1–11 together. **What does the Bible say about how men were living back before the Flood?** The wickedness of man was great in the earth, and every intent of the thoughts of his heart was only evil continually. The earth was corrupt and filled with violence. **What did God decide to do about it?** Destroy man and beast from the face of the earth. **Why did God decide to spare Noah and his family?** The Bible says that Noah was a just (righteous) man, perfect in his generations, and that he walked with God.

Verse 9 says, "These are the generations of Noah." Now, we know that Moses was the final author of the first five books of the Bible, right? But many people believe that Moses used written records that were passed down from the beginning to put together his book. This seems to be Noah's way of signing his name to what he just wrote. We've come across this phrase, "these are the generations of," twice before. Does anyone remember where?

Let's turn back to Genesis 2:4. Read Genesis 2:4. **And then let's read Genesis 5:1.** Read. **Whose name is given here?** Adam.

Right—Adam's name. This verse lets us know that Adam probably wrote the section before this verse. And then Noah picked up the story and wrote the section from here until we get to Genesis 6:9. There are more of these phrases later in Genesis, telling us that Moses likely used the writings of several people to put together the book we call Genesis. It would be like your father writing down what happened during his lifetime, and then signing it "this was the generation of . . . whatever your father's name is" (if you know the names of fathers of your students, insert some of them here). **And then you write down what happened during your lifetime and sign your name to it, and then pass it on to your children, and so on.**

Preparations for the Flood

Okay, let's go back to Genesis 6. Read Genesis 6:10–16.

Illustration 5-05. **The Lord has just told Noah how to build the Ark, although the Bible doesn't include a lot of specifics about it. There's a lot we don't know about what the Ark looked like, how it was built, what the inside was like, and so on. However, there are some people who are doing some research on this area.** [See www.WorldWideFlood.com for more information.]

Read Genesis 6:17. **So, what was the great catastrophe—the event that changed the whole surface of the earth?** A flood of water that covered the entire globe. **And why did God send a Flood?**

Illustration 5-06. It was a judgment on the sins of mankind at that time.

Read Genesis 6:18–7:7. **According to what we just read, what types of things did Noah take with him on the Ark?**

Illustration 5-07. His family—wife, three sons, and three daughters-in-law—two of every kind of land animal (cattle, creeping things), seven of the clean animals, two of every kind of bird, seven of the clean birds, and food.

Did Noah need to go out and collect all the animals? No; Genesis 6:20 indicates that the animals came to Noah. **Did Noah need to take fish with him on the Ark?** No; they were able to survive in the water (although many died).

The Size of the Ark

Some scientists estimate that there may have been around 16,000 individual animals that were on the Ark. That sounds like a lot, doesn't it? But the Ark was so big (it was bigger than a jumbo jet!) that all the animals could have fit on just one of the decks, with all their food and water, and have room left over for the animals to exercise!

Illustration 5-08. Note: It is estimated that the Ark was able to hold the equivalent of about 522 boxcars (rail freight wagons)!

Illustration 5-09. **In fact, the Ark was big enough to hold the dinosaurs that went on the Ark! So Noah wouldn't have needed to stuff them on the Ark, like this. The animals that God brought to Noah were most likely "teenagers" or younger ones that weren't fully grown. Perhaps Noah could have even had a dinosaur sitting on his shoulder as he walked around, like this!**

Illustration 5-10. **Some people draw pictures of the Ark that look like this.**

Illustration 5-11. **However, does this match the description of the Ark given in the Bible? What's wrong with this picture?** Discuss the problems with the cartoon Ark: not enough room, not sea worthy, etc. Pass out this week's student handout, and read *That's not the Ark . . . This is the Ark!* together.

The Lord Shut Him In

Read Genesis 7:8–16. **Who shut the door of the Ark after all the animals and Noah's family were aboard?** The Lord. **That's right, God shut the door of the Ark! How might this have been a comfort to Noah and his family?** It showed that God was (and still is) in control. He

was sending a flood to judge the wickedness of mankind, told Noah to build a boat to escape judgment, and kept them safe during the Flood by closing them in the Ark.

After God shut the door to the Ark, safely closing in Noah, his family, and the animals, the time of God's judgment on the sin of mankind had arrived. Only those who had obeyed God and entered the Ark were saved from God's judgment—the earth-covering Flood. After God shut the door, no one else was able to enter the Ark.

We can also think of the Ark of Noah's day as an example of how we can be saved from God's judgment on our sin. Just as Noah entered the door of the Ark, there is a door that we need to enter. Have the students turn to and read John 10:7–10. **Jesus said "I am the door. If anyone enters by Me, he will be saved." In a way, Jesus is our "Ark" of salvation, isn't He? When we repent of our sins and believe that He died and rose again in our place, He will save us from God's judgment on sin—just as He saved Noah from the floodwaters.**

Review and Prayer

Review the memory verse for this week: Genesis 7:23. Pray with your students, thanking God for preserving Noah and his family, and for providing Jesus as our "Ark" of salvation.

Discussion Questions

1. Why did God judge the entire earth during Noah's day?

    Answer: Because of the sin of mankind.

2. What types of animals were with Noah on the Ark?

    Answer: Two of every kind of land-dwelling, air-breathing creatures (seven of the clean) and birds.

Lesson 5

Activity Ideas

1. Use string (or paint on grass) to mark off the dimensions of the Ark: 510 ft long, 85 ft wide, 51 ft high (about 155 m long, 26 m wide, and 15.5 m high). Tie a helium-filled balloon to a string 51 ft (15.5 m) long and allow it to float to show how tall the Ark was.

2. Construct a timeline of events during the Flood, showing how long it rained, how long the Flood waters were on the earth, how long Noah and his family were on the Ark, etc. See "Flood Timeline" at the online Teacher's Resource Page for a detailed time line.

3. Assemble the *Noah's Ark Paper Model* as a class project.

4. Read the article entitled "Noah: the man who trusted God" as a supplement to the lesson. A link to this article is located at the online Teacher's Resource Page (www.AnswersInGenesis.org/go/AnswersForKids).

5. Noah's Ark cup game.

   Materials needed: L5a, 16 oz. blue plastic cups, half-size craft sticks, glue, crayons, 14-inch pieces of string, scissors, masking or painter's tape

   Print and make copies of L5a. Each child receives one set of illustrations (Noah, dinosaur, Ark), one blue cup, one piece of string, one half-size Popsicle stick. Have children color Noah, dinosaur and Ark and cut out. The Ark is glued to the side of the cup. One end of the string is taped to the side of the cup while the other end is glued to the Popsicle stick, which is then glued between Noah (on one side) and the dinosaur (on the other side of the stick). Let glue dry for a few minutes. The object is to get Noah and the dinosaur into the "Ark."

6. Print L5b and make copies for children to color.

Extension Activities

Global vs. local flood

Some people believe that the Flood was just a localized event rather than worldwide. Spend some time discovering why they believe this and the biblical and scientific problems with accepting this idea. How should we respond to people who claim the Flood was a local event in the Black Sea area? Make a list of reasons we know the Flood covered the whole earth. Draw pictures to illustrate various points in your list. See "Noah's Flood Covered the Whole Earth" at the online Teacher's Resource Page for more information.

Recommended Resources

Dinosaurs for Kids (book for children)

Dry Bones and Other Fossils (book for children)

In the Days of Noah (book for children)

Noah's Floating Animal Park (book for young children)

The Answers Book for Kids, volume 2 (book for children)

Science and the Bible, volumes 1, 3

Noah's Ark Paper Model

Available from www.AnswersBookstore or by calling 1-800-778-3390.

Notes

Catastrophe part 2

A GLOBAL FLOOD . . . c. 2348 BC

Scripture

Genesis 6–9:19

Memory Verse

Genesis 9:11

Lesson Truths

- God is holy and must judge sin and disobedience
- The Ark was a huge ship, adequate to house Noah's family and the animals, with plenty of space for food and supplies
- The Genesis Flood was an earth-covering event, forming most of the rock layers and fossils around the world
- Jesus is our "Ark" of salvation

Visuals & Materials

Fossils (look where rock layers are exposed—creek beds, road cuts, around housing developments, etc. There are also websites from which you can purchase fossils.); from CDs: Illustrations 6-00–6-09, Memory Verse graphic, *Billions of Dead Things* (song)

Preparation

1. Read "Worldwide Flood, Worldwide Evidence" at the online Teacher's Resource Page (www.AnswersInGenesis.org/go/AnswersForKids)
2. Study the Scripture passage for this week
3. Review the lesson before class so that you are familiar with the content
4. Pray that God will help your students understand God's judgment of sin and our need for Jesus—our "Ark" of salvation

Lesson 6

Lesson Overview

Many people believe that the vast number of sedimentary rock layers containing fossils found around the world formed over more than 500 million years. They believe that dinosaurs died out many millions of years before humans appeared on earth. However, the biblical record of history makes it clear that the earth has only existed for a few thousand years. Therefore, these rock layers must have formed within this time frame, i.e., within the past few thousand years. The earth-covering Catastrophe discussed in this lesson provides a basis for reconnecting the Bible to the real world of fossils and rock layers. The global Flood of Noah's day showcases God's righteous judgment on the sin of mankind and spotlights His merciful provision for salvation in the Ark.

Lesson Time

Welcome and Review

Welcome students to class, open in prayer, etc. Review the memory verse from last week.

Illustration 6-00. Last week we started learning about Catastrophe—the third C in the Seven C's of History. What was the catastrophe? The Flood of Noah's day. This week we are going to look at the Flood itself, and the impact it had on our world.

Floodwaters & Fossils

Read Genesis 7:11 together.

Illustration 6-01. Where did the Flood's water come from? From the "fountains of the great deep" (possibly oceanic and/or subterranean sources of water) and the "windows of heaven"/ "floodgates of the sky."

Let's read about what those waters did. Read Genesis 7:17–24 together. **What happened to the animals and people that weren't on the Ark?** They were drowned in the Flood.

Illustration 6-02. We can actually find the remains of these animals, plants, and sea creatures that died during the Flood, in the ground. All that water would have picked up lots of different things, such as sand or gravel, and laid them down in layers all over the earth. The animals were buried in some of those layers, and we find their remains as fossils today. Refer to the fossils that you've displayed, if applicable. [Note: This topic (fossils and rock layers) will be covered in more detail in a later lesson.]

Illustration 6-03. Some people believe that it takes a long, long time to form fossils. But that's not true—it just takes the right conditions—lots of water and lots of mud.

<u>Illustrations 6-04 to 6-07</u>. Go through these illustrations and explain that animals need to be buried quickly in order for them to fossilize. Read "Thinkin' about fossils" from the student handout together. Emphasize that only the Bible records the true history of the earth.

Rock Layers, Mountains, & Valleys

The mud and sediments in the water also formed many of the rock layers we find around the world today, such as those that we see exposed at Grand Canyon.

<u>Illustration 6-08</u>. **The catastrophe was so bad that everything was destroyed, including the Garden of Eden!** 2 Peter 3:6.

Read Genesis 8:1–5 and then Psalm 104:6–8. **These verses in Psalm 104 seem to tell us that at the end of the Flood, the ocean basins sank down and the mountains rose up—the floodwaters were collected in the ocean basins and many inland basins. This is when many of the mountains we have today formed. Did you know that on the tops of many of today's mountains (including Mt. Everest) we find lots of rock layers with fossils in them? That shows us that they were once under water, just like the Bible teaches!**

Some people believe that it has taken millions of years for the earth to look the way it does; however, we learned in this lesson that it takes lots of water (and earthquakes and volcanoes) and not very much time. Many of the rock formations and fossils that we find today formed just a few thousand years ago.

Read Genesis 8:6–9:7.

What did God make for Adam and Eve to eat in the beginning? Fruits and vegetables. **How many of you eat fruits and vegetables?** Wait for answers. **How many of you eat some kind of meat, as well—maybe hamburgers or chicken or steak?** Wait for answers. It's in this passage that God permits humans to eat meat, as well as the fruits and vegetables.

Global or Local?

Read Genesis 9:8–17 together. **Some people believe that the Bible teaches that the Flood we just studied was only a small flood. What covenant, or promise, did God establish in the verses we just read?** That He would never again flood the earth. **And what is the sign of God's promise?** The rainbow.

<u>Illustration 6-09</u>. **How many of you have ever heard about or experienced a flood?** Wait for answers. **Sometimes, people who live beside rivers have their houses flooded when it rains too much, or when the snow melts. So, if Noah's Flood were only a local event, as some people suggest, it would seem that God has broken His promise, wouldn't it?** Wait for answers.

In light of what we read about the Flood in the book of Genesis, what are some other problems with saying that Noah's Flood was only a local flood? Here are several you can discuss with your students:

*   If the Flood were local, why did Noah have to build an Ark? He could have walked to the other side of the mountains and missed it.

*   If the Flood were local, why did God send the animals to the Ark so they could escape death? There would have been other animals to reproduce that kind if these particular ones had died.

*   If the Flood were local, why was the Ark big enough to hold all the different kinds of vertebrate land animals? If only animald from that area were aboard, the Ark could have been much smaller.

*   If the Flood were local, why would birds have been sent on board? These could simply have winged across to a nearby mountain range.

*   If the Flood were local, how could the waters rise to 15 cubits (8 meters) above the mountains (Genesis 7:20)? Water seeks its own level. It couldn't rise to cover the local mountains while leaving the rest of the world untouched.

*   If the Flood were local, people who did not happen to be living in the vicinity would not be affected by it. They would have escaped God's judgment on sin. If this had happened, what did Christ mean when He likened the coming judgment of all men to the judgment of "all" men in the days of Noah (Matthew 24:37–39)? A partial judgment in Noah's day means a partial judgment to come.

God judged the sins of mankind by sending an earth-covering, global, world-wide flood to destroy those not safely on the Ark. The catastrophe of Noah's day was a result of sin and covered every part of the entire earth—not just a small part of it.

Review and Prayer

Review today's memory verse: Genesis 9:11. Pray with your students, thanking God that His Word is true, and that He is righteous, just, and forgiving.

Discussion Questions

1. How do we know the Flood covered the whole earth?

   Answer: Because the Bible says so: all the high hills under the whole heaven were covered (Genesis 7:18–20); God promised never again to flood the entire earth (Genesis 9:11–13), but we've had many local floods since then. See also "Noah's Flood Covered the Whole Earth" at the online Teacher's Resource Page.

2. How did this event change the world?

   Answer: It changed the earth's surface—formed rock layers, carved canyons, buried humans, animals, and plants, many of which turned into fossils.

3. What types of things can we see today that should remind us of God's judgment on sin?

   Answer: Rainbow, fossils, rock layers, canyons, mountains. Note: These things are not the result of God's creative handiwork, as many people teach, but most formed as a direct or indirect result of His judgment on sin. Although we can enjoy their beauty, we also need to keep in mind that God is very serious about sin and must punish disobedience.

Activity Ideas

1. Make a rainbow. Volume 1 (experiment 1) of *Science and the Bible* offers a simple way to make your own rainbow.

2. Make your own "fossils."

   Materials needed: Plaster of paris or play dough, paper plates or aluminum pie plates, objects to press into medium (leaves, dinosaur toys, etc.)

   Pour the plaster of paris into aluminum pie plates or paper plates (or pass out jars of play dough and a paper plate)—one plate or jar per child. Have children press objects into the plaster or play dough and lift them off, leaving the imprint behind. To emphasize that dinosaurs and humans lived together, imprint footprints from dinosaur toys and child's thumbprint. Allow to dry. Paint if desired.

3. Volume 3 (experiments 7, 27, 28) of *Science and the Bible* offer simple experiments that demonstrate different aspects of the worldwide Flood.

4. Use the Sculpt-A-Saur kit (available from answersbookstore.com) to sculpt a dinosaur head..

5. Add "Catastrophe" to your timeline (approximately 2348 BC). Have some students draw pictures of animals that were on the Ark, and others draw pictures of animals that were not on the Ark. Tape or glue the finished drawings to the timeline.

Lesson 6

Extension Activities

Ice Age

Learn more about the Ice Age, which occurred after the Flood. While evolutionists and other long-agers have great difficulty accounting for any Ice Age, the global Flood and its aftermath provided the warm oceans and cold continents necessary to generate the vast ice sheets that once covered extensive areas of our present-day continents (evidenced by remnant glaciers and U-shaped valleys). See the "Get Answers: Ice Age" section of the AiG website for more information (use the link at the online Teacher's Resource Page) and read *Life in the Great Ice Age*.

Geology/Paleontology

The earth's original geography would have been completely altered by the huge earth movements during the Flood. Many creation scientists believe that the continents were pushed to the present positions during the Flood. For more information, see the "Get Answers: Plate Tectonics" section of the AiG website (use the link at the online Teacher's Resource Page).

Spend some time studying how rocks and fossils form in more detail. What are the different types of rocks? What are the different ways remains are preserved? See *The Geology Book* and *Dry Bones and Other Fossils*. For an experiment that demonstrates how wood petrifies, click on the link at the online Teacher's Resource Page.

Recommended Resources

Dinosaurs for Kids (book for children)

Dry Bones and Other Fossils (book for children)

In the Days of Noah (book for children)

The Geology Book (book for older children)

Life in the Great Ice Age (book for children)

The Answers Book for Kids, volume 2 (book for children)

Science and the Bible, volumes 1, 3

Available from www.AnswersBookstore or by calling 1-800-778-3390.

Lesson 7

Confusion part 1

Scripture

Genesis 9:18–11:9

Memory Verse

Genesis 11:7–8

Visuals & Materials

World map, Sticky Tac; from CDs: Illustrations 7-00–7-08, Memory Verse graphic, *We're One Blood* (song)

Lesson Truths

- All people today are descendants of Noah and his three sons
- God brought a mulpicity of languages on the people at Babel, causing them to scatter over the earth
- The families that left Babel became the founders of many of the world's most ancient civilizations and gave rise to today's many people groups
- Since we are all descendants of Adam, we are all in need of a Savior

Preparation

1. Read "Are There Really Different Races?" at the online Teacher's Resource Page (www.AnswersInGenesis.org/go/AnswersForKids)
2. Go to www.AnswersInGenesis.org/go/case-against-racism, and choose a few of the men mentioned in the chart to discuss in class
3. Study the Scripture passage for this week
4. Review the lesson before class so that you are familiar with the content
5. Pray that your students can view all people as created in God's image

Lesson 7

Lesson Overview

Ever since Adam ate the fruit from the Tree of Knowledge of Good and Evil, man has rebelled against the Word of his Creator. Rebellion continues to be the theme of the lives of the descendants of Noah and his family. And God, because He is holy and just, must continue to punish this sin. Approximately 100 years after the Flood of Noah's day, in about 2242 BC, a group of people once again refused to listen and obey the Word of God. This event resulted in a breakup of the population and eventually resulted in the various people groups we have today. This also explains when the various language families first originated.

Lesson Time

Welcome and Review

Welcome students to class, open in prayer, etc. Review the memory verse from last week.

Illustration 7-00. **We've been learning that the Bible is the history book of the universe.**

Illustration 7-01. **It tells us about some major events that have affected the world, or will affect the world, in some way. Who can tell me what all seven events are? Remember, they all start with a C.** Creation, Corruption, Catastrophe, Confusion, Christ, Cross, Consummation.

Illustration 7-02. **Who can give me a summary of what we've learned so far?** Creation: God created the universe in six days and it was "very good." Corruption: it changed from "very good" to bad when Adam disobeyed. Catastrophe: the continued disobedience by Adam's descendants resulted in God judging their sin with a global Flood. Many of the rock layers and fossils we find today are a result of that catastrophe.

Origin of Languages

Do any of you speak a language other than English? Wait for answers—if you have students who speak an alternate language, ask them to say something for the class. Or if you know phrases in other languages, feel free to demonstrate for the students. **There are many different languages, aren't there? In this lesson we're going to learn why that is.**

Read Genesis 8:14–19 and 9:1.

Illustration 7-03. **What command did God give Noah and his family in this passage?** To be fruitful, multiply, and fill the earth. **Noah and his family had just come off the Ark, which had saved them from the watery catastrophe that God had used to judge the sin of the world. Do you think Noah's family learned to obey God?** Wait for discussion.

Disobedience and Idolatry

Read Genesis 11:1–4. **Does it sound like the descendants of Noah's sons learned from what Noah went through? Did they obey God's command to fill the earth?** No. **What did they do instead of obeying?**

Illustration 7-04. They built a tall tower that would keep them together so that they wouldn't be scattered. **Some people believe the tower may have looked something like this.**

Illustration 7-05. **Rather than using the tower to honor God who made the heavens, however, they used it to worship the heavens themselves. Do you think this pleased God?** No. Have students turn to Exodus 20, and choose one to read Exodus 20:1–3. **What does the first Commandment tell us?** To have no other god's before God—to worship Him alone. Turn to Deuteronomy 4:15–19 and read this with your students. **What did God warn the Israelites about in this passage?** To not worship any idols in the form of man or animals, and to not worship the heavens.

Can you think of people today who worship the stars? Astrologers and people who read horoscopes looking for guidance and direction, rather than trusting in God. **It's good for us to learn about the universe and the stars and our solar system, but we need to remember that God is the One who created it all, and give Him the glory for His creation.**

Continue reading with Genesis 11:5–9. **Why did God confuse the language?** So that they wouldn't be able to understand each other. **Because it was difficult to communicate, distrust developed and families began to move apart to other parts of the world. God used this method to get the people to stop building the Tower, and to carry out His command to fill the earth.**

Illustration 7-06. Read "The Land of Shinar 4,000 years ago" on the back page of the student handout.

Spreading Around the World

Illustration 7-07. Use this illustration, or spread out the map of the world and have the students gather around it. Point out where the tower was probably located—somewhere in Iraq. **From this point, the different family groups spread out. Genesis 10 gives us a list of the names of the fathers of some of the different families.** Turn to and read Genesis 10:1–5. **This chapter also tells who the sons of Ham and Shem were. Some people have been able to figure out where many of these families settled. Let's take a look at some of them.** Pick out a few of the men (such as Cush, Gomer, Asher, Tarshish, Mizrain, etc.) mentioned in the chart in the article "Noah, a Global Flood, and the Case Against Racism" (use the link at the online Teacher's Resource Page at www.AnswersInGenesis.org/go/AnswersForKids).

Write these names on separate pieces of paper and hand one to each student. As you discuss the individual, show on the map where they went, and why we assume those are their locations. Have student use Sticky Tac to stick the paper on the appropriate place on the map. Most descendants of Noah stayed on the continents of Europe, Asia, or Africa.

Review and Prayer

<u>Illustration 7-08</u>. **Adam and Eve were the first two people, and they had sons and daughters who multiplied and filled the earth. Then Noah and his family were the only ones left on the earth. His children multiplied and filled the earth, and eventually became the various people groups we have today. That means that everyone on the earth is related—I'm related to you, and you're related to me. No matter what we look like, we are all children of Adam.**

Review today's memory verse: Genesis 11:7–8. Pray with your students

Discussion Questions

1. How did this event (Confusion) affect the world?

    Answer: It gave rise to the various language families and people groups that are around today.

2. No matter what we look like or where we live, we're all related! Knowing this, how should we treat those around us?

    Answer: Allow children to respond. We should be kind to everyone and share the free gift of eternal life with them.

Activity Ideas

1. Some people believe the Tower of Babel may have been something like a ziggurat. Research people groups that used ziggurats—what did these structures look like? What was their use? Why would these structures, used by so many different people groups, look so similar and be used for the same thing? Draw pictures of what you find, or cut out or print out the illustrations and put them in a booklet. Include a short description of each illustration (where it was found, how big it was, etc.). Or make a model of a ziggurat out of craft sticks or wood.

2. Read through the front page of today's student handout.

3. Sword drill. God has given us the ability to communicate with Him and with others. Let's find out what the Bible (God's written communication to us) teaches about this topic. (In a sword drill, you have the children hold up their Bibles, closed, with one hand on each side of the Bible. You announce the verse, have them repeat it, and then say, "Go!" The first child to find the verse stands, and you call on them to read the verse. Feel free to modify this list.)

   Psalm 33:8–9 (God *spoke* His creation into existence); Proverbs 25:11; Proverbs 8:12–13; Proverbs 22:11; 2 Corinthians 6:3–10 (specifically verse 7); 1 Timothy 4:11–12; Titus 2:7–8; 1 Peter 3:9–10; Colossians 4:5–6; Ephesians 4:22–25; 1 Samuel 2:2–3; Psalm 12:1–4; Psalm 35:28; Psalm 40:9–11; Psalm 115:1–8; Psalm 145:20–21; Proverbs 20:15; Proverbs 31:8–9; Ecclesiastes 3:1–8; 1 Corinthians 13:1; Ephesians 5:19–20; James 1:19–20

Extension Activities

Anthropology

Read and study about the development and accomplishments of the early civilizations at the "Get Answers: History" section of the AiG website (use the link from the online Teacher's Resource Page). See also *Puzzle of Ancient Man*. Many people claim our early ancestors were "primitive." What do you think? Put together a list of the different accomplishments that you find.

Human anatomy

How has God designed us to talk? How are we able to hear what is spoken? Find out about which body parts are used to talk and hear (chapter 12 of *Body by Design* has a section on the ear) and how they all work together. See also "Talking Point" at the online Teacher's Resource Page.

Lesson 7

Recommended Resources

Body by Design (textbook for ages 13 and above)

Babel Explains Our Differences (wall chart from *Answers* magazine, April–June, 2008)

The Not So Super Skyscraper (children's book)

The Puzzle of Ancient Man (book for older children)

Unwrapping the Pharaohs (book for ages 15 and up)

The Tower of Babel Pop-Up and Read (book for young children)

Available from www.AnswersBookstore.com or by calling 1-800-778-3390.

Confusion part 2

WE'RE ALL RELATED! c. 2242 BC

Scripture

Genesis 9:18–11:9

Memory Verse

Acts 17:26

Visuals & Materials

World map, Sticky Tac; from CDs: Illustrations 8-00–8-04, L8a, Memory Verse graphic, *We're One Blood* (song)

Lesson Truths

- All people today are descendants of Noah and his three sons
- God brought a mulplicity of languages on the people at Babel, causing them to scatter over the earth
- The families that left Babel became the founders of many of the world's most ancient civilizations and gave rise to today's many people groups
- Since we are all descendants of Adam, we are all in need of a Savior

Preparation

1. Read "Kinver Caveman" at the online Teacher's Resource Page (www.AnswersInGenesis.org/go/AnswersForKids)
2. Study the Scripture passage for this week
3. Review the lesson before class so that you are familiar with the content
4. Pray that your students can see all people as created in God's image, descendants of Adam, and all in need of salvation through Christ

Lesson 8

Lesson Overview

Ever since Adam ate the fruit from the Tree of Knowledge of Good and Evil, man has rebelled against the Word of his Creator. Rebellion continues to be the theme of the lives of the descendants of Noah and his family. And God, because He is holy and just, must continue to punish this sin. Approximately 100 years after the Flood of Noah's day, in about 2242 BC, a group of people once again refused to listen and obey the Word of God. This event resulted in a breakup of the population and eventually resulted in the various people groups we have today. This also explains when the various language families first originated.

Lesson Time

Welcome and Review

Welcome students to class, open in prayer, etc. Review the memory verse from last week.

<u>Illustration 8-00</u>. **Do you remember what we talked about last week?** How Noah's descendants continued in disobedience to God, did not spread throughout the world, and began to build a large tower to worship the heavens. God brought confusion at the Tower of Babel, when he confused their languages. As a result, family groups left Babel and traveled to other parts of the world, settling new lands and starting new cultures.

Migrations

Spread out the map of the world that you used in the last lesson. **While most descendants of Noah stayed on the continents of Europe, Asia, or Africa, the descendants of these families later traveled to other parts of the world. How do you think they got to places like the Americas, Australia, or the Pacific Islands?** Wait for answers.

They probably built boats and set sail on an adventure to new places. Or they may have set out on foot to explore new areas and crossed land bridges between continents. This may have happened during the Ice Age.

Explain that during the Ice Age there were land bridges connecting Europe to the Americas providing routes of migration for people (and animals), and that others would have traveled on boats to Australia and other places. We'll learn more about the Ice Age in a later lesson. To learn more about the post-Flood world, read "Post-Flood World" at the online Teacher's Resource Page (use the link at www.AnswersInGenesis.org/go/AnswersForKids).

Flood Legends

If you moved from where you live now, what kinds of things would you take with you? Your favorite toys, your family, your favorite books or stories that your grandparents told you. **Well, the people who moved from the plain of Shinar also took things with them when they moved. Even more important than their possessions, they brought separate languages with them and stories about what happened to their grandfather Noah and what happened before that—in the very beginning. These different languages eventually developed into all the various languages we have today. And these different families eventually developed into all the different people groups we have today.**

In fact, all over the world, we find stories about what happened in the beginning and during the Flood—they're different from the true story in the Bible, but they also share many things in common.

As the people moved away from Babel, their descendants formed nations based primarily on the languages they shared in common. Through those languages, the story of the Flood was shared, until it became embedded in their cultural history.

Share these Flood stories from two different cultures with your class:

- Hawaiians have a flood story that tells of a time when, long after the death of the first man, the world became a wicked, terrible place. Only one good man was left, and his name was Nu-u. He made a great canoe with a house on it and filled it with animals. In this story, the waters came up over all the earth and killed all the people; only Nu-u and his family were saved.

- Another flood story is from China. It records that Fuhi, his wife, three sons, and three daughters escaped a great flood and were the only people alive on earth. After the great flood, they repopulated the world.

As the story of the Flood was verbally passed from one generation to the next, some aspects would have been lost or altered. And this is what has happened. However, as you can see from these two stores, each story shares remarkable similarities to the true account of Noah in the Bible.

<u>Illustration 8-01</u>. **We also find that many civilizations have built structures that look like the tower built at Babel.** [See Note 1 on page 65.]

Cavemen

Some of the families that went from Babel weren't as skilled in some areas as others were. How many of you have heard of "cavemen" before?

<u>Illustration 8-02</u>. Pass out today's student handouts and have students read *Caveman 101* together. *Caveman 101* points out that the so-called "cavemen" were merely men (and their families) trying to make the best of their new situation with the capabilities they possessed. And many people live in caves today—they're not such a bad place to live!

You may want to share with your students about the Kinver Cavemen or the amazing cave people of Malta. Links to these articles can be found on the online Teacher's Resource Page.

Review and Prayer

<u>Illustration 8-03</u>. **Adam and Eve were the first two people, and they had sons and daughters who multiplied and filled the earth. Then Noah and his family were the only ones left on the earth. His children multiplied and filled the earth, and eventually became the various people groups we have today. That means that everyone on the earth is related—I'm related to you, and you're related to me. No matter what we look like, we are all children of Adam.** Have students look up Acts 17:26. This is the memory verse for this week.

Review today's memory verse: Acts 17:26. Pray with your students.

Discussion Questions

1. If your family were suddenly cut off from the rest of civilization, what types of abilities would you have? Would you know how to build a brick home, or would you have to survive in caves or in houses made of wood? Would you know how to build a fire and kill and cook animals for food? Would you know how to make musical instruments or toys? Would you be able to make your own clothing?

2. Some people teach that marriage between people with different skin colors is wrong. Since we are all of "one blood," is there any such thing as "interracial marriage"?

   Answer: No.

3. Read 2 Corinthians 6:14. What is true "interracial marriage"?

   Answer: When a child of the last Adam (a Christian) marries a child of the first Adam (a non-Christian). See "Interracial Marriage: Is It Biblical?" at the online Teacher's Resource Page for a more thorough discussion of this.

Activity Ideas

1. Do the games on the back of today's student handout.

2. Print L8a and make copies for children to color.

3. Add "Confusion" to your time ine (approximately 2242 BC). Show **Illustration 8-04** ("hello" in various languages) and have students choose two or three to copy down on a sheet of paper. Have them draw a picture of a ziggurat (from **Illustration 8-01**) on the paper. Tape or glue the drawings to the timeline.

Extension Activities

Geology

We discussed caves in this lesson. How did they form? See the "Get Answers: Caves" section of the AiG website (use the link at the online Teacher's Resource Page). Use a concordance to find where the Bible mentions caves and those who lived in them.

Alternate languages

How do those who can't hear or speak communicate? Spend some time learning sign language.

Take a few weeks to learn the basics of a language other than your own: Spanish, French, German, Russian, Chinese, etc.

Recommended Resources

Body by Design (textbook for ages 13 and above)

Babel Explains Our Differences (wall chart from *Answers* magazine, April–June, 2008)

The Not So Super Skyscraper (children's book)

The Puzzle of Ancient Man (book for older children)

Unwrapping the Pharaohs (book for ages 15 and up)

The Tower of Babel Pop-Up and Read (book for young children)

Available from www.AnswersBookstore.com or by calling 1-800-778-3390.

Lesson 8

Notes

1. Today's languages have "descended" from those original ones. While linguists today can group languages into "families," they are unable to find linkages that might trace all languages back to a single common ancestral language—exactly what we would expect from the biblical account of confusion into distinct languages at Babel. See "More Than PIE: Babel Explains Distinct Language Families" at the online Teacher's Resource Page for additional information.

Christ

GOD BECOMES A MAN

Scripture

Genesis 3:15; Matthew 1:1–25; Luke 1:26–2:40; John 1:1–14

Memory Verse

Matthew 1:22–23

Visuals & Materials

World map; from CDs: Illustrations 9-00–9-07, L9a, Memory Verse graphic, *I've Got Good News!* (song)

Lesson Truths

- Old Testament sacrifices were only a temporary "covering" for sin
- The Law shows us our need for a Savior
- Throughout the Old Testament, God promised to send the Messiah
- Jesus Christ, the Creator, came as the long-awaited Savior

Preparation

1. Read "The Real Jesus" and "Ur Connects Babel to Today" at the online Teacher's Resource Page (www.AnswersInGenesis.org/go/AnswersForKids)
2. Study the Scripture passage for this week
3. Review the lesson before class so that you are familiar with the content
4. Pray that your students will understand who Jesus is and see their need for a Savior

Lesson 9

Lesson Overview

Who was Jesus Christ? Just a good teacher? A man of great morals? An interesting philosopher? Where did He come from? What did He accomplish? Jesus Christ is the central figure in history. Yet most people don't understand the real reason He came to earth or why He had to die. They don't realize that His coming was all part of God's eternal plan.

This lesson traces the promises of God about the coming Savior throughout history—from the time of Adam to the fulfillment in Jesus Christ. Children will learn that Adam's (and our) sin brought the need for a Savior, which God provided with His Son, 4,000 years later.

Lesson Time

Welcome and Review

Welcome students to class, open in prayer, etc. Review the memory verse from last week.

<u>Illustration 9-00</u>. **Over the past few lessons, we've been learning that the Bible is the history book of the universe—it tells us the history of the universe from the very beginning.**

<u>Illustration 9-01</u>. **There are seven words that help us remember the major events that have affected—or will affect—the world. Who remembers what those words are?** Creation, Corruption, Catastrophe, Confusion, Christ, Cross, Consummation.

<u>Illustration 9-02</u>. **Who remembers how creation affected the world?** Wait for answers. **Right—it tells us about the beginnings of the universe and all things in it. And how did the corruption event affect the universe?** Adam's disobedience changed the universe from "very good" to bad. **And what was the catastrophe that changed the world?** The worldwide Flood of Noah's day that formed many rock layers and fossils. **And how did the confusion at Babel change things?** This is when the various language families and people groups originated. **In this lesson, we're going to learn about the next C—Christ.**

Remember, after Adam disobeyed, God pronounced a curse on the serpent, on the ground, and on Adam and Eve. God also made a promise at that time. Let's read the promise He made. Turn to Genesis 3:15 and read together. **Throughout the rest of the Old Testament, God reminds His children of His promise to one day send someone who will defeat the serpent, who is the devil.**

In the lesson on "confusion," we learned about how the various nations came from Noah's sons. Today, we're going to do a quick overview of the Old Testament, from the time of Abraham up to Christ. We will follow the line of Noah's oldest son, Shem.

Abraham to Jacob

<u>Illustration 9-03.</u> Show the students the *From Creation to Christ!* chart that shows the geneaology from Adam to Christ, and briefly go through the list of Shem's descendents beginning in Genesis 11:10 and ending with Genesis 11:26. Continue to refer to the chart as you go through this lesson.

God chose a man named Abram and made a promise, called a "covenant," to him that he would be the father of a great nation, even though Abram had no children by his wife, Sarai. Read Genesis 12:1–3, 17:1–22 and 21:1–13. This could be another "C" you might want to use as a memory device—Covenant. **God kept His promise to Abram, and Sarah gave birth to Isaac.**

But then God asked Abram, whose name He changed to Abraham, to sacrifice Isaac. How would you feel if you were Abraham? God promised you a son and then took him away. Wait for answers. **Let's see what Abraham did.** Read Genesis 22:1–19 (or summarize the passage, if you need to).

The Apostle Paul later tells us that the "seed" or "offspring" mentioned in verse 18 refers to Jesus Christ. Turn to and read Galatians 3:16. **In other words, God promised Abraham that He would be the ancestor of the Messiah—the Promised One—and that through that Promised One all nations of the earth would be blessed.**

What does Abraham sacrificing his only son remind you of? Wait for answers. **When God provided the ram for Abraham to sacrifice instead of his son, He showed the way that He would one day provide His Son as the sacrifice for the sin of the world.**

God made the same promise to Isaac as He did to Abraham. Read Genesis 26:24. **And then again to Isaac's son, Jacob, who was the younger twin of Esau.** Read Genesis 28:10–16. **Jacob had twelve sons, each of whom received a blessing from Jacob.** Turn to Genesis 49:8–10. **In this passage, we learn that Jacob's son, Judah, would be the ancestor of the Messiah, and that his descendants would one day be kings.**

Moses and the Ten Commandments

Jacob's children lived in Egypt and eventually became slaves of the Egyptians. Over 400 years later, God raised Moses up to deliver the Israelites and take them back to the land God had promised to Abraham.

While Moses was leading the Israelites through the wilderness, God gave Moses the Law that God wanted the Israelites to live by. We're familiar with the Ten Commandments, aren't we? Read Exodus 20:1–17 with your students, explaining the Ten Commandments as you go along. This could be another "C" to help your students to remember biblical

history—Commandments. **But in addition to these Ten Commandments, there were over 600 laws that the Lord gave to Moses—these governed the lives and worship of the Israelites.** If your Bible has chapter/section headings, flip through Exodus 20 and the following chapters, including Leviticus, and point out some of the various laws (e.g., there were laws concerning relationships, laws about property, laws about fair play, laws about enemies, laws about feasts and sacrifices).

Why do you think God gave Moses all these laws? Wait for answers. Have students turn to and read Leviticus 11:45. **Many times throughout Leviticus, God repeats this phrase. God gave the Israelites the laws so that they could see what it was like to be holy and pure, just as God is. The Law also showed them that it was impossible for them on their own to be perfect. The book of James** (James 2:10) **tells us that even if we kept every part of the Law, but fell short in one part, it was the same as if we broke the whole Law. Does that seem harsh to you?** Wait for answers.

How many laws did Adam disobey before God punished him? Just one. **God is so holy and pure that He does not tolerate any disobedience at all, and He wants His children to be holy and pure, too.**

Do you remember what Adam and Eve did after they disobeyed?

Illustration 9-04. They tried to cover themselves with leaves. **Was God satisfied with their attempt to cover their sin?** No. **What did He do?**

Illustration 9-05. He killed at least one animal and made clothes for them to wear. This was the first time that an animal was sacrificed and its blood shed.

Do you think it would be possible for every person in Israel to obey every part of the law all the time? No. **Just like Adam and Eve, the Israelites needed a way to cover their sins. So, God gave Moses instructions on how to build a tabernacle, where priests could sacrifice animals on behalf of the people when they disobeyed the Law. The people were also to bring other offerings to the tabernacle, but any animal that they sacrificed had to be perfect—without blemish or defect.**

Judges and Kings

The Israelites wandered in the wilderness for 40 years until God led them into the land He had promised them—we call this place Israel today. On the world map, point out where Israel is located. **They were led by judges for a time, but then they wanted a king. The Lord chose a shepherd boy named David to be the king of His people. Remember the blessing Judah received—that he would be the father of kings? David was a great, great, great, great, great, great, great, great grandson of Judah. God also promised**

David something. Return to <u>Illustration 9-03</u>. Turn to and read 1 Chronicles 17:10–14. **God promised David that someone from his family would always sit on a throne.**

Throughout their history, the people of Israel continually looked for someone to come who would deliver them—the Law showed them they couldn't be perfect, and they waited for someone to come who would take away their sin and make them perfect.

God continued to give promises about the coming Savior. For example, God promised King Ahaz (point him out on the timeline, <u>Illustration 9-03</u>) **something through the prophet Isaiah.** Have students look up and read Isaiah 7:10–14. **And God promised Ahaz's son Hezekiah** (point him out on the timeline, <u>Illustration 9-03</u>) **that a messenger would go before the Promised One.** Look up Isaiah 40:3. **Do you know who that messenger was?** John the Baptist. **There are many other promises throughout the Old Testament like this, too.**

The Promised Messiah

Finally, the time came ("in the fullness of time" is says in Galatians 4:4) that God had chosen even before He created the world, and He sent His Son, Jesus Christ—the long awaited Messiah.

<u>Illustration 9-06</u>. **The life of Jesus the Messiah, the Creator-Redeemer, is recorded in four main books, which are part of the New Testament. The authors of these books were inspired by the Holy Spirit to record the events of Jesus's life.**

<u>Illustration 9-07</u>. **Luke was one of these men—he was actually a doctor who wrote down all that he heard about and saw.** Turn to and read Luke 1:26–32. **Remember the promise God gave to David—that someone would always be on his throne?** Point out David on the chart (<u>Illustration 9-03</u>), and then show that Jesus is a descendant of David. **Jesus Christ fulfilled that promise, since Jesus's parents were descendants of David, and Jesus would be the King forever.**

Continue reading Luke 1:33, and then point out Jacob on the timeline (<u>Illustration 9-03</u>). **Remember the promise that God gave to Abraham, Isaac, and Jacob—that all nations on the earth would be blessed through their offspring? This verse tells us that Jesus fulfilled God's promise to them—Jesus would be a blessing to all nations on earth.**

Continue reading Luke 1:34–38 and 2:1–24 together.

Now let's turn to the book written by a man named John and look at what he says about Jesus. Turn to and read John 1:1–5, 10–14. **John was a fisherman. What does he teach us about Jesus?** Jesus is the eternal God, and He is the Creator.

God loved His people so much that He provided a way for them to spend eternity with Him by sending His Son, Jesus Christ, who fulfilled every single promise that was made about His first appearance on earth!

Review the memory verse: Matthew 1:22–23. Pray with your students, thanking God for providing the promised Messiah, Jesus Christ, to make a way for us to spend eternity with our Creator.

Discussion Questions

1. Read Matthew 1:23, John 14:9, and Colossians 1:16. What do these verses teach us about Jesus Christ?

    Answer: They teach that Jesus is the Creator God. See the "Get Answers: Jesus Christ" section of the AiG website (use the link at the online Teacher's Resource Page).

2. Look up John 1:1–3, Colossians 1:15–17, Ephesians 3:9, and Hebrews 1:1–3. What do these verses teach us?

    Answer: They confirm that God is the Creator.

3. Sword drill! Look up the following verses. These references in the New Testament refer to historical events described in Genesis, showing that New Testament authors accepted Genesis as actual history.

    Matthew 19:5–6; 24:37–39; Mark 10:6–7; Luke 11:51; 17:26; Acts 17:24; Romans 5:12–19; 1 Corinthians 6:16; 11:8–9; 15:21, 45; 2 Corinthians 11:3; Ephesians 5:31; Colossians 1:16; 1 Timothy 2:13–14; Hebrews 1:10; 4:4, 10; 11:3–4; 1 Peter 3:20; 2 Peter 2:5; 3:5–6; Jude 11; Revelation 10:6; 20:2

4. How do we know the serpent is actually the devil?

    Answer: See Revelation 12:9.

5. How did this event affect the world?

    Answer: Jesus Christ is the Creator God who was born to the virgin Mary—His coming was the fulfillment of many promises and would provide a way for His people to be saved from their sins.

Activity Ideas

1. On the world map, trace the route Joseph and his family probably took from Bethlehem to Egypt to Nazareth.

2. Research the gifts given by the Magi to Jesus. What were they? What was their use? Draw pictures of what each may have looked like.

3. Jesus fulfilled many more prophecies than the ones we've listed on the *From Creation to Christ!* chart. What other fulfilled prophecies can you find? Make a list. See the "Get Answers: Jesus Christ" section of the AiG website.

4. Review this lesson by reading the *Do you know your Bible?* page, and the "Special women," "Problem solved," and "Prophecies" boxes on the *From Creation to Christ!* chart.

5. Print L9a and make copies for students to color.

6. Add Christ to your timeline (approximately 5–6 BC). Have students choose an aspect from today's lesson or the account of Christ's birth to illustrate (or write a summary about). Tape or glue the drawings or summaries to the timeline.

Lesson 9

Extension Activities

Archaeology

Research the various ways that archaeological finds have confirmed the Bible's teachings. See the "Get Answers: Archaeology" section of the AiG website (use the link from the online Teacher's Resource Page).

Bible

Continue learning about Jesus by using different passages throughout the gospels.

Matthew: Read Matthew 1:1–17, and have students compare the names listed in the genealogy with those in the *From Creation to Christ!* chart. You will notice that there are more men listed in the chart than are in Matthew's list. The explanation: Matthew was a Jewish tax collector and one of the 12 disciples of Jesus (Matthew 9:9; 10:3). Careful study of Matthew's book reveals that he wrote primarily for a Jewish readership, as he documents the Old Testament prophecies that Jesus, as the Messiah, fulfilled. This fulfillment of prophecy would have been particularly interesting to a Jew. Matthew emphasizes the kingly nature of Jesus (read through Matthew and make a list of the places you find this emphasis). He also shows that Jesus was descended from Abraham, the father of the Jews, through Joseph. Matthew's genealogy (1:1–17) from Abraham to Christ is intentionally incomplete—he selected just 3 groups of 14 men. There are other listings in the Old Testament which are complete and which help fill in the known "gaps" in Matthew's list (e.g., Genesis 5; Genesis 11; 1 Chronicles 3:11–12; 2 Kings 23:34; 24:6).

Mark: Mark was probably acquainted with Jesus because Mark's mother was the owner of the "upper room" where the last supper between Jesus and His disciples took place. Mark's account of Jesus's life is thought to emphasize the servanthood of Jesus (as you read through this book, make a list of the places you find this emphasis), and it was most likely written for Roman believers. Read Mark 5:21–42. Remember that death, disease, and sickness are not a permanent part of God's creation. They only came about after Adam sinned. In this passage, Jesus (the Creator God) shows His power over these things by healing Jairus's daughter and raising the daughter of the ruler of the synagogue from the dead.

Luke: Luke, the "beloved physician," addressed his account (and his second book, Acts) to a relatively unknown man, Theophilus, with an emphasis on the humanity of the Messiah (as you read through Luke, look for this emphasis). Luke's genealogy (3:23–38) is different from Matthew's because Luke traces Jesus's heritage through His mother, Mary (rather than through His earthly father, Joseph, as Matthew does). Luke's genealogy extends back to the father of us all—Adam. Read Luke 3:23–38 and compare the names given to those on the chart.

Here are a few reasons that Luke chose to present Mary's lineage:

- Luke's narrative mainly presents Mary's perspective, while Matthew presents Joseph's perspective. So readers of the original Greek would realize that these two narratives were intended to present Mary's and Joseph's lines respectively.

- Luke didn't mention Mary explicitly because rules for listing Jewish ancestry generally left out the mothers' names.

- A clear pointer to the fact that Luke gave Mary's line is that he put a definite article before all the names except Joseph's. Any Greek speaker would have understood that Heli must have been the father of Joseph's wife. Because the article is missing, the reader would insert the father's name, "Joseph," into the parenthesis "(as was supposed)" in Luke 3:23. So he would not read the sentence as "Jesus . . . being (as was supposed) the son of Joseph, the son of Heli," but as "Jesus . . . being son (as was supposed of Joseph) of Heli." (Note: the original Greek had no punctuation—or even spaces—between words.) Indeed, the Jewish Talmud—no friend of Christianity—dating from the first few centuries AD, calls Mary the "daughter of Heli," which could only be true if this is what Luke meant.

What about "Cainan"?

Luke (3:36) lists "Cainan" as the father of Shelah and the son of Arphaxad, yet Cainan's name is not listed in the genealogy of Genesis 11:12. Some have used this to say the Bible itself is mistaken and fallible.

We chose to omit this second "Cainan" in our list from Adam to Christ because several lines of evidence would indicate that it was not part of the original, inspired manuscripts, but probably resulted from a copyist's error. As a scribe was copying Luke's gospel, it is possible that he inadvertently added an extra Cainan as the father of Shelah. For more information, see "Contradictions: An Extra Cainan?" at the online Teacher's Resource Page.

John: John's book about the life of Christ highlights the deity of Christ and has a distinct evangelistic emphasis (John 20:30–31). Make a list of the titles John uses for Jesus and the ways he emphasizes the deity of Christ as you read this book.

Recommended Resources

The Answers Book for Kids, volumes 3 & 4 (books for children)

A Faith to Grow On (devotional book for children)

Messianic Christology (book for ages 13 and up)

What If Jesus Had Never Been Born? (DVD for ages 13 and up)

Available from www.AnswersBookstore.com or by calling 1-800-778-3390

Harmony of the Gospels (by A.T. Robertson, for ages 13 and up)

UP FROM THE GRAVE

Scripture

Luke 22–24
Matthew 26–28
Mark 14–16
John 18–21

Memory Verse

1 Corinthians 15:3–4

Visuals & Materials

From CDs: Illustrations 10-00–10-08, L10a, Memory Verse graphic, *I've Got Good News!* (song)

Lesson Truths

- Jesus died as the perfect sacrifice for our sin
- Jesus rose from the dead, conquering death and taking away the punishment for sin
- We must repent and place our faith in Christ to be saved

Preparation

1. Read "Why Did Jesus Have To Die?" at the online Teacher's Resource Page (www.AnswersInGenesis.org/go/AnswersForKids)
2. Study the Scripture passage for this week
3. Review the lesson before class so that you are familiar with the content
4. Pray that God will open the eyes of your students to see their need for a Savior, and that they will place their faith in Christ

Lesson Overview

Just as Adam and Eve tried to "cover up" their shame by sewing fig leaves together, many people today try to "cover up" their sin on their own. Some think that giving to the poor, attending church, being baptized, or living a good life will allow them entrance into Heaven. But sin (disobedience to the commands of God), any sin, separates us from the Holy Creator God, and nothing that we manufacture will allow us to live forever with God. For that, we need someone who is just like us—human—yet without sin, to pay the penalty for sin on our behalf. Jesus Christ—the perfect God-man—satisfied God's requirements, as the Creator Who is also our Savior. With this lesson, children will learn that the death of Jesus Christ paid the penalty for sin and that His resurrection showed His power over death, securing eternal salvation for those who believe.

Lesson Time

Welcome and Review

Welcome students to class, open in prayer, etc. Review the memory verse from last week.

<u>Illustration 10-00</u>. **Who remembers the special phrase that we've been using to describe the Bible?**

<u>Illustration 10-01</u>. **Right—and who remembers the seven big events that we've been learning about?** Creation, Corruption, Catastrophe, Confusion, Christ, Cross, Consummation.

<u>Illustration 10-02</u>. **Who can summarize Creation for me?** God created a "very good" world in six days. **And Corruption?** Adam disobeyed and God put a curse on the universe because of his disobedience. Death was the penalty for Adam's sin. **And Catastrophe?** God used an Ark to save Noah and his family from the Flood that He sent as a punishment for the sins of the world. **And Confusion?** God caused the people to separate by confusing their language. **And Christ?** Jesus Christ was the fulfillment of the promises God had made to people throughout the Old Testament, beginning with Adam. **Today, we'll be talking about the sixth C, Cross.**

Old Testament Sacrifices

<u>Illustration 10-03</u>. **Ever since God killed the first animal to make clothes for Adam and Eve, people offered animal sacrifices to God. From Cain and Abel to Abraham, Moses, and the people of Israel (who had a tabernacle in which to bring sacrifices)—all those**

who loved God made sacrifices to Him in order to cover their sins before a holy God. Have students turn to and read Hebrews 9:22.

The Bible tells us that blood must be shed to cover sins. But it also tells us that the people had to make sacrifices all the time—year after year, because they kept breaking the Law, and the blood of bulls and goats could never take away sin. Turn to and read Hebrews 10:1–4. **Are animals humans? No, not at all. Because animals aren't humans, their blood can only cover our sin, but it can't take it away completely. For that, we need someone who is human, but who is a perfect human.**

Over a thousand years after the Law was written, Paul explains the purpose of the Law a little more. Turn to Galatians 3:23–25 and read together. **What does Paul say was the purpose of the Law?** To bring us to Christ; to show us that people can't be perfect on their own and that they need someone to be perfect for them.

Jesus Lived a Perfect Life

We learned last week that Jesus was a descendant of Adam. He became a human like we are, and yet He never sinned. Jesus Christ obeyed every part of the Law—He lived an absolutely perfect life. Jesus did what Adam didn't do—obeyed God in every way. What happened when Adam was tempted? He disobeyed God's command (refer to Genesis 3). **Let's read about what happened when Jesus was tempted.** Read Matthew 4:1–11 and Hebrews 4:14–15 together. **Jesus obeyed His Father perfectly and never did anything wrong.**

Some people tried to find witnesses who saw Jesus do something wrong, but let's read what happened. Turn to and read Mark 14:53–62.

Because Jesus was perfect, He could be the perfect human sacrifice. He could take the punishment for sin once and for all. Turn to and read Hebrews 7:26–27.

Jesus Died and Rose Again

Let's read about when Jesus "offered Himself."

Illustration 10-04. Turn to and read Mark 15:16–39. **Did Jesus stay dead? No. Let's see what happened when His disciples went to look for Him in the tomb.**

Illustration 10-05. Turn to and read Luke 24:1–9, 36–53.

When Jesus died and rose again on the third day, He fulfilled the promise that God had given to Adam and Eve in the Garden of Eden over 4,000 years earlier—Jesus crushed the devil by conquering death and taking away the punishment for sin. He provided a way to have eternal life, rather than be eternally separated from God.

The Bible tells us that the names of those whose punishment has been taken away are written in a book called the Lamb's Book of Life.

Illustration 10-06. I know for certain that my name is written there, do you?

How We Can Be Saved

Let's look at how we can know for certain that our names are written in that Book of Life. Turn to and read Romans 6:23. Heaven is a free gift offered by God to all who will receive it, and because of our sin, there is nothing we can do to earn it or deserve it. Remember how Adam and Eve tried to cover their sin with leaves?

Illustration 10-07. Can you think of any ways that people try to cover up their sin today? Allow students to respond: some people believe that doing good works will override their bad ones, some believe that being baptized will save them, some believe going to church is enough to cover sin, etc.

Turn to and read Acts 20:21. Paul tells us here that we need to repent—or tell God we're sorry for our sins, and have faith in Jesus Christ. We need to believe that He is the Creator God and that He died in our place. Have students also look up Romans 10:9, John 14:6, and Acts 4:12.

The Bible teaches us about a real place—called the Lake of Fire—that was prepared for the devil and his angels. Those who refuse the gift of eternal life will also go there and be separated from God forever. Read Matthew 25:46, Mark 9:43–48, and Revelation 20:14–15.

If you would like to make sure that your name is written in the Book of Life, please talk to your parents (or me) after class today.

Jesus's Death and Resurrection

How do we know that Jesus died and rose again? The death and Resurrection of Jesus are not things that can be duplicated. They cannot be proven scientifically because they were one-time historical events. We know and understand what we do about Jesus Christ because of the words of Scripture. In the same way, the events of creation were one-time historical events—they cannot be proven

scientifically because they happened in the past. But God tells us in His Word that He created in six normal-length days, and He tells us that Jesus Christ (the God-man) died and rose again, so we can believe it because God never lies.

Did you know that some people don't believe what God says? They have made up different stories to try to explain why the tomb where Jesus was buried is now empty. Some people say that Jesus didn't really die on the Cross but just fainted, and that after He was buried, He woke up and then left. Can you think of anything wrong with this story? Try to get the students to think of and discuss the following: He would have had to unwrap Himself from the grave clothes, push aside the stone (which was too heavy to be moved by a single man) across the entrance to the tomb, and then walk past the soldiers outside. He would have been too weak to do this, and the guards would have stopped Him. Explain that, further, the Roman soldier pierced Him with a spear while He was still on the Cross, and the blood and water that flowed from this wound showed that He was truly dead.

Let's read about what some other people say. Turn to *Up from the grave He arose . . .* and begin reading with the second bullet point.

<u>Illustration 10-08</u>. **We discussed the catastrophe of Noah's day a few weeks ago. Jesus referred to this event while He was on the earth.** Have students turn to and read Matthew 24:37–39 and Luke 17:27. **Some of Jesus's followers also mention this event as true history in the books they wrote.** Read Hebrews 11:7; 1 Peter 3:20; 2 Peter 2:5, 3:6. Explain to your students the parallels between Noah's Ark and Jesus. **Both the account of Noah's Ark and Jesus are real history; both the Ark and Jesus provide escape from God's judgment; both the Ark and Jesus are God's only way of escape; just as many rejected the Ark as God's provision for escape from the Flood, so today many reject Jesus.**

End with the reminder that they can talk to their parents or that you're available to talk to them about how they can know for sure that they can escape God's judgment.

Review and Prayer

Review the memory verse for this week: 1 Corinthians 15:3–4. Pray with your students, thanking God for sending Jesus, Who paid the penalty for our sin on the Cross.

Lesson 10

Discussion Questions

1. Why did Jesus need to die on the Cross?

   Answer: To take away the sin introduced by Adam and to conquer death (a result of Adam's sin) so that we can have eternal life.

2. How do we know Christ rose from the dead?

   Answer: Ultimately because of the words of Scripture—God tells us in His Word that He rose from the dead. The gospel writers recorded for us eyewitness accounts of seeing Jesus after He had risen.

3. How did this event affect the world?

   Answer: Jesus's death and Resurrection paid the penalty for the sins of the world and provided a way for His people to be saved from their sins.

4. Why don't we offer animal sacrifices today, like the Israelites did?

   Answer: Because Jesus was the final sacrifice—He died and paid the penalty for sins, so that those who receive the free gift of eternal life can have forgiveness of sins and can be holy before a holy God.

Activity Ideas

1. Compare the First Adam and the Last Adam (Jesus Christ) by reading the front of the student handout. See "Why Did Jesus Have to Die?" at the online Teacher's Resource Page for more information.

2. Go over the *Do you know your Bible?* and *Let there be fun!* sections on the back of the student handout.

3. Use the "Two Trees of the Gospel" drawing activity to reinforce the reason Jesus came to die (you can find the link at the online Teacher's Resource Page).

4. Some people claim that the different accounts of the inscription written above Jesus's head on the Cross show that the Bible is fallible. However, read "Contradictions: Crossed Messages" for a possible answer to this charge (use the article link at the online Teacher's Resource Page).

5. Print L10a and make copies for children to color.

6. Add "Cross" to your timeline (around AD 30). Draw a large cross under the title.

Extension Activities

Church history

Trace the development of the church since the time Jesus returned to Heaven.

What did early church leaders believe about Genesis? See the "Get Answers: Genesis" section of the AiG website for help (use the link at the online Teacher's Resource Page). Choose two or three leaders and research their lives and work. Write summaries of what you find about each.

Spend some time finding out about the lives and testimonies of various Christian martyrs. *Foxe's Book of Martyrs* is a great resource for this.

History

What was the culture like during Jesus's day? Who was in power at that time? What did people wear at that time? What languages were spoken? What was going on in other parts of the world while Jesus was on earth? For help with this, consult the works of Flavius Josephus, a Jewish historian of the first century.

Recommended Resources

The Answers Book for Kids, volume 4 (book for children)

The Complete Works of Flavius Josephus (book for ages 15 and up)

Available at www.AnswersBookstore.com or by calling 1-800-778-3390.

Foxe's Book of Martyrs (book for ages 15 and up)

Notes

Lesson 11

Consummation

Back to Very Good

Scripture

Revelation 21–22

Memory Verse

Revelation 21:1

Visuals & Materials

From CDs: Illustrations 11-00–11-07, L11a, Memory Verse graphic, *The Seven C's of History* (song)

Lesson Truths

- One day God will create a new heaven and a new earth for His children
- Only those whose names are in the Lamb's Book of Life will be there
- Until Jesus returns, we are to carry out the Great Commission by sharing the gospel and making disciples

Preparation

1. Read "What Is the Gospel?" at the online Teacher's Resource Page (www.AnswersInGenesis. org/go/AnswersForKids)
2. Study the Scripture passage for this week
3. Review the lesson before class so that you are familiar with the content
4. Pray that your students will fully understand the gospel message and place their faith and trust in Christ

Lesson 11

Lesson Overview

In a previous lesson, we talked about the authors of the gospels. One of those authors, Luke, was a doctor—someone who provided help to those who are sick. In the very beginning of creation, doctors were not necessary because there was no such thing as disease or sickness. Adam and Eve were completely healthy. Because death and disease, thorns and thistles are only a temporary part of God's creation, they will one day be no more. In this lesson, children will learn about the last "C" of History—Consummation. This will take place in the future. God has promised a new heaven and earth for those who have received the free gift of eternal life, and eternity in the lake of fire for those who refuse the gift.

Lesson Time

Welcome and Review

Welcome students to class, open in prayer, etc. Review the memory verse from last week.

<u>Illustration 11-00</u>. **We've been learning that the Bible is the history book of the universe.**

<u>Illustration 11-01</u>. **It teaches us about seven events that affect the universe in some way.**

Who can tell me all seven events without looking? Creation, Corruption, Catastrophe, Confusion, Christ, Cross, Consummation.

<u>Illustration 11-02</u>. **The six events that we've studied so far have already taken place. Today, we're going to learn about the last C, which will happen sometime in the future. It's Consummation. Does anyone know what** *consummation* **means?**

Consummation means that everything is finished or completed, that it has reached its final goal.

After God created the world, what did He say about it?

<u>Illustration 11-03</u>. It was "very good." **God designed a world that would do what He wanted it to do—He had a purpose for each and every thing He created, and He designed it to fulfill that purpose. Today we see lots of things that aren't "very good." Why?** Because Adam disobeyed and brought death, disease, and corruption into the world.

<u>Illustration 11-04</u>. **This world is very different from the original world that God created. In fact, there are many jobs that we have today that Adam wouldn't have had to do**

while he was in the Garden of Eden. **Can you think of any?** Doctors, nurses, firefighters, police, judges, lawyers, surgeons, security guards, etc.

Let's see what Romans 8 says about the world. Turn to Romans 8:18–23. **These verses remind us that the entire universe is suffering from the curse of sin.**

Illustration 11-05. **But it also teaches us that we are waiting for something better to come.** Have students look up Acts 3:19–21. **God promises to restore all things—or make them like the way they were. But first, He is going to destroy the present heavens and earth.** Turn to 2 Peter 3:7–13. **During the time of Noah, what did God use to destroy the earth?** Water. **In the future, how will God destroy the heavens and earth?** With fire.

New Heaven and New Earth

After that, God is going to create a new heaven and earth. As we read about what it will be like, let's make a list of how it will be different from our present heaven and earth. Read Revelation 21:1–22:6.

Examples:

New Heavens and Earth	Present Heavens and Earth
No tears	Tears
No pain/suffering	Pain/suffering
No death	Death
No need for sun/moon to provide light	Sun/moon provide light
Day only	Day and night
Light provided by God Himself	Light provided by sun, moon, stars
Water of life	No water of life
Tree of life	No tree of life
Saints	Sinners and saints
Righteousness will dwell there	Sin is rampant now
No more curse of sin	Under the curse of sin
Complete health	Disease, sickness
Animals will get along and be vegetarians (Isaiah 11:6–9, 65:25 prophecies about a future time)	Animals do not get along and are not all vegetarian

This new heaven and new earth are only for those who have received the Creator's free gift of eternal life by repenting of their sins and believing in Jesus Christ—those whose names are written in the Lamb's Book of Life.

<u>Illustration 11-06</u>. **We will be able to eat from the Tree of Life (Revelation 22:14) just like Adam and Eve did in the beginning. We will enjoy being in a perfect place with God forever.** Pass out today's student handouts and have students turn to the back page. Read *Back to Very Good* together.

Let's read again what happens to those who don't receive this free gift. Read Revelation 20:11–15 together again.

Created in God's Image

We discussed in our lesson on creation that God created man in His own image, remember?

<u>Illustration 11-07</u>. **What are some things that show we're not just an animal but are created in God's image?** Wait for answers: creativity, language abilities, etc. **In the beginning, Adam and Eve were a "very good" reflection of God's image. But after they disobeyed, that changed. The sin in their lives (and in the lives of their children) corrupted God's image. But the good news is that when we receive the gift of eternal life, God begins restoring His image in our lives through the work of His Holy Spirit as we put off our old sinful ways and seek to become more like Christ who was the very image of God.** Read together Philippians 2:5–11; Romans 8:28–29; Colossians 3:8–10; Ephesians 4:22–24; 2 Corinthians 3:18.

The Great Commission

Until God brings about the new heaven and earth, He has given us something to do. Let's read about a job He gave to those who follow Him while they wait for His Second Coming. Read Matthew 28:18–20. **What are some ways we can carry out this Great Commission?** Wait for answers: share the gospel with friends and family, take mission trips (when older), write encouraging notes to missionaries your church supports, pray for missionaries, give to missions, hand out tracts and booklets with the gospel, etc.

For some people, obeying God's command to go into all the world involves learning another language. Remember how we learned about what happened at Babel, when God confused the languages? Today, we can help to overcome the language barriers that have come about since then by studying and learning different languages so that we can share the good news with other people groups. The Bible tells us that people from all tribes and nations will worship God. Read Revelations 7:9–10. **But Paul reminds us in Romans that we have the responsibility to tell others.** Read Romans 10:14–15.

Review and Prayer

Review the memory verse: Revelation 21:1. Pray with your students, thanking God that one day He will make a new heaven and a new earth where His children can live with Him forever.

Discussion Questions

1. List and describe each of the Seven C's of History.

    Answer: Creation (God created in six normal-length days); Corruption (sin corrupted God's "very good" world); Catastrophe (God judged the wickedness of mankind by sending an earth-covering Flood); Confusion (God confused the languages of the people at Babel so that they would fill the earth as He had commanded them to); Christ (Jesus Christ, the Creator God, stepped into history to become a man); Cross (Jesus came to redeem the world from sin by dying on the Cross and paying the penalty of death for those who receive Him); Consummation (in the future, the Curse will be removed and God will prepare a new heavens and earth for His children).

2. What things do we deal with now that we won't have to deal with in the new heavens and earth?

    Answer: For example, sickness, loss of loved ones.

3. How will this C (Consummation) affect the universe?

    Answer: The universe will be destroyed by fire and God will create a new heaven and earth.

Activity Ideas

1. Research the various precious stones mentioned in Revelation 21:18–21. What does each of the stones look like? How much are they worth today? Draw pictures of each one.

2. Review this topic with the drawing activity, "What Happened to God's Perfect Creation?" found at the online Teacher's Resource Page.

3. Read through the first page of the student handout.

4. Invite a missionary (from your church or elsewhere) to come speak to the children and share their testimony and what their mission work involves.

5. Volume 2 (experiment 24) of *Science and the Bible* contains a fun illustration of how we should not "keep the lid on" our faith, but should share it with others.

6. Print L11a and make copies for children to color.

7. Add "Consummation" to your timeline (some time in the future). Have students read the description of the Tree of Life in Revelation 22:1–2 and illustrate what they think the tree will look like. Tape or glue the drawings to the timeline.

Extension Activities

Christian stewardship

We are to be good stewards of what God has allowed us to use. Find out more about how we can be good stewards as we "occupy until He comes again" with unit 5 of *Exploring the World Around You*.

Missions

Spend some time learning about the various mission organizations your church supports. Find out more about your missionaries so that you can better pray for and support them in their work. Ask them to share their testimonies of how they decided to become missionaries. Make a small booklet with pictures of each missionary and descriptions of where they are and what they are doing and use it to remind you to pray for them.

Learn about "creation evangelism" by reading "Evangelism For the New Millennium" (a link to this article can be found at the online Teacher's Resource Page).

Recommended Resources

Exploring the World Around You (textbook for children)

Science and the Bible, volume 2

Available from www.AnswersBookstore.com or by calling 1-800-778-3390.

Lesson 12

Is There Really a God?

Scripture

Genesis 1:1

Memory Verse

Psalm 90:2

Visuals & Materials

Scrabble letters or magnetic letters arranged in a sentence "GOD IS LOVE" and another set of the same letters in no particular order, e.g., "ELIS OOD GV." Arrange and display the two sets before the children come into class (or use Illustrations 12-04 & 12-05); from CDs: Illustrations 12-00–12-05, Memory Verse graphic, *God's the Author of Creation* (song)

Lesson Truths

- Each person is specially made in God's image
- God created us with DNA that is specific for each person
- The information in our DNA had to come from an Intelligent Being; that person is God

Preparation

1. Read "Is There Really a God?" at the online Teacher's Resource Page (www.AnswersInGenesis.org/go/ AnswersForKids)
2. Study the Scripture passage for this week
3. Review the lesson before class so that you are familiar with the content
4. Pray that your students will understand that God created the information in our DNA and created them in His image

Lesson 12

Lesson Overview

We've probably all used the standard "design implies a Designer" argument as confirmation that God exists. However, evolutionists also agree that things appear "designed"—they attribute the apparent design to the effects of natural selection and mutations working on populations over millions of years. While it is beneficial to point out various "design features" in nature to confirm to children that there is a God, we also need to teach them the basics of another argument with this lesson (they can learn the details as they mature) so that in the future they're able to answer the evolutionist argument "of course it appears designed—it wouldn't be here if it didn't function well!" The material in this lesson is based on "information theory" (IT) and the study of genetics.

Lesson Time

Welcome and Review

Welcome students to class, open in prayer, etc. Review the memory verse from last week.

Many people don't trust the Bible to tell us the truth about the history of the world. They have lots of questions about God and the Bible. What kinds of questions do you have, or have you heard? Wait for answers. If they can't think of any questions, suggest questions like **"Is there really a God?"** and **"How old is the earth?"** and **"Did God really create in six actual days—or over periods of millions of years?"**

Over the next few weeks, we'll be learning what the Bible teaches and how to answer these questions so that when our friends ask us questions, or when we read something in our textbook, or hear something from our teacher, we'll know the truth and we'll be able to give answers.

Have your students turn to 1 Peter 3:15, and read the verse out loud. **This verse tells us that we need to be ready to give "a defense" for our faith. When people ask us questions, we need to be ready to answer them.**

Is There Really a God?

Ask, **Who can tell me what the first verse in the Bible is?** You may need to prompt them with **In the beginning . . . .** Wait for them to answer, or have them turn to Genesis 1:1. **Right! In the beginning, God created the heavens and the earth. The Bible tells us that *God* is the Creator of the universe.**

<u>Illustration 12-00</u>. **But some people don't believe that God exists. Do any of you know of anyone who doesn't believe God exists?** Wait for them to answer. **If you haven't already, you may one day meet someone who thinks this way. Today, we're going to learn one way to show how science supports the Bible's statement that God exists. We'll answer the question "Is there really a God?"**

Code Talkers

First, let me tell you a true story. In 1942, our country was involved in a war against Germany and Japan. It's important when fighting a war that the information we share with our fellow soldiers is kept a secret so that the enemy can't figure out what we're planning. To do this, the soldiers need a code system that the enemy can't decipher. Philip Johnston was the son of a missionary to the Navajo, a group of Native Americans who live in the Southwest. Philip could speak the Navajo language and knew that it was very complicated and that not many people could speak it. So he showed the Marines how to use the Navajo language to send and receive messages.

It worked like this: when a code talker got a message, he heard a string of Navajo words. He translated each of the words into English and then used just the first letter of the English words to form the message.

<u>Illustration 12-01</u>. **For example, what was being discussed if a code talker received the message, *tsah, wol-la-chee, ah-keh-di-glini, tsah-ah-dzoh*?** Wait for students to find the words and translate the message. **Right, he would know that the words were referring to the Navy, since *tsah* means needle, *wol-la-chee* means ant, *ah-keh-di-glini* means victor, and *tsah-ah-dzoh* means yucca. This code system was so complex that the enemy never figured it out, and many believe that without the Navajo code talkers we wouldn't have won the war!**

If you have time, ask **How would you spell your name using the Navajo code?** Allow students a few minutes to figure it out.

DNA

Just like the Marines needed a code to send information, our bodies have a code that sends information—in fact, every living thing has this code. It's much more complex than the Navajo code, and it's written with chemicals, rather than with words.

<u>Illustration 12-02</u>. **Inside each of us are special molecules called DNA** (which stands for deoxyribonucleic acid, if you want to mention that), **and it looks something like this. Our DNA stores the information needed to make you "you," in the form of a special code.**

Now, this coded information isn't very useful without something to translate it. That's what these special molecules are for.

Illustration 12-03. All of this machinery is in our cells and helps to make us who we are.

For example, the way the information is arranged in your DNA tells whether you're going to be a boy or a girl, whether you'll have blue eyes or green, whether your skin will be medium brown or very dark brown, whether you'll have brown hair or red hair, and so on.

What has the information stored in your DNA told *your* body to do? Wait for your students to answer. Encourage them with examples: my eyes are brown, my nose is pointy rather than round, my top lip is smaller than my bottom lip, my eyes are spaced far apart, etc.

Let's see your ears. Who has earlobes that are attached to the sides of your head? And who has earlobes that aren't attached? Now, who can curl their tongue in a *u*, like this? Demonstrate—if you're able! Now, put your hands together, like this. Interlace your fingers, naturally. Some of you have your right thumb on top, and some have your left thumb. Uncross your hands and try it so that your other thumb is on top. Demonstrate. Feels weird, doesn't it?

All these things are determined by the information stored in your DNA. And each of us is one-of-a-kind and special. In fact, the Bible tells us that we're wonderfully made (have students look up Psalm 139:14) and that we're made in God's very own image (have them read Genesis 1:26–27).

Source of Information

Now, where do you think all that information inside you came from? Wait for answers. Well, it's a combination of the DNA we received; some from our mom and some from our dad. And where did their information come from? From their parents and so on. Now, as that information is passed down from person to person, it changes—sometimes the copying process makes mistakes, or information gets switched around, and so on. But scientific observations indicate that no new information will come about naturally in your DNA. For instance, humans will never develop DNA information to grow feathers or a tail!

Illustration 12-04. For example, take a look at these letters. Use these two slides, or show the two sets of letter arrangements.

Which set tells you something? The set that spells out "GOD IS LOVE." How long would we have to wait to get the letters that don't spell something meaningful to change into the set of letters that do? It will never happen, unless someone with intelligence rearranges the letters into a meaningful pattern that gives us information. Like this. Rearrange

the letters to spell "God is love," or show <u>Illustration 12-05</u>. **What information does this pattern give us?** God is love.

So, if information comes from a greater source of intelligence, and if information can't be naturally added to the information stored in our DNA, then where did all the information for all living things come from in the first place? (They may say, "God!" at this point, but there's a bit more explanation needed.)

Well, it had to come from a source that has all intelligence and all information—a source that is infinite. The only source that we know of that fits this description is the God of the Bible! So, the Bible is totally correct when it says, "In the beginning, *God* **created the heavens and the earth." He filled the first creatures with enough information so that each could reproduce after their kind (dogs have puppies, cats have kittens, geese have goslings, etc.), and He put lots of information into Adam and Eve so that they could have many descendants without anyone being completely identical to the other.**

Today, we've learned that real science confirms that God exists.

Now we're going to do an activity that will help us to learn our verse for today. Turn to the "Deciphering the code" page in the handout and allow students to work for a few minutes. If you have time, you can read the "Of course I exist!" section of the handout.

Discussion Questions

1. What is the molecule called that helps to make us who we are?

   Answer: DNA

2. Where did our DNA come from?

   Answer: From our parents

3. Where did the information in Adam and Eve's DNA come from?

   Answer: The infinitely intelligent Creator God made it.

Activity Ideas

1. Telephone game. Have the students sit in a circle. Whisper into the ear of the one sitting by you something like *The quick brown fox jumped over the lazy red dog.* Say it only once. If they don't catch all of it, tell them to whisper into the ear of the person sitting beside them what they did hear, until the message makes it all the way to the last person. Have that student say out loud what he/she heard. It will likely have changed from what you originally said— sometimes drastically! The point of this game is that just as the information originated from an intelligent source but changed over time and lost information, so God is the originator of the information in all living things, but it changed as it was passed down from the original humans and animal kinds.

2. Family tree. On a large sheet of paper, begin with Adam and Eve at the top, then write the family line through Noah (from Genesis 5). Since you probably don't know which of Noah's sons were your student's ancestors, just draw a dotted line from Noah to the earliest ancestor they know about, and trace their family tree from there. If your students know what each person looked like, add a bit about some characteristics, and see if they can figure out where their blue eyes or other notable features came from!

3. Go over the other confirmations that God exists by reading through the "Is there really a God?" section of the handout.

Extension Activities

American history

Learn more about the Navajo, their history and the role the tribe played in World War II. Do they have any "creation" or "flood" legends?

Theology

We can learn a lot about God through His Word, but only He knows everything about Himself. We're going to have a "sword drill" so that we can learn more about God. (In a sword drill, you have the children hold up their Bibles, closed, with one hand on each side of the Bible. You announce the verse, have them repeat it, and then say, "Go!" The first child to find the verse stands, and you call on them to read the verse.) Feel free to add or subtract any verses as you have time or as you prefer:

Genesis 17:1 (*El shaddai* translated as "Almighty God" means the Sustaining God); Exodus 15:26 (the God who heals); Exodus 22:27 (gracious); Exodus 31:13 (the God who makes us holy); Isaiah 9:6 (Wonderful, Counselor, Mighty God, Everlasting Father, Prince of Peace); Isaiah 44:24 (the Creator); Isaiah 51:12 (the Comforter); Isaiah 60:16 (the Savior and Redeemer); Malachi 3:6 (Unchanging); Romans 15:33 (God of peace); 1 John 1:5 (God is light); 1 John 4:7–8 (God is love)

Codes

Learn Morse code and write Psalm 90:2 (or student's name, etc.) in Morse code. Or, get a long piece of yarn and, using long hollow tube macaroni (to represent the "dashes") and small hollow circular macaroni (to represent the "dots"), string the macaroni together, separating each "letter" by tying a knot in the string. Separate each "word" by tying several knots in the string. (Warning: do not let children eat uncooked macaroni. Small macaroni can be a choking hazard for young children.)

Or, have children make up their own code and write Psalm 90:2 or their names with it.

Lesson 12

Recommended Resources

The Answers Book for Kids, volume 3 (book for children)

A Faith to Grow On (devotional book for children)

Daddy, Is There Really a God? (book for children)

Digging Up the Past (devotional book for children)

Where Did God Come From? (DVD for high school—adult)

Available from www.AnswersBookstore.com, or call 1-800-778-3390.

Lesson 13

How Did We Get the Bible? part 1

Scripture

Selected passages

Memory Verse

2 Timothy 3:16

Visuals & Materials

"Books of the Bible Timeline" chart; from CDs: Illustrations 13-00—13-02, L13a (cut verse reference strips apart), L13b (one copy per child), L13c–e (cut apart each square), Memory Verse graphic, *You've Gotta Know the Bible* (song)

Lesson Truths

• God's general revelation (creation) is inferior to God's special revelation (Scripture)
• The Bible is inspired by God, Who cannot lie
• The Bible is God's Word, and we can trust it

Preparation

1. Read "Jesus Christ on the Infallibility of Scripture" at the online Teacher's Resource Page (www.AnswersInGenesis.org/go/AnswersForKids)
2. Study the Scripture passage for this week
3. Review the lesson before class so that you are familiar with the content
4. Pray that God will help your students to have full confidence in His Word

Lesson 13

Lesson Overview

If asked "Who wrote the Bible?" most churched kids will reply, "God!" But how many of us (including adults!) really understand how we got the Bible as we have it today, and how we can know it is *the* Word of God? This lesson explores in more detail the complex answers to these questions. It is vital that we understand why we accept that the Bible is "God-breathed" so that we can provide answers to the skeptics that challenge us on this point.

Lesson Time

Welcome and Review

Welcome students to class, open in prayer, etc. Review the memory verse from last week. Pass out the student handouts.

Last week we learned how to answer the question, "Is there really a God?" Do you remember what we discussed? Wait for answers. In necessary, briefly review the argument from Information Theory taught in last week's lesson.

<u>Illustration 13-00</u>. **Today, we're moving on to a different question: how did we get the Bible? Is it really God's Word? Have you ever thought about this question, or been asked this question?**

General vs. Special Revelation

Read Romans 1:19–20 with the children. Ask them, **What can the creation teach us about God?** Answers: He exists, and He is powerful. **Some people have a special name for God's creation—they call it general revelation. A revelation is something that is shown to us. In this case, God's creation is shown to us.**

While we can learn *some* things about God from the world around us, we are limited as to what we can learn.

Now choose a child to begin reading the first page of the student handout, and have a different child read each paragraph.

Ask, **What *can't* we learn about God just by studying the world around us?** Answers: The creation doesn't tell us how long ago God created, how long it took Him to create, that He created an originally "very good" world, that Adam's sin corrupted it, that the Creator came to earth, that Jesus rose from the dead, that we need to place our faith in Christ as Savior, that there will be a new heavens and earth, etc.

Remember when we studied about Corruption? **Although God created our world perfect, or "very good," it is now suffering from the curse of sin** (read, or have a student read, Romans 8:21–22). **So we cannot trust the world (or general revelation) to tell us the truth about the past, present, or future. This is why God gave us the Bible. The Bible is God's special revelation to us.**

The Bible Tells Us

Ask, **How do we know God wrote the Bible?** Wait for answers. **Well, there are several reasons:**

<u>Illustration 13-01</u> (or if you have a board available and want to, write "1. God says He wrote it."). **The first way we know God wrote it is that the Bible tells us.** Assign the following verses to various students to read when you call on them and discuss what each has to say about God inspiring the Bible: Exodus 24:4 (Moses didn't just make up stuff—he wrote down what the Lord told him to write); Exodus 34:27–28 (again, Moses wrote what the Lord commanded him to write); 2 Peter 3:15–16 (Peter is saying that Paul wrote his letters with "the wisdom God gave him"), and today's memory verse, 2 Timothy 3:16 tells us that Scripture is inspired or "God-breathed."

Let's see what these pairs of verses have to say on this topic. Compare the following pairs of verses, which show that the New Testament regards these statements in the Old Testament as made by God (distribute the strips of paper to the students from L13a): Psalm 2:1 (does this verse say that God wrote it? No, it's attributed to David) & Acts 4:24–25 (this verse says that God wrote it through David); Psalm 2:7 & Hebrews 1:5; Psalm 16:10 & Acts 13:32–35; Psalm 95:7 & Hebrews 3:7; Psalm 104:4 & Hebrews 1:7; Isaiah 55:3 & Acts 13:34.

One way we know the Bible was authored by God is that He tells us He wrote it.

The Bible's Internal Consistency

<u>Illustration 13-02</u> (or write on board). Pass out one copy of the "fish story" worksheet (L13b) to each student. Give them 1–2 minutes (depending on how many students you have and how much time you have) to write the next part of the story. When time is up, have the students pass their paper to the person on their right. Each student should read what is already written and then continue the story. Do this five times (more or less, depending on how much time you have). Announce the final time, and have the students finish the story. Then collect all the papers, and choose a few to read out loud.

Point out: **Even though we all started with the same sentence, we ended up with many differences because there were so many people working on our stories. Now, imagine writing our story with over 40 different men—and not just at one time like we did—**

but over a period of 1,600 years! This process should result in a pretty confusing story, shouldn't it? But that's how the Bible was written, and yet it has a consistent theme throughout and no inconsistencies between the various authors! This consistency shows that the writers were guided to record the message God wanted them to record.

Review and Prayer

Let's go over our memory verse for today: 2 Timothy 3:16.

Pray with your students, thanking God for giving us His perfect Word. **Next week we are going to look at the three more reasons how we know that God wrote the Bible.**

Discussion Questions

1. What does the phrase "All Scripture is God-breathed" mean?

   Answer: God the Holy Spirit guided the writers so that all of the very words they recorded in their own distinctive styles on the original scrolls were without error.

Activity Ideas

1. Study Genesis 1–3 and Revelation 21–22 to see the many parallels. Make a list of the items that are the same.

2. Discuss the "Books of the Bible Timeline." Go over how the books are divided, when each was written, and who wrote them.

3. Learn more about the authors of the Bible.

   Cut apart squares from L13c–e. Have the students match the authors with the books they wrote:

   > Moses (Genesis, Exodus, Leviticus, Numbers, Deuteronomy)
   > Joshua (Joshua)
   > David (many Psalms)
   > Solomon (Song of Solomon, Ecclesiastes, some Psalms, Proverbs)
   > Samuel (1 & 2 Samuel)
   > Ezra (Ezra, possibly 1 & 2 Chronicles and 1 & 2 Kings)
   > Jeremiah (Jeremiah, Lamentations)
   > Paul (Romans, 1 & 2 Corinthians, Galatians, Ephesians, Philippians, 1 & 2 Timothy, Titus, Philemon, possibly Hebrews)

   What jobs did each of these men perform? When did they live? (Use the "Books of the Bible Timeline" for help.)

Extension Activities

Church history

Since we discussed the Bible's survival throughout history, spend some time studying church history. How has the church grown and changed through the years?

Western civilization

The Bible's message has changed many civilizations. It is the basis of English common law, the American Bill of Rights, and the constitutions of great democracies such as the United Kingdom, the United States, Canada, Australia, and New Zealand.

Today, the message of the Bible still transforms. Animistic tribal groups in the Philippines are still being delivered from fear, and former cannibals in Papua New Guinea and Fiji now live in peace, all because of the gospel.

Ask for volunteers to do research online (with their parents permission) or in a library for copies of the various documents or histories of the countries, and discover the role the Bible played.

Literature / Art / Music

The Bible has inspired the noblest of literature—Shakespeare, Milton, Pope, Scott, Coleridge, and Kipling, to name a few—and the art of men such as Leonardo da Vinci, Michelangelo, Raphael, and Rembrandt. The Bible has inspired the exquisite music of Bach, Handel, Haydn, Mendelssohn, and Brahms.

Start a journey through various literary works, art pieces, and musical pieces and look for allusions to the Bible's teachings. Have each student choose an individual to research.

Recommended Resources

The Answers Book for Kids, volume 3 (book for children)

The Bible Comes Alive, volumes 1–3 (books for high school–adult)

Many Infallible Proofs (book for high school–adult)

Available from www.AnswersBookstore.com, or call 1-800-778-3390.

Notes

Lesson 14

How Did We Get the Bible? part 2

Scripture

2 Peter 1:20–21

Memory Verses

2 Peter 1:20–21

Visuals & Materials

"Books of the Bible Timeline" chart; from CD: Illustrations 14-00–14-05, L14a (cut verse reference strips apart), Memory Verse graphic, *You've Gotta Know the Bible* (song)

Lesson Truths

- God's general revelation (creation) is inferior to God's special revelation (Scripture)
- The Bible is inspired by God, Who cannot lie
- The Bible is God's Word, and we can trust it

Preparation

1. Read "Why 66?" at the online Teacher's Resource Page (www.AnswersInGenesis.org/go/AnswersForKids)
2. Study the Scripture passage for this week
3. Review the lesson before class so that you are familiar with the content
4. Pray that God will help your students to have full confidence in His Word

Lesson Overview

If asked "Who wrote the Bible?" most churched kids will reply, "God!" But how many of us (including adults!) really understand how we got the Bible as we have it today, and how we can know it is *the* Word of God? This lesson explores in more detail the complex answers to these questions. It is vital that we understand why we accept that the Bible is "God-breathed" so that we can provide answers to the skeptics that challenge us on this point.

Lesson Time

Welcome and Review

Welcome students to class, open in prayer, etc. Review the memory verse from last week.

Have them turn to 2 Peter 1:20–21 and read it together. **What does this verse tell us about how God's Word came to us?** The Bible authors did not write of their own will, but were moved by God's Holy Spirit. **This is our memory verse for this week.**

Illustration 14-00. **Last week we started talking about how we know that the Bible is God's Word. Do you remember what the first two reasons were?** The first way that we know the Bible was authored by God is that He tells us He wrote it. The second way is that, even though the Bible was written by more than 40 different men, over a period of 1,600 years, its message and theme is consistent throughout.

This week we are going to look at four more reasons why we can trust that the Bible is God's Word. For a chart you can print out depicting the accuracy of God's Word, see "God's Word Is True in Everything It Says" (use the link at the online Teacher's Resource Page).

Fulfilled Prophecy

Illustration 14-01 (or write on board). Ask, **Do you know what a prophecy is?** Wait for them to answer. It is a prediction of a future event. **Another way we can show that the Bible is the Word of God is because the Bible correctly predicts future events. Some say that there are over 2,000 prophecies in the Bible that have come true. These prophecies involve both individuals and nations, and many of them are very specific. We are going to look at a few of Old Testament prophecies and see how they were fulfilled in Jesus.**

Have students look up the following prophecies about Jesus and their fulfillment:

Prophecy	Given	Fulfilled
Born in Bethlehem	Micah 5:2	Matthew 2:1; Luke 2:4–7
Came at just the right time	Daniel 9:25–26	Galatians 4:4; Ephesians 1:10
Born of a virgin	Isaiah 7:14	Matthew 1:18–25; Luke 1:26–35
Enter Jerusalem on a donkey	Zecharaih 9:9	Matthew 21:1–11
Of the line of Abraham, Judah, and David	Genesis 12:1–3, 49:10; 2 Samuel 7:12–13	Matthew 1:1–3
Sold for 30 pieces of silver	Zecharaiah 11:12–13	Matthew 26:15, 27:3–10
Crucified with criminals	Isaiah 53:12	Matthew 27:38; Mark 15:27
Burial with the rich	Isaiah 53:9	Matthew 27:57–60; Luke 23:52–53

The Bible also contains specific prophecies about various cities and nations (e.g., Tyre, Sidon, Samaria, Gaza, Ashkelon, Moab, Ammon, Petra, Edom, Thebes, Memphis, Nineveh, Babylon, Chorazin, Bethsaida, Capernaum, Jerusalem). **And all of these prophecies came to pass as well.**

The probability of all these things coming to pass by chance is effectively zero, and yet they did come to pass. Do you know of other prophecies in the Bible that have come true?

Divine Preservation

Illustration 14-02 (or write on board). **The Bible has been amazingly preserved over the years—another sign that it has a divine origin. For example, over 1,500 years ago, one Roman emperor, named Diocletian, decided that he wanted Christianity to end. He ordered every Bible to be destroyed—burned—and he even built a column over the ashes of a Bible to celebrate his victory. Seems like that would be the end of the Bible, doesn't it? But 25 years later, a new emperor, named Constantine, had 50 new Bibles produced!**

And in the 1700s, a man named Voltaire hated God. He predicted that by the end of one hundred years, no more Bibles would be left on earth. He was obviously wrong! It seems like people have had a hard time destroying this collection of books, doesn't it? Today, the Bible is available in far more languages than any other book.

Scientifically Accurate

<u>Illustration 14-03</u> (or write on board). Pass out the set of Scripture references (L14a), and have the children look up the verses as you come to them. **Another way that we know the Bible was written by an all-knowing God is that it tells the truth about scientific things. For example, read Isaiah 40:22.** Have the student read Isaiah 40:22. **What does this teach us about the earth? Right—it's round—not flat, as some people have believed in the past.** (The Hebrew word is *khug*, which means sphericity or roundness.)

Have the student read Job 26:7. **What does this verse say about the earth? Right—it is suspended in space without support—just like we can observe today. Did you know that some people have believed that the earth rode around on the backs of giant turtles? Another group believed it rode on the backs of four elephants standing on the back of one giant turtle swimming in a sea of milk. Sounds silly, doesn't it? But the Bible tells us the truth.**

Over the years, people have thought that there were a certain number of stars—some thought 3,000; others, more; others, less. But today we know that there are too many stars to count. What does the Bible say about this (remember, this was written over 3,000 years ago!)? Have the student read Genesis 15:5. **Moses wrote that the stars were countless—just as we know they are today.**

Have the student read Psalm 8:8. **Matthew Maury was a man who loved God and who was born 200 years ago. He loved to study the Bible and believed that it was accurate in every area it touched on. When he found this verse in the Bible, he figured that there really must be paths through the sea, so he set out to discover them.**

<u>Illustration 14-04</u>. **And sure enough, he discovered several currents that run through the oceans—including the Gulf Stream, which runs down the east coast of America in the Atlantic Ocean. So, whether talking about science or history, the Bible has been shown to be accurate. This confirms that it is God's Word.**

Power to Change Lives

Illustration 14-05 (or write on board). **There are many other ways that we know the Bible was written by God, but we'll just cover one more. The Bible has a special message for humans—this message has the power to change lives. For example, there have been many stories of people who lived terrible lives—they were addicted to drugs or alcohol, and so on. But when they heard about the Good News and received the free gift of salvation, their lives were changed.**

Review and Prayer

Because God doesn't—can't!—lie, and because we know He wrote the Bible, we can trust it to tell us the truth about the things He wants us to know. Read "Did you know?" on the back of the student handout together to summarize why we can be confident that the Bible is God's Word. **Aren't you glad that God gave us His Word?**

Review the memory verse for this week: 2 Peter 1:20–21. Pray with your students, thanking God for His Word, and asking Him to help us believe it and live it for His glory.

Discussion Questions

1. Who can tell me one or two ways that we know the Bible was written by God?

    Answer: Accept various answers: the Bible tells us God wrote it; it is scientifically accurate, historically accurate, prophetically accurate; it has endured the "test of time"; has a life-changing message; has a consistent message; is the foundation of great nations; etc.

Activity Ideas

1. Go over the first page of the student handout, which defines the various words used for the Bible.

2. Discuss various other confirmations that the Bible was written by God. See Unit Studies below.

Lesson 14

Extension Activities

Archaeology

The Bible is historically accurate. Archaeological discoveries confirm the Bible's accounts. For example, archaeologists have found remains of the city of Jericho (have children locate Jericho on a map) that the Bible mentions. Burial sites of many biblical characters have been found, along with many of the man-made structures that the Bible mentions.

Spend some time researching the various archaeological confirmations of scriptural passages. See the "Get Answers: Archaeology" section of the AiG website for help (you can find the link at the online Teacher's Resource Page).

Bible characters

The Bible tells the truth about humans—it doesn't try to cover up their sinfulness but shows sinners just as they are. Even the "heroes of the faith" (Hebrews 11) have their failures recorded.

Look up the following verses to see how these "heroes" really lived. Make a list of the "heroes" as you go along. Can you think of any others to add to the list? Noah (Genesis 9:20–24), Moses (Numbers 20:7–12), David (2 Samuel 11), Elijah (1 Kings 19), and Peter (Matthew 26:74). On the other hand, the enemies of God's people are often praised—for example, Artaxerxes (Nehemiah 2), Darius the Mede (Daniel 6), and Julius (Acts 27:1–3). These are clear indications that the Bible was not written from a human perspective.

Recommended Resources

The Answers Book for Kids, volume 3 (book for children)

The Bible Comes Alive, volumes 1–3 (books for high school–adult)

Many Infallible Proofs (book for high school–adult)

Available from www.AnswersBookstore.com, or call 1-800-778-3390.

Lesson 15

How Old Is the Earth?

Scripture

Genesis 1–2, 5, 11–12
1 Kings 6, 11
Ezekiel 4

Memory verses

Isaiah 40:8

Visuals & Materials

Paper & pencils for
each child; from CDs:
Illustrations 15-00–15-11,
Memory Verse graphic

Lesson Truths

- God's has given us an eyewitness account of history in His Word
- We can calculate the approximate age of the earth from information given in the Bible
- The earth is approximately 6,000 years old, not billions of years old

Preparation

1. Read "Two Histories of Death" at the online Teacher's Resource Page (www.AnswersInGenesis. org/go/AnswersForKids)
2. Study the Scripture passage for this week
3. Review the lesson before class so that you are familiar with the content
4. Pray that your students will believe God's Word is true and begin to base all of their thinking on the Bible

Lesson 15

Lesson Overview

Since the Bible is God's written revelation to mankind, we should trust it to tell us the truth about every area it touches on—including the "age of the earth" issue. Many people believe the age of the universe is unimportant to Christianity and that "science" has proven that the universe is many billions of years old. However, there are limitations to what regular science (the science that gives us fast cars, fun foods, and rocketships to the moon) can tell us—it can't, for example, tell us what happened in the past, or when. For that, we need an accurate, reliable eyewitness account. The Bible is such an account. God has given us a written record of how He created (by the word of His mouth), how long He took to create (six days), and approximately how long ago He created (~6,000 years ago).

Not only does an earth "millions of years old" deny the plain teaching of Scripture, it also destroys the basis for the gospel message: the ancient earth idea is based on the thought that the fossil layers are a record of the animals that have lived and died over millions of years, while man has come on the scene only recently. However, this concept allows for death, disease, cancer, and suffering before the entrance of man, and thus before the entrance of man's sin. The Bible clearly teaches that death is God's punishment for sin and that Jesus Christ died to take away the punishment for sin. If death isn't the result of sin, then why did Jesus lay down His life? It's vital that we teach our children the truth about the "age" issue.

Lesson Time

Welcome and Review

Welcome students to class, open in prayer, etc. Review the memory verse from last week.

We've been learning how to answer questions that people ask about what the Bible teaches.

<u>Illustration 15-00</u>. **We've learned about God and the Bible, and today we're going to learn about the past.**

We Need an Eyewitness

<u>Illustration 15-01</u>. To introduce the lesson, show this illustration. Ask, **What do you think happened here? What happened to this village?** Allow various answers, then say (note: you can either explain this yourself or have the children read the back of the student handout), **Well, those are all good guesses, but I happen to have a written account of what really happened.**

The explanation goes like this: A few years ago, a man in India owned an elephant named Madhubala. He kept her chained to a tree. A bull elephant was wandering by one day and spotted her. It was love at first sight for the elephants. The bull elephant refused to leave Madhubala until the villagers began tossing firecrackers and flaming sticks at it. The elephant got angry and charged into the jungle. Later, he snuck back to Madhubala and broke her chains, and they both ran away. The owner wasn't happy about his missing elephant, so he tracked her down and brought her back to the village. This was a bad move on his part because the bull elephant soon showed up to claim his true love. He roared through the village in a rage, ramming through huts, tearing down anything in his way, and causing the people to run into the jungle. He freed Madhubala again, and the two ran off, never to return. That's an amazing story, isn't it? (Reference: www.snopes.com/critters/gnus/jumboluv.asp.)

Now, even if we did scientific tests on the jungle huts and detected some elephant blood in the wreckage or other things like that, we probably still wouldn't be able to figure out what really happened. The only way we could know what really happened is if we had a reliable eyewitness tell us what he saw.

In the same way, even though we can study the earth and the universe today, we can't use our scientific findings to figure out what happened in the past—or how long ago it happened—since we weren't there.

Illustration 15-02. For example, the fossils we find of dinosaurs or other animals don't come with attached tags saying how old they are.

Illustration 15-03. We can try to make up stories about what we *think* happened to them and when, but unless we have an eyewitness account to rely on, it will be impossible for us to know *exactly* what happened and when it happened.

Many people make statements about the beginning of the universe, claiming they know exactly when and how it all began. However, since they were not there, these statements are only stories of their beliefs about the past. There is only One alive today who was there in the beginning. Who was that? Right—God! And He tells us how He created and what has happened since then in His written Word, the Bible.

Last week we learned that the Bible is trustworthy. Who can remember some reasons why we can trust the Bible? (The Bible claims to be the Word of God, it is scientifically and archaeologically accurate, its prophecies have been fulfilled, its message changes lives, it has withstood the "test of time," and so on.) Who can quote last weeks memory verse, 2 Peter 1:20–21?

Calculating the Age of the Earth

How many of you have heard that the universe is billions of years old and that dinosaurs died out millions of years ago? Wait for answers. **I'm sure we've all heard that at one time or another—maybe from the movies or on TV or from our teachers at school. However, what you've heard isn't true. Today, we're going to learn the truth about how old the earth and universe are, by studying the Bible—the true history book of the universe.**

<u>Illustration 15-04</u>. **To do this, we'll each need some paper, a pencil, our Bibles, and our handouts.** (You may want to do the exercise on something large, such as a chalkboard, white board, or large piece of paper, so that the whole class can see and follow along, or use <u>Illustrations 15-05–15-11</u>.) **Turn to the front of your handout, and then make three columns on your paper labeled "verse," "event," and "age of earth (in years)," like this** (<u>Illustration 15-05</u> or demonstrate on the board). [Note: This chart is modeled after the one found in the article, "The Forgotten Archbishop." The link for this article can be found at the online Teacher's Resource Page.]

Okay, the very first event the Bible talks about is what? Right—God created in six days. Copy the first line from your handout onto your paper.

<u>Illustration 15-06</u>. **Now, we need to turn to Genesis 5. This chapter gives us the ages of Adam's descendants when each of their sons was born. So we'll add these up.** Go through the list found in Genesis 5, and write down the verse, name of the man, and his age when his son was born.

<u>Illustration 15-07</u>. **Now, let's do the same thing for the list in Genesis 11.**

<u>Illustration 15-08</u>. [Note that Abraham was not Terah's firstborn. Genesis 12:4 says Abraham was 75 when he left Haran—soon after Terah died at 205 (Genesis 11:32), and the difference (205–75) means Terah was actually 130 years old when Abraham was born, not 70. The latter figure refers to Terah's age when the oldest of the three sons mentioned was born, probably Haran.] **Abraham left Haran when he was 75.**

Then his descendants (the Israelites) stayed in Canaan and Egypt for a long time— remember that the children of Israel eventually became the slaves of the Egyptians until Moses delivered them? How long were they there? Have one child look up Exodus 12:40, and another Galatians 3:17. **Right—430 years. So we'll add that event to our list.**

<u>Illustration 15-09</u>. **Then Moses delivered them, and they went back to the Promised Land and lived there under the judges. Then they asked for a king, and Saul was chosen. He**

was replaced by David, followed by David's son Solomon. **When God allowed Solomon to build a temple, how many years was it after Israel left Egypt?** Look up 1 Kings 6:1 (It was in the 480th year, so it would have been 479 *full* years). **479 full years.**

Then the kingdom was divided between Solomon's son Rehoboam and Jeroboam, one of Solomon's officials, 37 years later. See 1 Kings 11:42. [Note: Solomon reigned 40 total years, but started building the temple in the third year of his reign, so 40–3=37.]

And then the Israelites were ruled by kings, and eventually the nation was taken into captivity because of their disobedience, and Jerusalem was destroyed 390 years later. See Ezekial 4:4–6. **From history, we know this happened around 584 BC.**

Illustration 15-10. **Our total so far is 4,003 years from the beginning of history. Our current calendar assumes that Jesus was born around 2,010 years ago** (His birth probably occurred around 5 or 6 BC, however), **so when we add 2,010** [please modify this date accordingly] **to 4,003, we get 6,013!**

Illustration 15-11. **So, the universe and the earth are around 6,013 years old—definitely** *not* **millions of years! Since God always tells the truth, we can trust His account of history (the Bible) to give us an accurate idea of how old the earth is!**

Review and Prayer

Let's go over our memory verse for this week: Isaiah 40:8. Review the memory verse with your students. Pray with them, thanking God that we can trust His Word to tell us the truth.

Discussion Questions

1. What do we need in order to figure out what happened in the past?

   Answer: A reliable eyewitness account

2. Why should we trust the Bible to tell us the truth about the past?

   Answer: Because God wrote it—He has always been there from the beginning and always tells the truth.

Activity Ideas

1. Science is a wonderful tool but it is limited when it comes to uncovering the past. The best way to figure out what happened in the past is to rely on an eyewitness account. *Science and the Bible*, volumes 1–3 (available from www.AnswersBookstore.com), offers great simple science experiments that you can conduct if you have the time.

Lesson 15

Extension Activities

Science

Spend some time studying the nature of science, the difference between operational science and origins science, and why science can only develop within a biblically-based worldview. Research some Bible-believing scientists of the past and present. For help, see the "Get Answers: Science" section of the AiG website and "Creation Scientists and Other Biographies of Interest" at the online Teacher's Resource Page (www.AnswersInGenesis.org/go/AnswersForKids).

History

To your timeline, add the dates you calculated in this lesson. Label the beginnings of some of the major civilizations: Egypt, Greece, Israel, China, etc. See the "Get Answers: History" section of the AiG website for help (the link to this section can be found at the online Teacher's Resource Page). James Ussher's *Annals of the World* (translated into English) makes for some interesting study and would be a helpful resource, as well. For an already completed timeline, see *Adams' Chart of History*. Both of these resources are available from www.AnswersBookstore.com.

Recommended Resources

Annals of the World (book for high school–adult)

Adams' Chart of History (chart for all ages)

Chronology of the Old Testament (book for high school–adult)

Science and the Bible, volumes 1–3 (books for children)

Available from www.AnswersBookstore.com, or call 1-800-778-3390.

Did God Create in 6 Days?

Scripture

Genesis 1

Memory Verse

Exodus 20:11

Visuals & Materials

Crayons/colored pencils; from CDs: Illustrations 16-00–16-03, L16a (one copy for each child), Memory Verse graphic, *In Six Days* (song)

Lesson Truths

- God created the universe in six ordinary days
- *Yom*, the Hebrew word for "day," means an ordinary day in the context of Genesis 1
- The earth is approximately 6,000 years old, not billions of years old

Preparation

1. Read "Did Jesus Say He Created in Six Days?" at the online Teacher's Resource Page (www.AnswersInGenesis.org/go/AnswersForKids)
2. Study the Scripture passage for this week
3. Review the lesson before class so that you are familiar with the content
4. Pray that your students will understand the necessity of believing in six literal days of creation

Lesson 16

Lesson Overview

Many Christians, in accommodating the secular "billions of years" idea about the age of the universe, attempt to fit the long ages somewhere in the beginning chapters of Genesis. Some do this by lengthening the days of Genesis 1 from normal-length days into periods of millions of years. However, this approach does not deal fairly with the Hebrew text, which clearly indicates that God created in six actual 24-hour days. Most churched children will already know how long God took to create, but they may not understand *how* they know—this lesson explores the Hebrew basis for "six days," and summarizes what God created on each day.

Lesson Time

Welcome and Review

Welcome students to class, open in prayer, etc. Review the memory verse from last week.

Over the past few weeks, we've learned how to answer questions like "Is there really a God?" "How do you know God wrote the Bible?" and "How old is the earth?" Today we're going to learn to answer a question about the days of creation.

Illustration 16-00. Have the students turn to Genesis 1 in their Bibles. They can follow along as you read Genesis 1 out loud, or you can have each student read several verses, or assign one student to be the "narrator" while another student reads what God says.

The Meaning of Day

After you've finished reading, ask, **Based on what we've just read, how long did God take to create?** Wait for answers, which should be "six days." If they say seven, remind them that He created in six days and rested on the seventh. Ask, **How do you know that?** Because that's what the Bible says. **But how do you know that each day was actually normal-length? What if they were really millions of years long?** Wait for answers: but it says six *days*.

But the word *day* can have different meanings—and it can sometimes refer to long periods of time. For example, look at this sentence and tell me the different ways *day* is used.

Illustration 16-01. Wait for them to answer. **The first "day" refers to the period of time when my grandfather lived, right? And the second "day" means actual 24-hour periods. The third "day" refers to the daylight portion of the day, right? So, the word *day* can mean different things.**

So, how do we know that Genesis 1 talks about real days? In fact, some people say that the days mentioned in Genesis 1 actually refer to long periods of time—millions of years. Today, we're going to learn one way to respond to these people to show them that the Bible means what it says. To do this, we need to learn just a little bit about the language the Old Testament was originally written in.

Who remembers who compiled the book of Genesis? Some may say God; if so, point out, Well, ultimately, God wrote the whole Bible, but whom did God use to write Genesis? Right—Moses! Now, Moses didn't speak English like we do. He was a Jew who spoke the Hebrew language—and that's the language he used to write his books. When Moses wrote Genesis, he chose a specific word to talk about the creation days.

The Meaning of Yom

Illustration 16-02. **This is what the Hebrew word for day looks like. Can anyone tell me how to say this? Well, it's pronounced** *yom* (rhymes with "home"), **and it's read from right to left. And just like with the English word for "day,"** *yom* **can mean different things.**

Illustration 16-03. **Can you see all the different meanings that** *yom* **has? In order to figure out what** *yom* **means in a certain passage, we need to look at the words around it—the context. Now, every time** *yom* **is used with a number elsewhere in the Old Testament, it always refers to an ordinary day.**

Let's look at how "day" is used in Genesis 1. Look at verses 5, 8, 13, 19, 23, and 31, and point out that each time, a number is used with "day."

Every time *yom* **is used with the phrase "evening and morning," it always means an ordinary day. Is "day" used with this phrase at all in Genesis 1?** Wait for them to look at the verses (5, 8, 13, 19, 23, 31). **Yes, it is—in fact, "day" is used with both a number** *and* **the phrase "evening and morning" each time Moses uses it, except where he refers to the daylight portion of the day in verse 5. So, we can be confident that God created in six actual days—not millions of years or over long indefinite periods of time—because the Bible tells us so. And actually, there are other words that Moses could have used if he had wanted to indicate that it was other than an ordinary day.**

Emphasize to the students that God could have created in six seconds, six years, six million years, or in no time at all. But He tells us He did it in six days, so we should believe what He says and not try to tell God how He did it.

Lesson 16

What God Created

Now we're going to go over briefly what God created on each of these days. Pass out the copies of L16a. Children can keep their Bibles open to Genesis 1 in case they need help remembering what God created on each day. [Note: This activity will take about 10–15 minutes—adapt it as you have time. These drawings don't need to be complicated. See "How to Draw the Six Days of Creation" at the online Teacher's Resource Page for ideas on how to do this activity. You can draw this along with the children, either on a board or onto an overhead transparency. Or, we have provided a video file of the basic drawings, which you can play on your computer. See the instructions on the Teacher Resource CD-ROM.]

Who can tell me the first verse in the Bible? Wait for someone to respond. **Right. Let's say it together—"In the beginning, God created the heavens and the earth." So let's write a number 1 in this circle, and then draw a circle—for the earth. What else did God create on the first day? Right—light. So we'll draw some light rays in this corner. And evening and morning were the first day, and God said everything was good.**

On the second day, God took the watery blob that was the earth, separated the waters above from the waters below. This was the day that God created the *atmosphere* **in between the waters above and below. Who knows what the atmosphere is?** Allow them to answer, if they know. **Everyone take a deep breath. That stuff that you just breathed in is part of the atmosphere that God created for us. He knew that when He created the living things a few days later, they would need to be able to breathe. So, put a number 2 in this circle, and draw the waters below, and put a few clouds in the sky to show the atmosphere.**

On the third day, God said, "Let dry ground appear." So let's put a 3 in this circle and draw some dry ground. And then what did God create on the ground? Wait for answers. **Right—plants and trees of all kinds. So let's draw some plants and trees. Perhaps add some grass and a few flowering plants. He created the plants and trees because He knew that the living things would need something to eat.**

[Note: A different colored marker would be nice for this half of the lesson, especially if you've only used one color up to this point. A second color makes it possible to separate what was made on the first three days from those things made on the last three days of creation.]

On the fourth day, what did God create? Wait for answers. **Right—the sun** (draw it near the number one)**, moon** (a small circle on the opposite side of the earth from the sun)**, stars** (draw little "asterisk"-type stars around in space) **and planets** (draw small circles around in space—you can put rings on Saturn and make Jupiter a little larger than the other planets, and so on)**. And don't forget to put the number 4 in this circle.**

On the fifth day—let's put a 5 in this circle—God said, "Let the air bring forth living creatures." What kinds of animals live in the air? Let them answer—be sure they know this includes flying reptiles like pterodactyls and flying mammals like bats. Little m's are sufficient to represent flying creatures (unless you're a proficient artist!)—you can make them different colors to represent the different colors of birds. **And God said, Let the waters bring forth living creatures. What types of animals live in the water?** Let them respond (e.g., whales, octopi, starfish, coral, sea turtles, plesiosaurs, sharks and trout). Be sure they know this includes swimming reptiles like plesiosaurs. Fish are easy to draw, along with an octopus (circle with eight lines), jellyfish (circle with squiggly lines coming off the bottom of the circle), etc.

Let's put a 6 in this circle and talk about what God created on the sixth day. God said, "Let the earth bring forth animals after their kind." What kinds of animals live on the land? Allow them to respond (e.g., dinosaurs, lizards, cats, dogs, rabbits, deer, bears, sheep, cattle and elephants). Be sure they know this list includes dinosaurs. Draw a simple dog and dinosaur. **And then God took dust and created His most special creation—right, Adam! And then He took Adam's rib and created . . . Eve, right!** Draw two stick figures. Give the children time to finish drawing. Feel free to add any animals that you want to. Don't worry about not being an artist—have fun with this (laugh at your own drawings), and the kids will, too. **And God looked at His completed creation and said everything is what? Right—"very good"!**

Lesson 16

Review and Prayer

Review the memory verse for this week: Exodus 20:11. Pray with your students, praising God for His wonderful creation.

Discussion Questions

1. What does Exodus 20:11 say about how long God took to create?

   Answer: It says He created everything in six days.

2. What does the Bible teach about the length of the creation days?

   Answer: It teaches that they were regular-length—approximately 24 hours long.

3. Why did God create in six days and rest for one?

   Answer: It was a pattern for us to follow—to work for six days and rest for one.

4. What is the Hebrew word that God used for the word *day*?

   Answer: *Yom*

Activity Ideas

1. Have the students read the "Think about it!" section in the student handout, and then do the word search.

Extension Activities

Language

Children are able to learn other languages relatively quickly. Find out if there are any elders or others in your church (or elsewhere) who are familiar with the Hebrew and Greek languages, and ask them if they would be willing to teach you some of the basics (perhaps just the alphabet) of each language.

Recommended Resources

The Answers Book for Kids, volume 1 (book for children)

Six Short Days, One Big Adventure! (DVD for children)

The Six Days of Creation (DVD for high school–adult)

Available from www.AnswersBookstore.com, or call 1-800-778-3390.

Notes

How About a Date? part 1

Scripture

Psalm 33

Memory verse

Psalm 33:6

Lesson Truths

- Many people believe the earth is billions of years old because they reject the Bible's history
- Carbon dating is used to "date" once-living things as tens of thousands of years old
- There are many problems with carbon dating

Visuals & Materials

Optional: A small living plant, a rock, a fossilized bone
Optional: Fruits and vegetables—you can use them as a snack during or after class.
Optional: examples of headlines (discussing "millions of years") from your local paper or school textbooks
From CDs: Illustrations 17-00–17-10, Memory Verse graphic, *I Believe* (song)

Preparation

1. Read "Doesn't Carbon-14 Dating Disprove the Bible?" at the online Teacher's Resource Page (www.AnswersInGenesis.org/go/AnswersForKids)
2. Study the Scripture passage for this week
3. Review the lesson before class so that you are familiar with the content
4. Pray that your students will understand that God is Creator and will glorify Him by believing in His Word

Lesson 17

Lesson Overview

We've learned in previous lessons that the Bible teaches that God created in six days approximately 6,000 years ago. But the majority of the world insists that the earth is millions and billions of years old because they reject what the Bible teaches. One of the main methods used to determine the age of once-living things is carbon dating. To determine the ages of igneous (volcanic) rocks and the associated sedimentary rocks, other radiometric methods are used. However, there are assumptions involved in each of these methods, and these methods are known not to work on rocks of known ages. This lesson (and the following one), while a bit on the technical side, will teach your students how the methods are supposed to work, what assumptions are involved in the various methods, and how the Word of God can be trusted.

Lesson Time

Welcome and Review

Welcome students to class, open in prayer, etc. Review the memory verse from last week.

Ask, **Who can tell me how old the earth is?** Wait for someone to answer. **Right—we learned a few weeks ago that God created it around 6,000 years ago. And who can tell me how long it took God to create?** Wait for answers—six days. **Right—how do you know that?** Wait for answers—because God used the Hebrew word *yom*, which, in context, refers to actual days. **We've learned to answer these questions over the past few weeks.**

Illustration 17-00. **Now we're going to learn how to answer another question that people have.**

Millions of Years

I have here a picture of some newspaper clippings that tell a very different story about the age of the earth.

Illustration 17-01. Have some of the students read what the headlines say. **Millions of years is a long time, isn't it? Much, much longer than 6,000 years.**

Illustration 17-02 (point out all the zeroes behind the "1" and compare that to the number of zeroes behind the "6").

Why do you think people have come up with ages different from what the Bible teaches? Wait for answers. **Because they don't believe the Bible—that's right. They want to figure out things on their own. Since they don't believe the Bible's account of the history of the**

universe, they've come up with other ways to confirm their ideas of how old things are and when things happened in the past.

The world believes that rocks and fossils formed over millions of years. The next two weeks, we're going to examine some of the methods used to find ages for things like bones and rock layers so that, when you read things like this (Illustration 17-01), either in the newspaper or in school books, you'll know the truth behind the reports. To do this, we're going to learn a little about geology and a little about chemistry. We'll answer the question "What is carbon dating?"

Dating Methods

First, let me ask you a question. What is the difference between these two things?

Illustrations 17-03. Show this illustration or bring in a rock and a fossilized bone if you have access to them. Wait for answers—try to get them to say that the bone was once part of something that was once alive, while the rock was never alive. **Right—the bone was part of an animal that was once alive, but the rock was never living. Seems kind of basic, doesn't it? But it's important to realize the difference because one method is used to find a date for once-living things—that's the one we'll talk about today, while another method is used to find an age for rocks—we'll talk about that one next class time.**

First, though, let's review.

Illustration 17-04. **We mentioned before that when scientists dig up a bone, they don't find tags attached saying, "Hi! I'm 65 million years old." There are lots of instruments scientists can use to figure out other things, such as how much the bone weighs, its color, what types of chemicals are in it and its size. But there isn't an instrument that a scientist can stick into a bone to directly measure how old it is.**

Instead, they use some guesswork and a method called carbon dating.

How Carbon Dating Works

Carbon is a substance that is found in all living things (including humans and animals)—it's the black stuff that's left over after you burn wood. Diamonds are made of carbon. The graphite in your pencils is, too. Carbon comes in different forms. One form occurs naturally and is called carbon-12. Another type of carbon forms today primarily in the atmosphere from processes acting on nitrogen, and is called carbon-14. Both of these combine with oxygen to form carbon dioxide, which we breathe out—everyone breathe out—and which plants take in.

<u>Illustration 17-05.</u> Show this illustration or display your living plant and fruits and vegetables. **Okay, you can breathe in again now.**

When a cow, for instance, eats grass or when we eat fruits and vegetables, our bodies absorb the carbon (both carbon-12 and carbon-14) in the plant.

<u>Illustration 17-06.</u> Allow children to start eating fruits and veggies, if you want. **We continue to do this as long as we're living and eating. However, when the cow dies, it stops taking in carbon.**

<u>Illustration 17-07.</u> **Why? Right, because it stops eating! Now, the amount of carbon-12 in the cow's body stays the same after death, but the amount of carbon-14 decreases, because it turns back into nitrogen. As time goes on, the amount of carbon-14 continues to decrease until nothing is left, which is supposedly around 50,000 years later.**

<u>Illustration 17-08.</u> **When a paleontologist finds the bone of the cow (or any other animal), she can measure the amounts of carbon-12 and carbon-14 it contains. Based on how much carbon-14 is left and how much carbon-12 is present, she can supposedly calculate when the animal died. Does that make sense to you? Any questions so far?**

Wait for questions and try to answer them, if you're able. If not, tell them you'll get back to them with the answer next week, and feel free to email AiG at info2@AnswersInGenesis.org (or visit the "Get Answers: Radiometric Dating" section of the AiG website. You can find a link at the online Teacher's Resource Page at www.AnswersinGenesis.org/go/AnswersForKids).

Problems With Carbon Dating

So, this sounds like a good way to figure out the ages of bones or plants, doesn't it? But, there are some problems. Can you think of anything that might cause a problem with this method? Wait for answers, if they offer any.

Okay, well, one problem is that plants can tell the difference between carbon dioxide with carbon-12 and carbon dioxide with carbon-14. They don't like the carbon-14 as much, so they don't take in as much of it as we might expect. And different plants take in different amounts.

<u>Illustration 17-09.</u> **So, if there wasn't as much carbon-14 in the plant, or animal that ate the plant, when it died as the scientist assumed, what would this do to the apparent age? It would change it. In fact, it would make it appear as if more carbon-14 had decreased than actually did, so the bone or leaf would appear *older* than it really is.**

Any event or happening that changes the amount of carbon-14 or carbon-12 will affect the apparent age of an animal that lives or dies around the time of the event. Now, when this is understood, a scientist can try to interpret the result of the dating technique within a biblical time frame, but the results cannot be used to *prove* the age of once-living things.

<u>Illustration 17-10</u>. So, the next time you read a headline like this or read something in your textbooks, you can know that they're not telling the truth, and that God's Word is the true history of the universe.

Read Psalm 33 with your students. Discuss with them that God is the sovereign Creator, and that it is He who upholds the universe by His power. Rather than inventing our own ideas about the world, we should submit ourselves to God and His Word.

Review and Prayer

Next week, we'll discuss how scientists attempt to find the age of rocks.

Review the memory verse for this week: Psalm 33:6. Pray with your students.

Discussion Questions

1. Why do people say the earth is millions or billions of years old?

    Answer: Some may not know what the Bible teaches; others simply don't want to listen to what the Bible teaches.

2. What is the element that we talked about today that is in all living things?

    Answer: Carbon

3. What are the two forms of carbon we talked about?

    Answer: Carbon-12 and carbon-14

4. What happens to the carbon-14 in an animal or plant after it dies?

    Answer: It converts back into nitrogen.

5. What are some things we can do when we read things that talk about "millions of years"?

    Answer: You may want to write a polite letter to the editor of the paper or textbook, explaining the truth about radiometric dating methods (perhaps enclosing an article or two from the AiG website). What other ideas can you think of?

Lesson 17

Activity Ideas

1. Bring in some "hour glasses" from the kitchen and table games, with different times (30 seconds, 1 minute, 30 minutes, etc.). Before class, let the sand fall a variety of distances (and lay down the glasses so that no more falls until your activity). Then set up the glasses in front of the class and ask the students to guess how long the sand has been falling.

   When they're done guessing, tell them they're all "wrong" because they were *assuming* that the top began full and they were *assuming* that the sand falls at the same rate. But what if they don't know how much sand there was at the beginning, and what if the sand fell at different rates in the past? Modern carbon dating has the same problem. They don't know about the levels and rates of change before, during and after the Flood.

Extension Activities

Math (for older children)

Spend some time discussing ratios (for appropriate ages).

Botany

Spend some time studying the plant cycle: how plants contribute oxygen to the air and how they absorb carbon dioxide. See unit 3 of *Exploring the World Around You*

Geology

Study how diamonds form. For more information, see "Diamonds—Evidence of Explosive Geological Processes" at the online Teacher's Resource Page.

Recommended Resources

Dinosaurs of Eden (book for children)

Does Carbon Dating Disprove the Bible? (booklet for high school–adult)

Dry Bones and Other Fossils (book for children)

Exploring the World Around You (book for children)

Available from www.AnswersBookstore.com, or call 1-800-778-3390.

Lesson 18

How About a Date? part 2

Scripture

2 Peter 3:1–7

Memory Verse

2 Peter 3:5–6

Visuals & Materials

Candle—burned for an hour or two before class time, and burning before class begins; from CDs: Illustrations 18-00–18-14, Memory Verse graphic, *I Believe* (song)

Lesson Truths

- Experiments in the present can't figure out what happened in the past; we need an eyewitness for that
- Radiometric dating is used to "date" rocks to millions of years old
- Radiometric dating methods have many problems, and rocks of recent origin have been "dated" at millions of years

Preparation

1. Read "Does Radiometric Dating Prove the Earth Is Old?" at the online Teacher's Resource Page (www.AnswersInGenesis.org/go/AnswersForKids)
2. Study the Scripture passage for this week
3. Review the lesson before class so that you are familiar with the content
4. Pray that your students will believe God's Word and not be taken captive by man's philosophies and ideas

Lesson 18

Lesson Overview

We've learned in previous lessons that the Bible teaches that God created in six days approximately 6,000 years ago. But the majority of the world insists that the earth is millions and billions of years old because they reject what the Bible teaches. One of the main methods used to determine the age of once-living things is carbon dating. To determine the ages of igneous (volcanic) rocks and the associated sedimentary rocks, other radiometric methods are used. However, there are assumptions involved in each of these methods, and these methods are known not to provide accurate ages for rocks of known ages. This lesson (like the previous one), while a bit on the technical side, will teach your students how the methods are supposed to work, the assumptions involved in the various methods, and the trustworthiness of the Word of God.

Lesson Time

Welcome and Review

Warning: Never leave a burning candle unattended, and do not allow children near the candle.

The night before class begins, burn the candle (preferably a taper candle) in a candle holder for an hour or two, enough so that the wax begins to drip down the sides and starts to pool in the holder. Then, before class starts, light the candle and set it in a safe place—out of reach of the children. When class begins, carefully set the candle in front of you.

Welcome students to class, open in prayer, etc. Review the memory verse from last week.

A Burning Candle

Who can tell me when this candle started burning? Wait for answers. **It's hard to tell, isn't it, since you haven't been around the whole time it's been burning, right? But you know that it's been burning at least since class started, because you've observed it burning since you got here. Do you think you could figure out how long it's been burning? How?** Wait for answers: measure how fast it's burning now, how much wax is dripping down the side, and how much is in the holder, and then calculate.

Right—by conducting some scientific experiments *in the present* we can try to figure out what happened in the past. However, because you weren't there when the candle started burning, you can't know for sure what happened, right? For instance, what if the candle burned faster in the past? Would that change your conclusion? Or what if the flame were blown out and then relit—would that change your ideas on when it

started burning? Or what if some of the dripping wax has been scraped off, or added? That would also affect your conclusion, wouldn't it? And a breeze would make the candle drip faster.

What you need is an eyewitness—someone who was there when the candle was lit, and who has been around the whole time the candle has been burning to observe it. In fact, *I* am an eyewitness to the burning candle. I lit it last night and let it burn for two hours, then blew it out, and then lit it again right before class! So it's been burning for about two hours—but not all at the same time.

Illustration 18-00. Today we're going to continue our study of the age of the earth that we started last week. Just as we studied the candle to try to figure out how long it has been burning, scientists study certain kinds of rocks to try to figure out how long they've been around. Today, we're going to learn how they do this.

Listening to God's Word

For a long time—in fact, beginning with the first two people, Adam and Eve—people have chosen not to listen to the Word of God. How did Adam and Eve choose not to listen to God's Word? Wait for answers. Right—Adam chose to disobey God's command to not eat from the Tree of the Knowledge of Good and Evil. Ever since that time, people have tried to figure out things on their own. They refuse to read and study and listen to God's Word.

In fact, our Scripture passage for today talks about some of these people. Have students look up 2 Peter 3 and read verses 1–7. What do these verses teach us about those who deny what God says? Right—they *choose* to do so—they are *willingly ignorant*. Let's memorize verses 5 and 6. Go over these verses with your students.

Illustration 18-01. We've learned that the Bible is the history book of the universe, remember? It gives us the history of the universe that God chose to let us know. And a few weeks ago, we learned that the universe is how old? Wait for answers. Right—about 6,000 years old.

But some people refuse to learn from the history book of the universe, and instead choose to make up their own history. These people believe the universe is billions of years old; that's a long time—much, much longer than 6,000 years. They believe that it takes a very long time for rocks and fossils to form. In order to support their ideas, they've come up with methods that supposedly give results that say the earth really *is* billions of years old. Today we're going to learn what's wrong with these methods.

Measuring Age

<u>Illustration 18-02</u>. Last time, we talked about carbon dating—a method used on bones and other remains of things that were once alive. But carbon dating can give ages of up to a few thousand years at most. Today, we're going to investigate the methods that supposedly show *rocks* are millions and billions of years old, and we're going to figure out what's wrong with these methods. Now this gets a bit technical, but I'm sure we'll be able to understand it.

<u>Illustration 18-03</u>. First, let's start with an easy question. Who can tell me what this is? Wait for answers. **Right—a volcano. Now, when a volcano erupts, it releases hot molten rock called what?** Wait for answer. **Right—lava. The lava comes from deep inside the earth, and after it leaves the volcano it eventually hardens into rock. The lava is made of some special elements that are radioactive. This means that one type of element changes into another. And we can measure how long it takes for one element to change into another.**

<u>Illustration 18-04</u>. **It's kind of like this glass—the white sand in the top changes into blue sand as it passes through this section of the glass. Let's say we find this glass in a room, and it has this much white sand and this much blue sand** (point to the illustration), **and we want to know how long ago the sand started changing. How do you think we could figure it out?** Wait for students to answer.

Well, we need to do some detective work, since we don't have a tool that can directly measure the glass's age. For instance, we could measure the rate the sand is currently changing, right? And then we could measure how much blue sand there is, and how much white sand, and based on those measurements, we could figure out how long it's been changing.

Seems pretty simple, doesn't it? However, since we haven't been around since the sand started changing, we don't know its history.

<u>Illustration 18-05</u>. **For example, what would happen to the age if someone added blue sand to the bottom at the beginning?** Wait for answers.

<u>Illustration 18-06</u>. **If there is more blue sand in the bottom, then it would seem that the sand has been changing longer than it actually has, right? And what would happen if in the past, the sand changed faster? Right—it would again seem older than it is.**

Radiometric Dating

Now, let's get back to lava. When the lava hardens into rock, the special elements inside it begin to change.

Illustration 18-07. Scientists can measure how long it takes for the first element "a" to change into "b." In some cases, the change is very slow. It would take millions of years for half of "a" to change into "b" at today's rates. The scientists then measure how much of "a" and "b" are in a rock sample. Based on those measurements, they supposedly can figure out how long the rock has been around, right?

Well, just like with our hourglass, there are things we don't know about the rock, since we weren't around when it formed. For instance, what if "a" changed into "b" a lot faster in the past? Or what if a lot of "b" were already in the rock when it formed? Both of these things would make the rock seem a lot older than it really is, wouldn't they? In fact, creation scientists have discovered evidence that indicates that the change rates were actually much faster in the past! And they've also found out that in some cases, a lot of element "b" was in the rock when it formed!

Dating Errors

What happens when we test this method on rocks that we already know the age of?

Illustration 18-08. Mount St. Helens blew its top in the early 1980s. How long ago was that? Right—over 25 years ago. A few years ago, some scientists took some rock samples from these explosions and had them tested. And the results were that the rocks were between 340,000 and over 2 million years old! Something's wrong, isn't it?

Another scientist arranged for some tests on rocks from a volcano in New Zealand that erupted around 50 years ago. The results of those tests were that the rocks were over 3 million years old! Something is even more wrong, isn't it?

Illustration 18-09. So, the next time we hear that something is so many millions of years old—maybe on the news, in the newspaper, or in our textbooks—we can know that those ages aren't correct. Just as we needed an eyewitness to figure out the burning candle mystery, we need an eyewitness to tell us about the past.

Illustration 18-10. The Bible is the true history book of the universe, and we can trust it to tell us the truth—that the earth is only around 6,000 years old—not millions.

Review and Prayer

Let's go over our memory verse (2 Peter 3:5–6) for this week again together. You may want to write each word of the verse on a small stone and then have the students put the stones in the correct order. Or, lay the stones out in order and have the children read the verse together, removing one stone after each reading. Pray with your students.

Discussion Questions

1. Review how the radiometric dating methods are supposed to work—use the hourglass illustrations (see "Radiometric Dating: Back to Basics" at the online Teacher's Resource Page).

2. What are the three assumptions behind radiometric dating methods?

   Answer: 1) None of element "b" was present when the rock formed; 2) There was no gain or loss of element "a" or "b"; 3) The rate that element "a" changes into element "b" has been constant.

3. How can we know if what we're learning and hearing from other people is correct?

   Answer: We need to study the Bible and learn what it says and then test what others are saying against what the Bible teaches.

Activity Ideas

1. If you have time during class, you can explore some of the many methods that yield ages more in line with what the Bible teaches—and against the "millions of years" idea (or you can have the students do some research on their own—the "Get Answers: Young Age Evidences" section of the AiG website has a great amount of information. Use the link at the online Teacher's Resource Page).

   We've seen that carbon dating and radiometric dating methods don't say that the earth is millions of years old. When the results are interpreted according to the Bible, these methods confirm the biblical teaching. In fact, there are many other methods that scientists use that also confirm the Bible. Let's take a quick look at some of these.

   a. Salty oceans (<u>Illustration 18-11</u>)—**How many of you have ever been to the ocean?** Wait for answers. **What does ocean water taste like?** Wait for answers—some should know that it's salty. **Right—it's salty, definitely not something you'd want to drink, is it? In fact, the oceans are getting saltier every year. This happens because all of the rivers and underground streams carry salt from the earth into the oceans, and the salt doesn't easily leave the oceans once it's there. The major way the salt leaves the ocean is through the salt spray. Since we can measure how much salt is already in the ocean, and the rate at which the salt is still coming in, we can work out how long the ocean has been around. In fact, scientists have found that the oceans' age is perfectly in line with what the Bible teaches about the age of the earth!** See "When I hear . . ." at the online Teacher's Resource Page for more information.

b. Fast-forming rocks—**We mentioned that some people believe that it takes a long time for rocks to form. However, people have found many examples of fast-forming rock. For example, this clock (**Illustration 18-12**) is completely encased in rock—it didn't take a long time for that rock to form, did it? Probably just a few dozen years at most.**

Illustration 18-13. **And here's a picture of rock that formed inside a pipe in less than three months!**

Examples like these show it doesn't take a long time at all to form rock! See the "Get Answers: Geology" section of the AiG website for more information. A link can be found on the online Teacher's Resource Page (www.AnswersInGenesis.org/go/AnswersForKids).

c. Rapid geological formations—**How many of you have ever been through a cave before?** Wait for answers. **If you have, then you've probably seen stalactites hanging from the ceiling and stalagmites growing up from the floor. The world believes it takes a long time—many thousands of years—for these things to form. However, here's a picture of a stalagmite (**Illustration 18-14**) growing around a bottle that was left in a cave around 50 years ago—didn't take that long, did it?** See the "Get Answers: Caves" section of the AiG website for more information. A link can be found on the online Teacher's Resource Page.

Extension Activities

Geology

Spend some time studying how various rocks form (sedimentary, igneous, metamorphic, etc.). *The Geology Book*, available from www.AnswersBookstore.com, is a helpful resource.

Volcanoes

Spend some time learning about volcanoes: where they're found, what happens during an eruption, the different types of lava, etc.

Recommended Resources

Rock Strata, Fossils, and the Flood (DVD for high school–adult)

The Geology Book (book for high school)

Life in the Great Ice Age (book for children)

Available from www.AnswersBookstore.com, or call 1-800-778-3390.

Notes

Lesson 19

What Is Compromise?

Scripture

Selected passages

Memory Verse

Romans 12:2

Lesson Truths

- Compromise can be a good thing, but compromising the Word of God is never good
- Compromise positions on Genesis undermine the clear teaching of God's Word
- Death entered the world as a result of Adam's sin and is the "last enemy" to be destroyed; it has not always been part of God's "very good" creation

Visuals & Materials

Cup of oil and cup of water—unmixed; from CDs: Illustrations 19-00–19-02, Memory Verse graphic

Preparation

1. Read "Two Histories of Death" at the online Teacher's Resource Page (www.AnswersInGenesis.org/go/AnswersForKids)
2. Study the Scripture passage for this week
3. Review the lesson before class so that you are familiar with the content
4. Pray that God will help your students see the importance of taking His Word as written and not compromise with the ideas of the world

Lesson 19

Lesson Overview

In spite of what the Bible teaches about the age of the earth and the days of creation, many people would rather listen to the teachings of the world. They believe the naturalistic ideas that the earth is billions of years old, and attempt to twist the Bible into teaching this as well. Some throw millions of years in between Genesis 1:1 and 1:2 (the gap theory), others believe the days of Genesis 1 were long periods of time over which God progressively created new creatures (progressive creation), and still others believe God used evolutionary processes to bring about His creation (theistic evolution).

However, there is a serious theological problem with any view that attempts to accommodate the "millions of years" idea with biblical teachings. These views assume that death, disease, and suffering have been a part of the creation from the very beginning—long before humans entered the scene, and therefore before Adam sinned. This removes death as a punishment for sin and thus removes the need for Christ to take away the punishment for our sin—death is no longer the "last enemy" (1 Corinthians 15:26). This lesson explores what compromise is and why it is wrong to use the world's teachings to explain the Bible.

Lesson Time

Welcome and Review

Welcome students to class, open in prayer, etc. Review the memory verse from last week.

The last two weeks we have been talking about how secular scientists try to determine the age of fossils. Many Christians have accepted these ideas despite what the Bible says.

What Is Compromise?

<u>Illustration 19-00</u>. Pass out student handouts. **Today we're going to talk about something called *compromise*.** Choose a student to read the first paragraph about compromise from the front of the student handout. Then have them direct their attention back toward you.

Here's an example of a compromise. Let's say your parents give you and your sister a choice of where you want to go for dinner. You want to go to Pizza Hut, and she wants to go to McDonald's. Your parents give you fifteen minutes to decide, and finally, after discussing it, you both agree on eating at Subway.

Who compromised in this situation? Wait for answers. **Right, both you and your sister compromised.**

What was given up? Wait for answers. **Right—you gave up going to Pizza Hut and your sister gave up going to McDonald's.**

Was there anything wrong with this compromise? Wait for answers. **No, there wasn't anything wrong with the compromise—you both still got to eat, just not at your favorite places.**

Here's another example. Cicily and Theresa are shopping in the mall. They both find some earrings that they really like (or, if you're teaching a class of boys, Kameel and Micah and a small army knife), **but they don't have enough money to buy them. Cicily decides to put a pair in her pocket and urges Theresa to do the same thing. After all, it's only a pair of earrings, she says; nobody will ever miss them. Theresa knows that the Bible teaches stealing is wrong, but after listening to her friend, she decides to also put a pair of the earrings in her pocket and walk out of the store.**

In this situation, who compromised? Wait for answers. **Right, Theresa did.**

What did Theresa give up? Wait for answers. **She gave up what she knew the Bible taught was the right thing to do.**

Was there anything wrong with her compromise? Wait for answers. **Yes, in this situation there was something wrong—she disobeyed God's command and broke the law by taking something that she hadn't paid for and that didn't belong to her.**

Can you think of some times when you had to compromise? Wait for answers. Allow children to role-play some situations they come up with, if you have time.

The First Compromise

Sometimes it's okay to compromise, and sometimes it's not. Let's read about the very first person to compromise. Can anyone guess who that was? Wait for answers. Have the students turn the back of the student handout. Assign individuals to read Romans 5:12; Psalm 119:140; 2 Timothy 3:16–17, and Psalm 119:128, and then have them read the verses as you come to them while you (or someone you assign) read "Do you know when compromise began?"

When we don't follow the Word of God and instead use what the world says, the compromise is wrong and displeases God. The Bible teaches that we shouldn't allow the world to influence us. Let's read our memory verse for today. Have students look up and read Romans 12:2.

Compromising Genesis

Over the past couple months we've learned that the Bible teaches that the earth is only about 6,000 years old and that God created in six actual days. Who remembers the Hebrew word the Bible uses for the word *day?* Wait for answers: *yom*.

However, the world teaches that the earth is millions and billions of years old. And we learned that there are scientific problems with these ideas. Yet some people believe they can combine a belief in the Bible with a belief in the idea that the earth is very old. Today we're going to learn about some ways that people do this and the problems these compromises cause.

We'll need to do some comparisons today, so let's begin by opening our Bibles to Genesis 1. Because the Word of God is perfect, we need to compare everything we hear to what the Bible says.

Literal Days, Not Long Ages

Illustration 19-01. We've already taken a brief look at what happened on each of the six days, and here's a chart showing an overview of the Bible's account of what happened when. Briefly go through the chart with the students.

Illustration 19-02. Now let's take a look at the timeline of those who believe the earth is billions of years old. Briefly go over the chart with the students.

In order to get the Bible to teach that the universe is billions of years old, some people say that the days in Genesis weren't regular-length days. They believe they were long periods of time and that God created different things over those periods to replace other animals that became extinct. Who can tell me what extinction is? Wait for answers. Right—extinction happens when all of a type of animal dies out.

However, we learned in a previous lesson that the days can't be anything other than ordinary-length days because of the words God used to write Genesis 1. So what these people say can't be right, can it? Wait for answers—definitely not.

Different Views of Earth History

Secondly, let's compare the order of each view of history. How is this timeline (Illustration 19-02) different from what the Bible teaches? Let the students discuss the differences.

So, the Bible definitely teaches that God created in six days and that the order of what God created is different from what the world teaches.

Entrance of Death

There's one more very important thing I want you to think about as we compare these two views of history. Take another look at this (Illustration 19-02) **timeline. According to this time, when did things start dying?** Wait for answers—encourage students to see that things began dying right from the beginning—long before humans entered the scene. **Right—death was around long before humans ever entered the scene.**

Now let's look at what the Bible teaches. According to the Bible, why did things start dying? Look up Genesis 2:17 and 3:6, 19, 22–24. Wait for answers—encourage them to see that death began after Adam sinned; in fact, death was the punishment for his sin. **Right— things started dying because Adam disobeyed God's command not to eat from the Tree of Knowledge of Good and Evil—when he compromised. Death was the punishment for his disobedience. In fact, death is the punishment for** *our* **disobedience.** Have someone read Romans 5:12; 6:23. **And it's the reason that Jesus came to Earth and died on the Cross—His death paid the penalty for sin.**

Adam's sin not only affected *humans,* **it also affected the entire world.** Have a student read Romans 8:22. **According to the Bible, after God finished creating, He declared everything to be what?** Wait for answers. **Right—everything was "very good." It was perfect. Do you think God would say that death, diseases (like cancer), and suffering are good things?** No, but those who believe this view of history (Illustration 19-02) believe this. **However, this certainly isn't what the Bible teaches, is it?**

Adam's sin also affected the animals. In the beginning, animals and humans ate plants for their food, rather than each other (Genesis 1:29–30). **And the Bible tells us that in the future, things will be like they were in the beginning. Let's read about what the Bible teaches the animals will be like.** Read Isaiah 11:6–9; 65:25. **That's certainly different from what we see today, isn't it? But those who believe that the earth is millions of years old, believe that animals have always eaten each other. But that's not what the Bible teaches.**

A Bad Compromise

No, it's very clear that those who believe that the Bible teaches the earth is millions of years old have made a bad compromise, haven't they? It's like mixing these two things. Show cup of oil and cup of water. **Let me show you what happens when you try to mix oil and water.** Pour oil into water. **They just don't mix, do they? It's the same with millions of years and the Bible—the two ideas just don't mix. The Bible is clear that the earth is around 6,000 years old and that God created in six actual days. And many scientific experiments confirm this biblical teaching.**

The "millions of years" people are giving up what the Bible says and accepting what the world teaches. The Bible teaches that we shouldn't be caught up with what the world has to say.

Review and Prayer

Review the memory verse for today: Romans 12:2. Pray with your students.

If you have time, you can let them complete the maze on the back of the student handout.

Discussion Questions

1. What is compromise? Is it always a good idea to compromise?

   Answer: Compromise is a settlement of differences in which each side makes a concession. Compromise is often a good idea and helpful when we can't agree on something, but when it comes to the Word of God, Christians must not compromise with unbiblical ideas, such as evolution and millions of years.

2. Why is it wrong to compromise with what the world teaches about the history of the universe?

   Answer: Because it isn't what the Bible teaches—the Bible teaches a completely different view of history. Compromise puts death before Adam sinned. True science confirms the earth is young—not old. We need to allow God's Word to teach us and not try to change it.

3. Why do we experience so much death and suffering in the world today?

   Answer: Adam's sin brought death and suffering into the world, and each of us also sinned, in Adam. Death is the punishment for sin.

Activity Ideas

1. Spend some time researching the various "compromise" positions: gap theory, theistic evolution, progressive creation, day-age idea, etc. Learn what each teaches and the scientific and theological problems associated with each. See the "Get Answers: Creation Compromises" section of the AiG website for additional information. Use the link from the online Teacher's Resource Page.

Recommended Resources

The Great Turning Point (book for high school–adult)

The New Answers Book 1 (book for high school–adult)

Available from www.AnswersBookstore.com, or call 1-800-778-3390.

Answers for Kids
BIBLE CURRICULUM

Lesson 20

Where Did Humans Come From? part 1

Scripture

Genesis 1:24–31
Genesis 2:4–7, 18–24
Psalm 139:13–16

Memory Verse

Psalm 139:14

Visuals & Materials

From CDs: Illustrations 20-00–20-08, L20a, Memory Verse graphic, *I Don't Believe in Evolution* (song)

Lesson Truths

- Secular scientists tell us that humans evolved from ape-like creatures over millions of years
- The Bible tells us that God created animals and man separately, and that man in created in God's image
- We are valuable in God's sight, since we are created in His image

Preparation

1. Read "Man: The Image of God" at the online Teacher's Resource page (www.AnswersInGenesis.org/go/AnswersForKids)
2. Study the Scripture passage for this week
3. Review the lesson before class so that you are familiar with the content
4. Pray that your students will recognize that they are created in God's image and not just highly evolved animals

Lesson 20

Lesson Overview

Either overtly in school or subtly through cartoons and movies, children are taught fairly early that we are related to animals and share a common ancestor with apes. As adults, we often hear in the popular press of a new find that "proves" we came from an ape-like creature. However, the truth is that humans were created by God separately from animals and in His image. This lesson explores the biblical and scientific answers to the question "where did humans come from?" It helps children learn to think critically about secular claims about our past.

Lesson Time

Welcome and Review

Welcome students to class, open in prayer, etc. Review the memory verse from last week.

<u>Illustration 20-00.</u> **How many of you have ever seen the movies** *Ice Age* **or** *Dinosaur*? Allow children to respond.

As much as we may enjoy watching movies and television programs such as these, we need to be aware that they are not telling us the truth about what happened in the past.

<u>Illustration 20-01.</u> **Over the next few weeks we'll be continuing to learn about the true history of the universe that God has revealed to us in the Bible. As we learn about what the Bible and science teach us, we'll find out how to answer many questions that people ask about the past: Where did we come from? What about the dinosaurs? Why do we look so different from each other?**

Different Interpretations of the Same Evidence

Let's start this lesson by thinking about what we've heard about where we come from. Have you ever heard that we share an ancestor with apes and monkeys, or that millions of years ago apemen wandered the earth? Maybe someone has told you that you're just another animal. Allow children to respond. They may have read something in a textbook or seen something on television or in a movie.

In this lesson, we're going to learn what the Bible teaches about where we came from and how we can respond when we hear claims like these.

<u>Illustration 20-02.</u> **First, let's take a look at this picture. How many of you see an old woman in this picture?** Wait for answers. **And how many of you see a young woman?**

Wait for answers. Then point out the old woman and young woman, for those who couldn't see them.

There are two different ways to view this picture, aren't there? It's the same picture, but depending on how you look at it, you can see something different.

The world around us is like that, too. For example, two people can look at the same fossil and come to completely different conclusions about what it means. Note: a fossil is any evidence of past life found in a rock.

This happens because people have different ideas of why the world is the way it is. They believe different things about what happened in the past. There are two main ideas about the history of our universe.

Biblical History

<u>Illustration 20-03.</u> **The first idea comes from the collection of 66 books that we call the Bible. Who wrote the Bible?** Wait for answers. God used over 40 different men to write down what He wanted them to record.

<u>Illustration 20-04.</u> **Let's briefly review the Seven C's of History:**

Creation: God created all things in six actual days around 6,000 years ago. Everything was very good.

Corruption: Adam disobeyed, and his disobedience changed the entire world.

Catastrophe: God sent a globe-covering Flood as a judgment for the sin of mankind.

Confusion: God confused the people's languages at Babel, causing the various family groups to go their separate ways.

Christ: God sent His Son, Jesus Christ, to earth to become a human so that He could live a perfect life in obedience to the Father.

Cross: Jesus died on the Cross for the sin of mankind.

Consummation: One day all things will be "very good" again for those who have received the free gift of eternal life.

<u>Illustration 20-05.</u> **Those who accept this view use the Bible to help them make sense of the world around them.**

Evolutionary View of History

<u>Illustration 20-06.</u> **The other idea comes from those who don't believe the Bible. This view says that the universe came into being on its own, and that countless millions of years ago a single-celled creature appeared on earth. This was supposedly our first ancestor, which we share with all living things. Over the years, this creature's descendants gradually changed into the wide variety of animals and plants that we see today. Eventually, humans came from an ape-like creature.**

<u>Illustration 20-07.</u> **Those who accept this view use evolutionary ideas to help them make sense of the world around them.**

That's a quick summary of the two main ideas about the past. They're very different, aren't they? How do we know which view is the correct one? Allow children to respond.

It would be helpful if someone who witnessed, or who was involved in, past events recorded what happened, wouldn't it?

Do you know anyone who has been around from the beginning, and whom you would trust to tell you the truth? Wait for answers. **Correct—God! God is eternal, which means He doesn't have a beginning or end. He has always existed. And God always tells the truth. So we can trust His account of history to be completely accurate.**

Where has God recorded His account of history? Wait for answers. **Right—in the Bible! So, in order to learn about why the world is the way it is, we need to study the Bible.**

What Does God Say?

Let's take a closer look at how the Bible answers our question for today, "Where did we come from?"

Read Genesis 1:24–31; 2:4–7, 18–24 together.

<u>Illustration 20-08.</u> **The Bible teaches that humans were made in whose image?** We were created in the image of God. We were made in the image of the holy, eternal, Creator God, not in the image of ape-like creatures.

How did God make the animals? He spoke, and the land produced living creatures according to their kinds (Genesis 1:24–25).

Compare that to how God made man. What is different? Allow children to respond. Encourage them to see that God formed man directly from the dust and breathed into him the breath of life (Genesis 2:7), whereas He commanded the earth to bring forth the animals (Genesis 1:24). Note that the Bible teaches that Adam was a special creation of the Lord; Adam was not created from a pre-existing animal.

Another difference between animals and humans is that Eve was created from Adam's side (Genesis 2:21–22). None of the female animals were created from the sides of the male animals. Also, God made humans in His image (Genesis 1:26)—He didn't do this for the animals. An additional point of difference between animals and humans is that, when Jesus came to earth, He came as a man, not an animal, and He died for men, not animals.

So what's the answer to today's question, "Where did humans come from?" We were created by God in His image.

In the Image of God

Read Genesis 1:26–27 again. Ask your students, **What does it mean to be "made in the image of God"?** See "Man: The Image of God" at the online Teacher's Resource Page. Here is an excerpt from the article to help with your discussion:

> The main impact of the image is that God endues man with some of his divine attributes, thereby separating and making him different from the beasts. What are these special Godlike qualities which man is permitted to share? I shall mention six: language, creativity, love, holiness, immortality, and freedom. You will probably be able to add to this list. All can be summed up by saying that man, like God, has an intelligence, a mind.

Review and Prayer

Let's look at our Scripture passage for today, Psalm 139:13–16. Have students read it together, and have them begin memorizing verse 14.

Discussion Questions

1. What do the following Bible verses teach about our purpose on earth? Genesis 1:26; Micah 6:8; Ecclesiastes 12:13.

   Answer: We are to be careful stewards of the earth, its resources and the animals and plants. We are to act justly, love mercy, and walk humbly with God. We are to fear God and keep His commandments. Discuss some practical ways that you and your students can fulfill our God-given purpose on earth.

2. How are humans different from animals?

   Answer: Humans are made in the image of God. We possess the ability to communicate in complex sentences and via the written word, to make tools to create beautiful works of art, to love God and others, to live forever (either in heaven or hell).

Lesson 20

Activity Ideas

1. Read the student handout for this week with your students.

2. Use a tangram to demonstrate the human ability to be creative (one aspect that separates us from animals). See *Science and the Bible*, volume 2, experiment 18 (or look up "tangram" on the Internet). Print L20a and make a copy for each student. Cut the square into seven pieces along the lines. Challenge students to creatively use the pieces to construct different shapes (animals, flowers, letters, numbers, people, etc.), making sure the pieces touch, don't overlap, and lie flat. What else can you find out about how to make a tangram and its history? See also *Tangram Puzzles* (by Chris Crawford), and *Tangrams: 330 Puzzles* (by Ronald Read) for design ideas.

Extension Activities

Language Arts

The ability to speak and write using a complex grammatical system sets us apart from animals. One way that we can express ourselves through writing is poetry. Choose three different types of poetry to study. Have students write a poem in each style on the following topics: the differences between animals and humans, what it means to be created in the image of God, what it means to be fearfully and wonderfully made. For an overview of different types of poetry, see "Types of Poetry?" at the online Teacher's Resource Page.

Recommended Resources

The Answers Book for Kids, volume 1 (book for children)

Bones of Contention (book for older children)

Puzzle of Ancient Man (book for ages 15 and up)

Where Did Humans Come From? part 2

Scripture

Selected passages
Psalm 100

Memory Verse

Psalm 100:3

Visuals & Materials

From CDs: Illustrations 21-00–21-09, L21a, L21b, Memory Verse graphic, *I Don't Believe in Evolution* (song)

Lesson Truths

- Secular scientists tell us that humans evolved from ape-like creatures over millions of years
- The Bible tells us that God created animals and man separately, and that man in created in God's image
- We are valuable in God's sight, since we are created in His image

Preparation

1. Read "Did Humans Really Evolve from Ape-like Creatures?" at the online Teacher's Resource Page (www.AnswersInGenesis.org/go/AnswersForKids)
2. Study the Scripture passage for this week
3. Review the lesson before class so that you are familiar with the content
4. Pray that your students will accept the Bible's history as true

Lesson 21

Lesson Overview

Either overtly in school or subtly through cartoons and movies, children are taught fairly early that we are related to animals and share a common ancestor with apes. As adults, we often hear in the popular press of a new find that "proves" we came from an ape-like creature. However, the truth is that humans were created by God separately from animals and in His image. This lesson explores the biblical and scientific answers to the question "where did humans come from?" It helps children learn to think critically about secular claims about our past.

Lesson Time

Welcome and Review

Welcome students to class, open in prayer, etc. Review the memory verse from last week.

Illustration 21-00. Last week we learned how man was created differently from the animals. We saw that the evolutionary view of history is vastly different from the biblical view. Today, we are going to look more closely at how different humans are from animals, and we'll see that there is a huge gulf between humans and animals.

Some Similarities

Illustration 21-01. The people who believe this evolutionary view of history believe we came from animals, and that we are just another type of animal. They believe that the many similarities between us and apes show that we were once apes. The Bible tells us that we were created in the image of God. We are not just another type of animal. We are fearfully and wonderfully made in the image of God.

Illustration 21-02. It's true that there are some similarities. Let's look at some of them. Discuss some similarities: two eyes, two ears, nose, mouth, teeth, hands with opposable thumbs (thumbs that help us grip an object), arms, legs, heart, stomach, eat some of the same foods, breathe, have backbones, give birth to live young, etc.

The Bible teaches that the same God created animals and humans, doesn't it? So, we might expect to find some of the same types of features among animals and humans. However, the Bible is also clear that God created us differently.

Big Differences

Illustration 21-03. We've already looked at a few ways that the Bible teaches animals and humans are different. Let's look at a few more. **Can you think of any other differences between apes and people?** Apes don't have a complex language system, don't drive cars,

don't build computers, don't make or play musical instruments, and aren't creative. They don't go to church to learn about God, don't have friends over to play board games or watch a television program, don't have birthday parties or celebrate Christmas, can't have a relationship with God, don't choose which outfit to wear, don't go shopping for groceries or new shoes, etc. God gave humans dominion over the animals (Genesis 1:28).

What Does the Bible Say About Communication?

Let's look at what the Bible say about how we are to use our ability to communicate? Have children look up the following passages in a "sword drill." (This is not an exhaustive list—please modify as necessary.) Have the children hold up their Bibles (closed), with one hand on each side of the Bible. Announce the verse, have children repeat it, and say, "Go!" The first child to find the verse stands and reads the verse when called on.

Psalm 16:8–10, 35:27–28, 37:30, 119:171–172, 150:6; Proverbs 4:24, 6:16–19, 10:11, 10:13, 10:19–21, 12:13–14, 12:18–19, 12:22, 13:3, 15:1–2, 15:23, 16:13, 16:23–24, 16:28, 17:27–28, 18:21, 20:19, 21:23, 24:26, 25:11, 26:18–26, 27:2; Ephesians 4:17–32; Colossians 3:1–17; James 3:3–12

Based on these passages, discuss with your students how God communicates with us and how are we to communicate with our Creator.

So-called Apemen

<u>Illustration 21-04.</u> **The people who believe this view of history also believe that they have found evidence that we have evolved from ape-like creatures over millions of years. They claim that they have found bones of supposed "apemen" that show how we've changed over the years.**

<u>Illustration 21-05.</u> **They often use pictures like this to illustrate the evolution of man.**

<u>Illustration 21-06.</u> **But we need to keep in mind that pictures like these are only an illusion. That means that they aren't real. They were drawn by somebody who didn't believe the Bible's account of history.**

<u>Illustration 21-07.</u> **We also need to keep in mind that when people find bones, the bones don't come with attached tags that say, "Hi, I'm an apeman!" The bones need to be carefully studied to find out what type of creature they belonged to.**

Let's take a look at some of the more famous so-called apemen, and find out the truth behind the illusions.

Pass out the student handout for this week and read the "Looking a Little Closer" page together. You may also want to discuss how the movies mentioned previously (*Ice Age,*

Dinosaur, Curious George, or any other movie or television program) portray human ancestors and why this portrayal isn't correct. See the online Teacher's Resource Page for links to movie reviews of *Dinosaur* and *Ice Age.*

If you have time, go over the various so-called "missing links" listed below. What are they now known to be? What other alleged ancestors of humans have you heard about? What have these turned out to be? They have all been shown to be either an ape, a human, or a hoax. (For help, visit the "Get Answers: Anthropology" section of the AiG website. You can find a link on the online Teacher's Resource Page. Or read *Bones of Contention* by Marvin Lubenow, or *Skeletons in Your Closet* by Gary Parker.)

- Cro-Magnon man – an extinct people group of Europe and Eastern Asia; fully human but often misinterpreted as missing links in human evolution

- Piltdown man – fraudulent "prehuman" fossil consisting of the skull cap of a modern human and the jaw and teeth of an orangutan; this hoax fooled the scientific establishment for over 50 years

- Nebraska man – an "apeman" from the 1920s, which consisted of a single tooth; later discovered to be an extinct pig

- *Ardipithecus ramidus* – a quadrupedal ape with relatively little in common with humans

- *Homo habilis* – an alleged transitional form from apes to humans that turns out to be an assemblage of at least three different species, and which resembles Lucy—a small chimp-like creature

- *Homo erectus* – an extinct human people group; fully human but often misinterpreted as missing links in human evolution

- *Ramapithecus* – once widely regarded as the ancestor of humans, it has now been realized that it is merely an extinct type of orangutan (an ape)

Review and Prayer

<u>Illustration 21-08.</u> **The Bible explains the truth about where humans came from, and we can trust it. When we hear something that doesn't agree with what the Bible teaches, we need to closely examine what was actually found. Sometimes, we may need to wait a few years to find out what type of bones they really are, but we can be certain that God's Word—which never changes—is true.**

Read Psalm 100 together. Verse 3 is the memory verse for this week. Pray with your students, thanking God for giving us true history in His Word.

Discussion Questions

1. On which day of the Creation Week did God create apes and monkeys?

   Answer: Day 6—the same day that God created humans.

2. Have scientists found any real "apemen"?

   Answer: No! They have found either apes or men, but nothing in between.

Activity Ideas

1. Read "The Evidence" page from the student handout. The point of this page is that sometimes something we see on television (or read in a book or magazine) might make us doubt whether the Bible is true. But later on, we find that what we were taught was wrong, and we shouldn't have doubted God's Word. Instead, we should have doubted what the people on television or in the book were saying.

2. Take a trip to the zoo and visit the primate enclosure. Look for similarities and differences between the primates (monkeys, chimps, gorillas, etc.) and humans.

3. Print out L21a and L21b. Make copies for children to color.

4. Create a collage based on the similarities and differences between humans and apes that we've learned about. Find pictures (in old magazines, for example) or draw pictures of apes and humans doing activities that accentuate the differences between us and animals. For example, picture of a chimp and a human next to a picture of an airplane—which one would fly the plane? Orangutan and human beside a computer—which one built it? Gorilla and human beside a store—which one goes shopping for clothes and food? Monkey and human beside a church—which one can have a relationship with God? Write across the top of your collage, "I am not just an animal—I was created in the image of God!"

   Some people will point out that both apes and humans use tools (see "Gorillas and Tools?" at the online Teacher's Resource Page). However, only humans use tools to make tools! Additionally, animals throughout the world use tools. What examples of this can you find? Draw or cut out pictures of a variety of animals using tools. Add these to your collage.

   Another difference between humans and apes or monkeys is the shape of our feet (see **Illustration 21-09**). Non-human primates have feet with opposable thumbs (digits used for grasping or climbing). On the collage (or on separate pieces of paper) make prints of each child's hands and feet, using finger paints. Have each child sign and date his prints.

Lesson 21

Extension Activities

History

Find out who may have been behind the famous Piltdown man hoax. Was it Charles Dawson, Sir Arthur Keith, Sir Arthur Conan Doyle, Martin A.C. Hinton, or someone else? Write a short essay detailing your findings.

There have been several other apemen hoaxes in the past. Find out more about the Minnesota Iceman hoax. For help, see the "Get Answers: Anthropology" section of the AiG website (a link can be found at the online Teacher's Resource Page).

Science

There have been some claims that animals have learned to talk. Read the articles on the "Get Answers: Linguistics" section of the AiG website (a link can be found at the online Teacher's Resource Page).

How does the human vocal tract differ from the vocal tract of most animals? See the articles on the vocal tract and larynx using the links at the online Teacher's Resource Page (www.AnswersInGenesis.org/go/AnswersForKids).

Although animals and birds may not communicate as we do, they are able to communicate with others of their kind. Visit the "Get Answers: Design Features" section of the AiG website (a link can be found at the online Teacher's Resource Page). Find out how the following communicate: honey bees, ruffled grouse, chameleons, ants. How do other animals communicate?

Recommended Resources

The Answers Book for Kids, volume 1 (book for children)

Bones of Contention (book for older children)

Puzzle of Ancient Man (book for ages 15 and up)

Have Animals Evolved? part 1

Scripture

Genesis 1:11–13, 20–25

Memory Verse

Genesis 1:25

Visuals & Materials

From CDs: Illustrations 22-00–22-11, L22a, Memory Verse graphic, *I Don't Believe in Evolution* (song)

Lesson Truths

- Secular scientists tell us that all animals have descended from a common ancestor
- The Bible teaches that God created animals to reproduce according to their "kind"
- The study of genetics confirms that animals only reproduce within their kind, and one kind of animal cannot turn into another kind

Preparation

1. Read "Zonkeys, Ligers, and Wolphins, Oh My!" at the online Teacher's Resource Page (www. AnswersInGenesis.org/go/AnswersForKids)
2. Study the Scripture passage for this week
3. Review the lesson before class so that you are familiar with the content
4. Pray that your students will understand that God created animals according to their kind and that they did not evolve from a common ancestor

Lesson 22

Lesson Overview

Children are continually bombarded with the message that evolution is true: plants and animals have evolved over millions of years into the abundant variety that we have today. However, the Word of God relates a very different history. God created various kinds of animals to reproduce and fill the earth. Although there is great variety within each kind of animal and plant, one kind does not change into another kind. In this lesson, students will learn that molecules-to-man evolution is biblically and scientifically impossible.

Lesson Time

Welcome and Review

Welcome students to class, open in prayer, etc. Review the memory verse from last week.

The last two weeks we talked about where humans came from. We learned that we didn't evolve from apes, but God created us specially in His image, to worship and serve Him.

During this lesson series, we are learning how to answer some of the questions that Christians are asked. Briefly review the main points of the previous lessons (radiometric dating, where humans came from, compromise positions, etc.).

Have Animals Evolved?

<u>Illustration 22-00.</u> **In today's lesson, we're going to learn how to answer the question "Have animals evolved?" How many of you have heard that over time, one kind of animal has changed into another kind?** Allow students to discuss what they've heard and what they think. Many nature programs (e.g., those on the *National Geographic*, *Discovery Channel*, and *Animal Planet* channels) and books showcase the alleged evolution of certain animals (fish, amphibians, dinosaurs, birds, whales, horses, etc.).

This idea is called *evolution* and it was made popular in the 1800s by a man named Charles Darwin. How many of you have heard of him?

<u>Illustration 22-01.</u> **Some people believe that life began a long time ago in a sea of chemicals that organized themselves. Evolution is the idea that over millions of years, one kind of animal turned into another kind. Eventually, the abundant variety of life we have today came about. But is this really a true story? We've**

already seen that humans were created in the image of God and have not evolved from ape-like creatures. But what about the animals? We learned that after Adam sinned, the diet of the animals changed. But can one kind of animal really change into a completely different kind?

After Their Kind

To find the answer, we're going to look at what the Bible and science have to say on this topic.

Illustration 22-02. We'll start with what the Bible teaches, since God has revealed to us in His Word what happened in the beginning.

Illustration 22-03. From the Bible, we know that God is the Creator. And that the beginning of creation was about 6,000 years ago—not millions of years!

Illustration 22-04. Let's review what God created in the beginning. On which day did God create the various kinds of plants? Allow students to respond: Day 3. Read Genesis 1:11–13. Emphasize that God created plants according to their various kinds. This means that each kind of plant would produce more of its kind, with much variety within the kind.

Illustration 22-05. For example, the many varieties of cherry and plum trees that we have today are probably descendants of the same created kind. Even though they may look very different, and the fruit may taste different, these varieties of trees are in the same family, and probably share the same ancestor.

Illustration 22-06. What did God create on Day 5? Allow students to respond: sea and flying creatures.

Read Genesis 1:20–23. Emphasize that God created sea creatures according to their kinds, and flying creatures according to their kinds. This means that each kind of flying creature would produce more like themselves, with much variety within the kind. Although we can't say for sure which of today's sea and flying creatures are descendants of the same original created kinds, scientists think that in many cases the animals grouped into the same "family" or "genus" may be members of the same kind. In many cases, members from the same kind are able to mate with each other (although the inability for different species to produce offspring in the wild or even in captivity doesn't necessarily mean they are not part of the same kind).

Illustration 22-07. For example, there are over 1,000 species of bats, but all are probably members of the same created bat kind.

<u>Illustration 22-08.</u> **The various kinds of sea creatures would produce more sea creatures like themselves. For example, there are more than 350 species of sharks. Yet they are probably all descendants of the original created shark kind.**

<u>Illustration 22-09.</u> **On Day 6, God created the various kinds of land animals.** Read Genesis 1:24–25. Emphasize that God created the various kinds of land animals to reproduce after their kinds. This means that each kind of land animal would produce more of its kind, with much variety within the kind. **The Hebrew word** *min* **is the word translated as** *kind.* **Although we can't say for sure which of today's animals are descendants of the same original created kind, scientists think that in many cases the animals grouped into the same "family" or "genus" may be members of the same kind. In many cases, members from the same kind are able to mate with each other (although the inability for different species to produce offspring doesn't necessarily mean they are not part of the same kind).**

For example, the dog kind would produce a great variety of dogs, including wolves, jackals, and coyotes. What are some other "kinds" of land animals God created? Wait for response. Answers might include horse kind, cat kind, elephant kind, rabbit kind, kangaroo kind, giraffe kind, tortoise kind, bear kind, deer kind, to name just a few.

<u>Illustration 22-10.</u> **From studying the Bible, we also learn that two of every kind of air-breathing land animal and bird (seven of some) survived the worldwide Flood on the Ark. Many of the sea creatures were able to survive in the water.**

<u>Illustration 22-11.</u> **These animals refilled the earth after the Flood.**

From the Bible, we learn that God created animals and plants after their kinds, which means that they will produce others like themselves. But the Bible does not teach that one kind can turn into a completely different kind. For example, over time a fish can't eventually turn into a frog. In fact, today we observe animals and plants reproducing according to their kinds, don't we?

Next week we are going to look at what scientists have learned since the time of Darwin, and how real science confirms what the Bible says.

Review the memory verse for this lesson: Genesis 1:25.

Discussion Questions

1. How is the evolution story different from what the Bible says?

    Answers: Evolutionists believe that all life forms evolved from a common ancestor over millions of years. The Bible teaches that God created each kind of animal separately around 6,000 years ago.

Activity Ideas

1. The Bible mentions quite a few of God's creatures by name. A list of crafts associated with some of the animals mentioned in the Bible is available online at "Animals of the Bible Crafts" (use the link at the online Teacher's Resource Page). Choose one animal. Have students look up biblical references to this animal and draw a picture of the animal. Discuss some of the "design features" this animal exhibits (for ideas, visit the "Get Answers: Design Features" section of the AiG website at the online Teacher's Resource Page). Have students list some of these features on their drawing, along with the day that God created the original kind.

2. Play Bible-animals charades. Print L22a. Cut along lines. Give each child a slip of paper with the organism name and Bible reference. Have the student look up the verse and read it out loud, acting out the organism mentioned, rather than saying the name while reading the verse. Other students can guess what is being acted out.

3. Have students read through the student handout.

Extension Activities

Language Arts

Choose a favorite animal that you might see while visiting a zoo near you. Write your own "zoo guide" entry for this animal that is free of evolutionary and "millions of years" content. Include a picture of the animal, on which day God created its ancestral kind, some "fun facts," and evidence of design.

Bible

Put together a book of animals that are mentioned in the Bible. Find a picture to go with each entry. Include the biblical reference, and if appropriate, list a lesson that you can learn from the animal. For some ideas, see "Animals of the Bible" (a link to this page can be found at the online Teacher's Resource Page).

Recommended Resources

The Answers Book for Kids, volume 1 (book for children)

Creation: Facts of Life (book for teens and adults)

Zoo Guide (book for children)

Aquarium Guide (book for children)

Notes

Have Animals Evolved? part 2

Scripture

Revelation 4:9–11

Memory Verse

Psalm 104:24

Visuals & Materials

From CDs: Illustrations 23-00–23-11, Memory Verse graphic, *I Don't Believe in Evolution* (song)

Lesson Truths

- Secular scientists tell us that all animals have descended from a common ancestor
- The Bible teaches that God created animals to reproduce according to their "kind"
- The study of genetics confirms that animals only reproduce within their kind, and one kind of animal cannot turn into another kind

Preparation

1. Read "DNA: The Language of Life" at the online Teacher's Resource Page (www.AnswersInGenesis.org/go/AnswersForKids)
2. Study the Scripture passage for this week
3. Review the lesson before class so that you are familiar with the content
4. Pray that your students will understand the complexity of living things and how that points to a loving Creator

Lesson 23

Lesson Overview

Children are continually bombarded with the message that evolution is true: plants and animals have evolved over millions of years into the abundant variety that we have today. However, the Word of God relates a very different history. God created various kinds of animals to reproduce and fill the earth. Although there is great variety within each kind of animal and plant, one kind does not change into another kind. In this lesson, students will learn that molecules-to-man evolution is biblically and scientifically impossible.

Lesson Time

Welcome and Review

Welcome students to class, open in prayer, etc. Review the memory verse from last week.

Read Revelation 4:9–11 to the class. **This is a picture of worship that is taking place in heaven. Who is worshiping God here?** The four living creatures and the twenty-four elders. **For what are they praising God?** Because God is the Creator and has created all things. **What are some things that God created?** Allow students to respond. **He created the earth, the sun, moon, and stars, the oceans, the air we breathe, and us. He also created all the living things around us—all the plants and animals.**

Illustration 23-00. Last week we started to answer the question, "Have animals evolved?" We saw that God's Word states that He created plants and animals according to their kinds. This means that each kind was to reproduce after its own kind.

Today we are going to look at the science that supports and confirms what the Bible says—that animals only reproduce the same kind of animal; one kind does not turn into another kind.

DNA and Dogs

Let's take a look at what scientists have discovered.

Illustration 23-01. Scientists have found that inside plants and all living things is a special large molecule called DNA (which stands for "deoxyribonucleic acid"). DNA carries the recipe that tells each plant and living thing what to look like, how to grow, and so on. Parents pass a combination of their DNA on to their children.

Illustration 23-02. To understand what this means, we'll use the dog kind as an example. Scientists have found that all dogs are descended from a wolf-type dog, which may have

looked something like the ones pictured here. This is probably the type of dog that was on the Ark with Noah.

Illustration 23-03. From these original dogs came many more dogs. So the dogs we have today don't look exactly like the original dogs that God created, but they are still part of the dog kind.

Do some of you have dogs? What breed of dog? Allow children to respond. Do these all look the same? No, some are large, some are small, they have different features—but they are all still dogs!

Illustration 23-04. As the DNA has been combined and passed down over the years, the recipe from the original dogs has produced a wide variety of dogs: dogs with short legs and small bodies (pugs), dogs with short legs and long bodies (Welsh corgis), dogs with longer legs and large bodies (deerhounds), dogs with longer legs and thin bodies (dalmatians), dogs with thicker fur (collies), dogs with longer fur (lhasa apsos).

Even though they may look very different, they are all still obviously dogs. They are all part of the dog kind. Many of the different varieties are able to mate with other varieties.

Illustration 23-05. We can use a cake mix to help explain this. From one basic recipe, we can get a variety of different desserts. We could make a large round cake, square cakes, cupcakes, bundt cakes, and so on. Even though they may look very different, they were all made using the same basic recipe. There is a limit, however, to what the cake mix and recipe can make, isn't there? Using the cake recipe and mix, could you ever make lasagna?

Allow children to respond: no, the recipe and ingredients for lasagna are different. You would have to add a lot of new information to the cake recipe, and change most of the existing recipe, as well as gain new ingredients to make lasagna.

Mutations and Natural Selection

Illustration 23-06. Just as there is a limit to what the cake mix can produce, there is a limit to what the DNA recipe within the dog kind can produce. Dogs cannot grow fins or gills like a fish, or wings and feathers like a bird because dog DNA doesn't carry the recipe for these features.

Some people say this could happen through a series of small changes in the DNA. In fact, small changes in DNA do happen due to mutations. Mutatations are mistakes that occur in the DNA.

Sometimes, some members of a created kind are not able to survive in their environment. Natural selection is the process by which animals die out when they aren't able to adapt to their surroundings. Those members of the created kind that have the ability to adapt are able to survive and reproduce more animals like themselves.

Illustration 23-07. For example, which variety of dogs do you think would be more likely to survive in the arctic, where it's cold and snowy? Those with short, dark fur, or those with thicker, white fur? Allow students to respond: those with thick, white fur, like the Arctic Wolf has. Those with thick fur are able to stand the cold better, and those with white fur are able to blend in with the snow. So if a group of dogs traveled to the Arctic, those that already have thick, white fur would be more likely to survive and reproduce pups like themselves. The other varieties would die from exposure to the cold, from not being able to sneak up on their prey, or from being preyed upon by larger animals.

Which varieties of dogs would be better able to survive in hotter climates? Those with shorter, thin fur, with colors (dark brown, tan, etc.) that enable them to blend into the grasslands, like the jackal has.

In some cases, a new species may eventually form. However, this illustrates variation within a kind, not molecules-to-man evolution. God created the original animal kinds with much diversity in their DNA, so that as they reproduced and filled the earth after the Flood, their descendants were able to adapt to many different environments. Natural selection may bring about a new species of animal, but it cannot generate a new kind of animal.

Limits to Change

Although mutations and natural selection occur, scientists have not found a way that whole new recipes can be added by natural processes to DNA.

This is true for the other kinds of animals and plants, too. On its own, a fish could never develop the DNA recipe for lungs, legs, and arms and turn into an amphibian. A dinosaur could never turn into a bird. And a cow could never turn into a whale. Each kind will simply continue to reproduce more of its kind.

Illustrations 23-08 to 23-10. Let's look at a few examples of animals reproducing according to their kinds. These illustrations show the variety within the horse kind, the chicken kind, and the ceratopsian kind (one of the 50 or so kinds of dinosaurs).

In the beginning, God created each kind with the right mix of DNA to produce much variety within the kind. Those animals and birds that survived the Flood on the Ark were the ancestors of today's variety. Scientists have confirmed that animals reproduce according to their kinds!

Transitional Forms?

<u>Illustration 23-11.</u> Sometimes we might hear that someone has found the fossil of a transitional form. Transitional forms are the remains of animals or plants that were supposedly in the process of transitioning, or changing, from one kind to another. In fact, if the story of evolution were true, we should expect to find thousands of transitional forms in the fossil record. However, scientists have only found a very few, and these are highly questionable fossils.

For example, some scientists say they have found fossils of "feathered dinosaurs." However, some scientists who have carefully studied the evidence have shown that, in some cases, the dinosaurs don't actually have feathers. In other cases, the "feathered dinosaurs" have turned out to be true birds! And in at least one case, the entire supposed transitional form was found to be a fake, produced by some very clever Chinese farmers (e.g., the infamous Archaeoraptor, see *National Geographic* 196 no. 5: 98–107, November 1999 and *National Geographic*, Forum section, March 2000).

Some of the creatures that we find in the fossil record may seem bizarre or strange to us. For example, it's not impossible that God may have programmed the DNA of some of the creatures that we call dinosaurs to produce feathers (although to-date, no dinosaur fossils with true feathers have been found). But when we hear about "transitional forms," we need to remember it is biblically and scientifically impossible for one kind of animal to turn into another kind. Instead, we can know that the creature is a descendant of one of the kinds God originally made. It's not evolving!

Review and Prayer

God has created, and cares for, an amazing variety of animals on this earth. Read Psalm 104 and praise God for his creation and care together as a class. Review the memory verse for this lesson: Psalm 104:24.

Lesson 23

Discussion Questions

1. How does natural selection work? Does this process cause one kind of animal to change into another?

    Answer: Natural selection is the process whereby animals with favorable traits for survival in a specific environment live to reproduce, and animals that have negative survival traits die off and don't reproduce. This process results in a net loss of information, and cannot be the source of molecules-to-man evolution.

Activity Ideas

1. Put together a "Created Kind" collage. See the Science section below for more information.

2. Have students read the student handout.

Extension Activities

History

Where did evolutionary ideas come from? Although Charles Darwin was one of the most famous evolutionists, he was not the first person to put forward ideas that molecules have turned into men over millions of years. Trace the development of evolutionary ideas over the centuries. Compile a timeline that highlights some of the major developments in evolutionary hypotheses. Find out who Edward Blyth was and his significance to this question. For help, see the "Get Answers: History" section of the AiG website. A link can be found at the online Teacher's Resource Page.

Science

Find out more about the relatively new science of baraminology—the study of the created kinds. What does the existence of ligers and zonkeys indicate? See the "Get Answers: Created Kinds" section of the AiG website. A link can be found at the online Teacher's Resource Page.

In most cases, the biblical "kind" is probably not the same as what we call a "species" today. If two animals or two plants can mate and produce a truly fertilized egg, then they must belong to (i.e., have descended from) the same original created kind. For example, if the interbreeding animals are from different genera (plural of genus) within one family, it suggests that the whole family might have come from one created kind. If animals that can successfully mate are from genera in different families within the same order, it suggests that

the whole order may have derived from the original created kind. However, in most cases, the kind is usually at the family level, not the order level.

On the other hand, if two species will not hybridize (mate together and produce a viable offspring), it does not necessarily prove that they are not originally from the same kind.

Tigers and lions have been known to reproduce together, producing ligers or tigons. Many believe that all of today's cats (panthers, lions, tigers, domestic, etc.) came from an original cat kind. Find pictures of all these different cats. Combine their features to come up with one idea of what that original cat kind may have looked like.

North American buffalo and cattle have produced offspring. And other types of cattle have mated together. Find pictures of the various cow types. What do you think the original "cow" kind looked like?

Donkeys and horses mate to produce mules, while other horse types (zebras and donkeys, zebras and horses) have also produced offspring. What do you think the original horse kind may have looked like?

Camels and llamas have successfully crossbred. Combine the features of llamas, camels, alpacas, guanaco, and vicuna—how do you think this "kind" looked?

Also consider an elephant kind (Asian and African elephants, mammoths, mastodons; see "The Elephant Kind" at the online Teacher's Resource Page), a dog kind (all the varieties of dogs, including wolves, dingoes, coyotes, etc.), and a bear kind (polar, grizzly, panda, etc.).

Recommended Resources

The Answers Book for Kids, volume 1 (book for children)

Creation: Facts of Life (book for teens and adults)

Zoo Guide (book for children)

Aquarium Guide (book for children)

Notes

What About Dinosaurs? part 1

Scripture

Job 40:15–24

Memory Verse

Job 40:15–17

Visuals & Materials

From CDs: Illustrations 24-00–24-31, L24a, L24b, L24c, Memory Verse graphic, *Behemoth is a Dinosaur* (song)

Lesson Truths

- The media and secular scientists tell us that dinosaurs lived and died out millions of years ago, and that they evolved into birds
- From the Bible, we can learn that God created various dinosaur kinds and other animal kinds during the Creation Week 6,000 years ago
- Both science and history confirm that dinosaurs and man lived at the same time

Preparation

1. Read "What Really Happened to the Dinosaurs?" at the online Teacher's Resource Page (www. AnswersInGenesis.org/go/AnswersForKids)
2. Study the Scripture passage for this week
3. Review the lesson before class so that you are familiar with the content
4. Pray that your students will develop a biblical view of dinosaurs (and of everything else!)

Lesson 24

Lesson Overview

Children are fascinated by the ferocious beasts featured in movies and books. Perhaps more than any other creature, dinosaurs are used to promote the idea that the earth is many millions of years old. This lesson explores a biblical view of dinosaurs and dinosaur-like creatures (e.g., swimming reptiles [plesiosaurs, etc.], and flying reptiles [pteranodons, etc.]).

Lesson Time

Welcome and Review

Welcome students to class, open in prayer, etc. Review the memory verse from last week.

During this series of lessons, we've been learning how to answer some questions that people ask about Christianity and the Bible. The last two weeks we looked at the question, "Have animals evolved?" Briefly review the content of the previous lessons.

Dinosaur Misinformation

<u>Illustration 24-00.</u> **Although we've mentioned dinosaurs in previous lessons, this week we're going to focus specifically on these creatures. Our question for today is "What about dinosaurs?" We've probably seen quite a few movies or television programs about these amazing creatures, or read about them in books. But most of what we've heard isn't true. Let's take a look at a few examples.**

[Note: If you have a DVD of *Dinosaur* or any of the *Land Before Time* movies, show a short clip to your class, especially one that mentions millions of years. Discuss what these movies teach about dinosaurs. If you don't have a DVD, then use the next two illustrations.]

<u>Illustration 24-01.</u> **How many of you have seen or heard about the** *Land Before Time* **movies? One of the main themes of these movies is that dinosaurs lived and died millions of years ago—long before humans were around.**

<u>Illustration 24-02.</u> **In the Disney movie** *Dinosaur,* **we learn that many dinosaurs died when a meteor struck the earth millions of years ago.**

<u>Illustration 24-03.</u> **Signs in most museums and zoos tell us that dinosaurs have evolved into birds over millions of years.**

However, as we'll learn today, these things are simply *not* **true.**

The Biblical View of Dinosaurs

Illustration 24-04. **We've learned that the Bible is God's Word to us. It is the history book of the universe.**

Illustration 24-05. **We need to allow the Bible to help us understand the true history about dinosaurs, so that when we watch these movies or read books, we can tell the difference between truth and lies. Just like we use the Seven C's of History to guide our thinking about earth history, today and next week we are going to learn about the seven ages of dinosaurs; they all start with the letter F: Formed, Fearless, Fallen, Flood, Faded, Found, and Fiction.**

Formed

Illustration 24-06. **Let's start with the first F—Formed. In the beginning, God created the heavens and the earth.**

Illustration 24-07. **How many days did God take to create everything?** Six days. He rested on the seventh.

Illustration 24-08. **On the fifth day, what kinds of animals did God create?** Discuss some of the sea and flying creatures that God created on this day (fish, octopi, sea cucumbers, bats, birds, etc.).

Illustrations 24-09 & 24-10. **God also created different kinds of dinosaur-like creatures on Day 5.** Technically, the different kinds of dinosaurs are animals that lived on the land and would have been created on Day 6, although creatures such as the plesiosaur and pteranodon are often considered "dinosaur-like," and would have been created on Day 5. **God said that everything He created on this day was "good" (Genesis 1:21).**

Illustration 24-11. **On the sixth day, what did God create?** Discuss some of the various kinds of land animals (cats, elephants, dogs, etc.), and remind students that this was the day that God created the first two humans.

Illustrations 24-12 & 24-13. **Since dinosaurs are land animals, God also created the different dinosaur kinds on Day 6, along with the other land animals and humans.** There may have been as many as 50 different kinds of dinosaurs, e.g., ceratopsians, tyrannosaurs.

Fearless

Illustration 24-14. **When God finished His creative acts, He declared that His completed creation was "very good." It was perfect and complete, and much different from our world today.**

Illustration 24-15. Remember, the animals didn't eat each other (or people!). Instead, they ate the fruits and plants that God had created for them. See Genesis 1:29–30. **Adam and Eve would have had nothing to fear from dinosaurs—even the *T. rex*.**

This is the second F—Fearless. Even though many of the dinosaurs were large, and later became meat-eaters, originally Adam and Eve had nothing to fear from them, or from any other animal.

Illustration 24-16. We know from carefully studying the Bible that God created the heavens and the earth around 6,000 years ago. Even though some movies or books might say that dinosaurs lived and died many millions of years ago, this is simply not true.

Illustration 24-17. We've already discussed why some dinosaurs changed from eating only plants to dining on other animals for their supper.

Fallen

Illustration 24-18. The third F stand for Fallen. This helps to explain what happened to God's "very good" creation. Who can tell me what happened? Allow students to briefly review how Adam and Eve's disobedience to the command of God affected the world and animals, specifically. **Animals, including dinosaurs, were under God's Curse and were affected by the Fall of man. After this time, dinosaurs began to eat other animals.**

Flood

Illustration 24-19. Adam and Eve's children and grandchildren continued to disobey their Creator, and after many years, God judged their sinfulness by destroying the earth with water—a global Flood. That's the fourth F—Flood.

Illustration 24-20. God chose Noah to build an Ark, which would carry Noah's family and representatives of the (land-dwelling, air-breathing) animal and bird kinds safely through the earth-covering Flood. Since dinosaurs are classified as "land animals," the various dinosaur kinds were represented on the Ark. The flying reptile kinds were also on the Ark.

Illustration 24-21. Some people claim that dinosaurs were too big to fit on the Ark. However, the Ark was quite large, and many dinosaurs were quite small—the average size being that of a sheep. The Ark had plenty of space for all the animals, plus their food and water.

Illustration 24-22. Additionally, although some dinosaurs were quite large, God probably brought the younger, smaller dinosaurs to the Ark. After all, they were to

repopulate the earth after the Flood, so it would make sense to have young animals with their whole lives ahead of them.

<u>Illustration 24-23.</u> The dinosaurs and others animals that were not on the Ark were caught up in the floodwaters that covered the earth as a result of the fountains of the great deep breaking up and forty days of rain.

<u>Illustrations 24-24 & 24-25.</u> Many dinosaurs tried to escape the rising floodwaters by running to higher ground. They left behind many tracks that show their attempt to escape the water. Some had even laid eggs just before the floodwaters reached their area. However, there was no escape for the dinosaurs or any of the other animals that were not on the Ark. Eventually, the water buried the dinosaurs in mud, and covered their trackways and eggs with layers of sediments. Even the highest hills were covered by the Flood. In recent years, scientists have discovered some of the bones, tracks, and eggs of those dinosaurs that didn't survive the Flood. These are called fossils. For more information, see "In the Footsteps of Giants" at the online Teacher's Resource Page (www. AnswersInGenesis.org/go/AnswersForKids).

Remember, these fossils are not millions of years old, as you might have heard. They are around 4,300 years old, at the most. In fact, scientists have found something that confirms the bones can't be millions of years old. They found that some dinosaur bones still contain what appears to be preserved soft tissue—blood vessels, blood cells, and proteins. Scientific tests have shown that this soft tissue couldn't have lasted for millions of years! For more information, see "The Scrambling Continues" at the online Teacher's Resource Page).

<u>Illustration 24-26.</u> About a year after Noah and his family entered the Ark, the floodwaters began to go down. Finally, the Ark landed in the mountains of Ararat. God told Noah and his family and the animals to get off the Ark and to spread out and fill the earth. God promised to never again flood the entire earth with water. The rainbows we see today remind us of this covenant (promise).

Well, if dinosaurs came off the Ark as well, then they must have lived with man—right? Well, does the Bible say anything about dinosaurs? Allow children to respond.

A man named Job recorded his experience with an animal called *behemoth*. Let's read about it in the Bible.

Read Job 40:15–24 together. **How does the Bible describe behemoth's tail?** It has a tail like a cedar tree (40:17).

<u>Illustration 24-27.</u> This is a picture of a cedar tree. Do you see how large it is?

<u>Illustration 24-28–24-31.</u> **Some people (and some Bible commentaries) claim that the behemoth Job mentions was merely an elephant or a hippopotamus. However, neither of these animals has a tail like a cedar tree. But dinosaurs such as an *Apatosaurus* do!**

Review and Prayer

We can trust what the Bible says. Next week we are going to learn the final three F's of dinsour history: Faded, Found and Fiction.

Work on today's memory verses: Job 40:15, 17. Pray with your students.

Discussion Questions

1. Dinosaurs are "missionary lizards." What do you think is meant by the term "missionary lizards"? How can you use dinosaurs as a witnessing tool to your friends or neighbors?

    Answer: The term "missionary lizards" refers to using the topic of dinosaurs as a witnessing tool. We can use dinosaurs as a way to engage people in conversation and to present the gospel to them. We can do this by showing people that the Bible actually explains dinosaurs and makes sense of the evidence we find around the world. When discussing dinosaurs, we can talk about death (after all, dinosaur fossils are dead!), and why death came into the world (because of Adam's sin). This can lead into a discussion of the gospel.

    We can also talk about the Flood of Noah's day in relation to dinosaurs: the Flood buried billions of creatures including dinosaurs, and thus is the main cause of most dinosaur fossils. And when discussing the Flood, the vital matter of salvation can also be covered: Noah's Ark is a picture of salvation in Christ, and just as Noah had to go through a doorway to be saved, so each one of us must go through a doorway—the Lord Jesus Christ (John 10:9).

    Allow students to discuss some ways they can use dinosaurs to share the gospel with others (for example, passing out "dinosaur cards," available from www.AnswersBookstore.com).

Activity Ideas

1. Print L24a and make copies for children to color.

2. Play "pin the tail on behemoth." Print, color, and then laminate L24b (you may want to enlarge this picture by hand or on a copier). Print L24c and make copies for children to color.

3. Purchase the Sculpt-A-Saur kits from AnswersBookstore.com and make sculpted dinosaur heads.

Extension Activities

Language Arts

Write a short essay that describes your favorite dinosaur. How big did it grow? What was its post-Fall diet? What would you have done if you met this dinosaur while taking a walk?

Recommended Resources

After the Flood by Bill Cooper (book or teens and adults)

D is for Dinosaur by Ken Ham (book for children)

Dinosaurs for Kids by Ken Ham (book for children)

Dinosaurs by Design by Duane Gish (book for children)

Dinosaurs, Genesis, and the Gospel (DVD for children)

Dinosaurs of Eden by Ken Ham (book for children)

God's Dinosaurs (activity books for children)

The Great Dinosaur Mystery Solved! by Ken Ham (book for teens and adults)

When Dragons' Hearts Were Good by Buddy Davis (book for children)

Notes

Lesson 25

What About Dinosaurs? part 2

Scripture

Job 41:1–34

Memory Verse

Job 41:1–2

Visuals & Materials

From CDs: Illustrations 25-00 –25-13, "Drawing Dinosaurs" (movies), Memory Verse graphic, *Behemoth is a Dinosaur* (song)

Lesson Truths

- The media and secular scientists tell us that dinosaurs lived and died out millions of years ago, and that they evolved into birds
- From the Bible, we can learn that God created various dinosaur kinds and other animal kinds during the Creation Week 6,000 years ago
- Both science and history confirm that dinosaurs and man lived at the same time

Preparation

1. Read "Thunderbirds" at the online Teacher's Resource Page (www.AnswersInGenesis.org/go/ AnswersForKids)
2. Study the Scripture passage for this week
3. Review the lesson before class so that you are familiar with the content
4. Pray that your students won't be led astray by the world's version of history but will hold to what the Bible teaches

Lesson 25

Lesson Overview

Children are fascinated by the ferocious beasts featured in movies and books. Perhaps more than any other creature, dinosaurs are used to promote the idea that the earth is many millions of years old. This lesson explores a biblical view of dinosaurs and dinosaur-like creatures (e.g., swimming reptiles [plesiosaurs, etc.], and flying reptiles [pteranodons, etc.]).

Lesson Time

Welcome and Review

Welcome students to class, open in prayer, etc. Review the memory verse from last week.

Illustration 25-00. **Last week we started looking at dinosaurs—where they came from, why they died out, and so on. While movies and the secular world give us one view of dinosaurs, the Bible paints a completely different picture. And why should we trust what the Bible says?** Because the Bible is the Word of God, Who cannot lie; He was an eyewitness to the events.

I introduced you to the Seven F's of dinosaur history. Do you remember what they were? Formed, Fearless, Fallen, Flood, Faded, Found, and Fiction. Last week we looked at the first four F's. Who can summarize them for me? Formed—God created the flying reptiles and "sea monsters" on Day Five of Creation Week, while he formed the land dinosaurs on Day Six, along with the other animals and man. Fearless—Dinosaurs, and other animals, were originally vegetarian, and they did not eath other animals or man. There was nothing to fear from dinosaurs. Fallen—Adam disobeyed God, which brought a curse on the world, including on animals. Dinosaurs were created as vegetarians, but after the Fall, they began to eat one another. Flood—God brought a worldwide Flood upon the earth to judge mankind's sin. Representatives of the land-dwelling, air-breathing land animals and birds were brought on the Ark; this would have included flying reptiles and dinosaurs. The rest were drowned in the Flood, and many were fossilized as a result. The book of Job tells us of behemoth—probably a large dinosaur such as an apatosaurus.

Illustration 25-01. **After the Flood, Noah's descendants didn't spread out and fill the earth as God had commanded, but instead they built a great tower to make a name for themselves and worship false gods. What did God do to them? Right—God confused the language of the people, and they began to spread out around the world.**

Many of the people groups that spread out over the earth have stories that describe their encounters with the animals we call dinosaurs (or dinosaur-like) today. However, they gave the creatures names like "dragon," "thunderbird," "behemoth," and "leviathan," instead of "dinosaur." Remember how Job described behemoth? Take this opportunity to review last week's memory verse: Job 40:15, 17

Illustration 25-02. Well Job also describes an animal he calls "leviathan." Read Job 41. The description of this creature that Job gives is similar to the dinosaur-like sea animal we call *Kronosaurus*.

Illustrations 25-03 & 25-04. Other people groups also have their own accounts of encounters with what may be dinosaurs. For example, the Australian Aborigines have described a creature they call the "bunyip." This may refer to what we call the *Edmontosaurus*.

Illustration 25-05. The Chinese people also have many tales about dragons. Such stories are found around the world.

Illustrations 25-06 & 25-07. Other groups of people drew pictures of the animals they saw. For example, one group of people drew a picture of an animal that looks similar to a dinosaur, while another group drew a picture of an animal that looks similar to a flying reptile like a pteranodon.

So if the dinosaurs survived the Flood and at one time lived with people, why aren't there any around today? People have different ideas of what happened to the dinosaurs.

Some people believe that some dinosaurs eventually turned into birds.

Illustration 25-08. However, we know that this simply isn't true for a number of reasons. First, God created birds on Day 5—a day *before* He created the dinosaurs. Scientists have also found that there are differences in the lung structure of dinosaurs and birds, and differences between scales and feathers. If you hear that dinosaurs have evolved into birds, you know the truth: dinosaurs have always been dinosaurs, and birds have always been birds.

Illustration 25-09. Some people believe that dinosaurs disappeared when a giant asteroid or meteorite hit the earth. In fact, the movie *Dinosaur* presents this idea. However, there are many scientific problems with this idea. For more information, see the "Get Answers: Dinosaurs" section of the AiG website. A link can be found at the online Teacher's Resource Page.

Faded

<u>Illustration 25-10.</u> **The simple reason that the dinosaurs are no longer around is that they died. In fact, animals continue to go extinct even today. Some scientists have estimated that several species go extinct every day. There are several reasons that dinosaurs (and animals today) may have died out over time. What do you think they are?** These reasons include that humans continued to hunt and kill them, their habitat changed and they were unable to adjust to changes, and their source of food became scarce.

What happens when a story is passed along from one person to another over a long time? The details of the story change. Well, this is what happened with man's stories about dinosaurs. And this is the next F—Faded.

<u>Illustration 25-11.</u> **Man's encounters with dinosaurs faded from memory, and they turned into myths and legends of dragons. We don't know when the last dinosaur died out, but it was probably after the middle ages, when we have many stories of knights killing "dragons," like the story of St. George.**

Found

<u>Illustration 25-12.</u> **The next F of dinsoaur history is Found. It was in the 1700s when dinosaur bones were first found, and it wasn't until 1841 that the term** *dinosaur* **was used to describe these animals. Many people believe that these animals lived and died out millions of years ago, but the Bible tells us the true history of dinosaurs.**

Fiction

<u>Illustration 25-13.</u> **As we discussed, many scientists today have invented stories about dinosaur history based on an evolutionary worldview, rather than on the Bible. They tell us that dinosaurs lived and died out millions of years ago, and that they evolved into birds. We know from the Bible that these stories are not true; they are nothing more than fiction. And that's the final F of the age of dinosaurs—Fiction.**

Review and Prayer

It can be fun to watch movies or read books about dinosaurs, but we need to think carefully about what we are learning, and we need to have the Bible as the foundation for our thinking about everything—even about dinosaurs!

Review today's memory verses: Job 41:1–2. Pray with your students.

Discussion Questions

1. How do we know that dinosaurs lived with people?

   Answer: God created land animals on the same day that He created people (Day 6). As land animals, dinosaurs were part of those creatures that God created on Day 6, alongside of man. Additionally, the many dragon legends and cave drawings seem to confirm that dinosaurs were contemporaries of humans.

2. When you see in a movie or read in a book about dinosaurs dying out millions of years ago, or changing into birds, how can you respond?

   Answer: Allow for individual responses. We can know these things aren't true, based on what the Bible teaches.

Activity Ideas

1. Bake and decorate dinosaur cookies, using the cookie-type of your choice. Arrange a dozen cookies on a paper plate decorated with non-toxic markers or crayons and cover with colored plastic wrap. Include a dinosaur card (available from www.AnswersBookstore.com) and deliver the cookies to friends or neighbors.

2. Use the movies on the CD (or your own artistic ability!) to help children draw a dinosaur, swimming reptile, or flying reptile.

3. Make your own Chinese dragon. See "Chinese New Year Dragon" at the online Teacher's Resource Page for instructions.

4. Complete the puzzles on the back of the student handout.

Lesson 25

Extension Activities

History

Find out more about some of the many dragon legends that are told around the world. Compare Chinese dragons to British dragons. What was the terror of Nerluc? What type of dragon did St. George slay? Which people group told stories of the bunyip? Which Native American tribes reported encounters with thunderbirds? What was the Piasa bird? What is the connection between dragons and the Ishtar Gate? What happened to the cooper who met with winged dragons in Lucerne, Switzerland?

In a three-ring binder, compile summaries (or copies of pages from books) of dragon legends, organized according to the country of origin. Draw a picture of each dragon based on the description given in the legend.

Links to online articles to help you in your research can be found at the online Teacher's Resource Page (www.AnswersInGenesis.org/go/AnswersForKids).

Science

There are many differences between reptiles and birds. Find out how the following systems differ between the two types of creatures: respiratory, circulatory, excretory. In addition, find out how scales differ from feathers. How does embryonic development of most reptiles differ from embryonic development in most birds?

Bible

Have children draw a picture of the behemoth and leviathan, based on the descriptions of these beasts given in Job 40 and 41.

Recommended Resources

After the Flood by Bill Cooper (book or teens and adults)

D is for Dinosaur by Ken Ham (book for children)

Dinosaurs for Kids by Ken Ham (book for children)

Dinosaurs by Design by Duane Gish (book for children)

Dinosaurs, Genesis, and the Gospel (DVD for children)

Dinosaurs of Eden by Ken Ham (book for children)

God's Dinosaurs (activity books for children)

The Great Dinosaur Mystery Solved! by Ken Ham (book for teens and adults)

When Dragons' Hearts Were Good by Buddy Davis (book for children)

Notes

Why Are Snakes So Scary?

Scripture

Selected passages

Memory Verse

Genesis 3:14

Visuals & Materials

From CDs: Illustrations 26-00–26-20, L26a, Memory Verse graphic, *The Seven C's of History* (song)

Lesson Truths

- God originally created snakes (and all animals) to be vegetarians
- As a result of the Fall and God's Curse on creation, animals now have defense-attack structures to kill others and defend themselves
- We also are under the Curse of death and eternal separation from God. We all must come to Christ for forgiveness of sin and eternal life

Preparation

1. Read "Designed to Kill in a Fallen World" at the online Teacher's Resource Page (www. AnswersInGenesis.org/go/AnswersForKids)
2. Study the Scripture passage for this week
3. Review the lesson before class so that you are familiar with the content
4. Pray that your students will understand the significance of the Fall and come to Christ for their salvation

Lesson 26

Lesson Overview

Too often, the world that we see today is understood to be the same world that God initially created. However, this is *not* the same world that Adam and Eve first lived in. Genesis 1 and 2 paint a picture of a beautiful, "very good" world in which life flourished and peace was the norm. Genesis 3 tells us what changed the original creation into the cursed world that we live in today. This lesson explores some of the effects of the Curse (Genesis 3), and offers some insights into how animals became skilled hunters, rather than the veggie-lovers that God created them to be (Genesis 1:29–30). It is vital that we teach our children the truth about the origin of death and suffering so that they do not lay the blame for our cursed world at the feet of the Creator, as so many have done in the past.

Lesson Time

Welcome and Review

Welcome students to class, open in prayer, etc. Review the memory verse from last week.

Illustration 26-00. Note: You may not want to show the title slide at the beginning of class, since it is introduced in illustration 26-05. **During this lesson series, we are learning how to answer some of the questions that Christians are asked.**

Illustration 26-01. **The last couple weeks we learned about dinosaurs, and how to answer questions about them from the Bible. Who can remember the seven F's of dinosaur history?** Formed, Fearless, Fallen, Flood, Faded, Found, Fiction.

Illustration 26-02. **Today, we will learn how to answer another question. We'll be learning more about the second C in the Seven C's of History—Corruption.**

Illustration 26-03. **How many of you like snakes?** Allow children to express their feelings about snakes (and feel free to express yours as well!). Some children may like snakes, although most will consider them scary.

Illustration 26-04. **Most people are afraid of snakes, aren't they? Why do you think most people have ophidiophobia (the fear of snakes)?** Allow children to respond: because some snakes are venomous (although not all snakes are venomous), etc.

Illustration 26-05. **Today we are going to answer the question: Why are snakes (and other animals) so scary?**

God's Original Creation

<u>Illustration 26-06.</u> **Let's begin by remembering what the world was like in the very beginning. In the beginning God created the heavens and the earth in six, normal-length days. When He was finished, He said everything was . . . .** Allow children to say "very good." **God's original creation was perfect. It was complete and just the way God wanted it.**

<u>Illustration 26-07.</u> **God had created plants, fruits, and vegetables for all the animals and humans to eat (Genesis 1:29–30). Even animals that we think of as primarily eating meat, like this dinosaur, would have eaten only fruits and vegetables in the beginning.**

<u>Illustration 26-08.</u> **Adam and Eve would have enjoyed hanging out with dinosaurs or snakes—animals that we consider "scary." Their world was very different from the world we live in today. Snakes and spiders weren't venomous (as we see today, not all snakes and spiders are venomous), and lions weren't ferocious meat-eaters. Other animals didn't need to defend themselves from attack.** Allow children to mention other animals that are scary today or that are adept at defending themselves against attack. Remind them that in the beginning all animals were peaceful and vegetarian.

Effects of God's Curse

<u>Illustration 26-09.</u> **However, everything changed when Adam and Eve disobeyed a command the Lord had given them. Who remembers what the command was?** Allow children to respond: God had told Adam to eat from any tree in the Garden, except the Tree of the Knowledge of Good and Evil (Genesis 2:15–17).

<u>Illustration 26-10.</u> **Their sin (and ours) corrupted the entire creation.** Read Romans 8:22 together.

<u>Illustration 26-11.</u> **Let's look at two of the changes that took place.** Read Genesis 3:14–18 together. **God placed a curse on the serpent, and the serpent now had to crawl on his belly and eat dust. The second change that we read about occurred in the plants: God cursed the ground and caused it to produce thorns and thistles. It was no longer an easy task for Adam to live off the produce of the ground.**

Our memory verse for this week comes from this passage: Genesis 3:14. Let's read Genesis 3:14–15 again. Read the passage together. **In verse 15, God gives Adam and Eve (and us) a promise that one day someone would come ("the seed of the woman"), who would crush the head of the serpent (Satan). Who was this person?** Wait for answers. **That's right! Jesus came to defeat Satan, and to reverse the effects of the Curse. Remember when we studied about the seventh "C" of history? In the Consummation, God will reverse the Curse, and there will no longer be death, disease, or suffering.**

Now these changes we read about that occurred from God's curse may help to explain why snakes slither on the ground (we don't know for certain that the serpent was a snake, but most people assume that it was), and why we prick our fingers on thorns when picking a rose, if we're not careful. But our question for today is "why are snakes (and other animals) so scary?"

How Did Animals Change?

Theologians (people who study the Bible) have several ideas about how to answer this question.

Illustration 26-12. **The first idea is that the things that animals use to attack other animals today (or to defend against attacks) had different functions before Adam sinned. And over time, the features have been modified for different uses. For example,** T. rex **(and other animals) may have used his sharp teeth to chomp on vegetables.**

Illustration 26-13. **Another example is found in the bat kind. Even though vampire bats drink blood today, most species of bats feed on insects or fruit. Before the Fall, the original bat kinds may have used their teeth to pierce fruit or drink nectar from plants. Over time, some of the bats have developed a taste for blood, using their sharp teeth to pierce animal skin instead of fruits.** See "The Dracula Connection to a Young Earth" at the online Teacher's Resource Page for more information.

Illustration 26-14. **Another example is the piranha. What are piranhas known for?** Allow children to respond: they are thought to be fearsome, flesh-eating fish. **However, another fish, called the** pacu, **is a member of the piranha kind, but it primarily feeds on plants and fruit that falls from trees near the rivers. In fact, piranhas have also been observed to feed on vegetation at times. It may be that in the beginning, the original piranha kind used its teeth to bite and tear plants. Over time, some of the species of piranha have learned to use their teeth to eat other things.** See "Piranhas, the Feared Fish" at the online Teacher's Resource Page for more information.

Illustration 26-15. **And yet another example is found among the cat kind. One lioness, named "Little Tyke," refused to eat any type of meat. Instead, she enjoyed feasting on cooked grains, raw eggs, and milk. Another lioness has "adopted" several baby antelopes over the years. Rather than trying to eat them, as we might expect, this lion has tried to protect these babies from other predators. It may be that the descendants of the original cat kinds have developed a taste for foods other than fruits and veggies over the years.** See "No Taste for Meat?" at the online Teacher's Resource Page for more information.

<u>Illustration 26-16.</u> Another idea about why animals are the way they are is that God "redesigned" many of the animals after Adam sinned and God cursed His creation. We've already seen that the serpent changed and that plants began to grow thorns. In addition, it became difficult for women to bear and bring up their children (Genesis 3:16). This may have been when God changed some kinds of snakes so that their fangs would inject venom into their prey (not all snakes are venomous—many are quite harmless). Perhaps God also changed some of the features in other animals at this time.

Yet another possibility is that, because He knew that Adam would sin, God programmed the DNA of living things with information for these defense-attack structures during the original Creation Week. And then, this information was somehow "switched on" at the Fall.

Review and Prayer

So, why are snakes so scary?

<u>Illustration 26-17.</u> We've discussed several answers to this question. Although the Bible doesn't say for sure, the bottom line is because of Adam's sin (and yours and mine), we are no longer living in a perfect, "very good" world.

<u>Illustration 26-18.</u> God has placed a curse on this world.

<u>Illustration 26-19.</u> But there is good news! God tells us in His Word that things won't always be this way. Our Creator has promised to restore His Creation to the way it was in the very beginning. Read Acts 3:21, Isaiah 11:6–9, and Revelation 21:4 together. Discuss what these verses teach: lambs, wolves, leopards, children, bears, calves, and snakes will all dwell together peacefully; lions will once again be plant-eaters. There will be no more death or mourning or crying or pain.

<u>Illustration 26-20.</u> This future paradise is only for those whose names are written in the Lamb's Book of Life—those who have received the free gift of eternal life. Discuss how children can know for certain that their names are written in the Lamb's Book of Life: Romans 3:23, 6:23, 10:9–10.

Review the memory verse for this lesson: Genesis 3:14. Pray with your students, thanking God for salvation from the Curse, and for eternal life forever with Him.

Lesson 26

Discussion Questions

1. Read the "*Did you know?*" page in the student handout. What kinds of things do you see around you that remind you of a "very good" world? What kinds of things remind you that we are living in a sin-cursed world?

   Answer: Allow for individual responses.

2. In the very beginning, Adam and Eve were never sad and were never in any pain. What things today make you sad or cause you pain? What does the Bible promise to those who believe in Christ Jesus as their Lord and Savior?

   Answer: Allow for individual responses. The Bible promises that we will one day live in a place were there is no crying or pain (Revelation 21:4).

3. Read Genesis 3:17–19. How was the ground affected by Adam's sin? What things do you see today that remind you of the curse God placed on the ground?

   Answer: Thorns and thistles are part of the Curse. It became difficult for Adam (and his descendants) to get food from the ground. Allow for individual responses.

Activity Ideas

1. Print L26a (one copy for each child). Have children color the earth and draw a horizontal line across the middle of the paper. On the top half of the paper, write words that describe the earth before the Fall (e.g., "very good," tearless, joyful, full of life, beautiful, peaceful, vegetarian diet, etc.). On the bottom half, write words that describe the post-Fall world (e.g., sinful, death, disease, suffering, sadness, crying, carnivory, thorns, thistles, etc.).

2. Put together two news segments: a pre-Fall segment (what news stories would Adam and Eve have reported to each other in the days before they sinned?) and a post-Fall segment (what news stories would Adam and Eve have reported to each other or their children in the days and years following their sin and the subsequent curse on the creation?).

3. Visit the *After Eden* cartoon site (a link is on the online Teacher's Resource Page) and use some of the *After Eden* cartoons to illustrate other effects of the Fall and to compare life before and after Eden. Have students illustrate their own "After Eden" cartoon.

Extension Activities

History

Ever since Adam and Eve sinned and God cursed His creation, people have tried to counteract the effects of the Curse (in temporary ways). In fact, Jesus said that those who overcame sin's curse were blessed. For example, those who try to restore peace between people are blessed (Matthew 5:9). And Jesus performed many miracles that healed people of diseases (products of the Curse), and even raised people from the dead (sin's ultimate curse)!

Louis Pasteur was a Bible-believing scientist whose work helped to (temporarily) overcome some of sin's effects. When did Pasteur live? What did he do? What did he believe about the Bible? How has his work influenced our quality of life today? Find out more by reading "Louis Pasteur at the online Teacher's Resource Page.

Joseph Lister was another scientist whose work was anti-curse. When did he live? What did he contribute to the field of medicine? Find out more by reading "Joseph Lister" at the online Teacher's Resource Page.

Language Arts

Imagine you were Adam and Eve. Write an essay on what it might have been like to live in the Garden of Eden, when everything was perfect. What would you have seen? What would you *not* have seen? What jobs did Adam and Eve have? What jobs would they *not* have had?

Science

The Bible teaches that part of God's curse on the serpent was that it would eat dust. Is this really true? Scientists have found that snakes do, in a sense, eat dust! Find out how by researching how snakes use their Jacobson's organ. See "Contradictions: Left in the Dust" at the online Teacher's Resource Page.

Recommended Resources

The Answers Book for Kids, volume 1 (book for children)

Why is Keiko Sick? (book for children)

The Day the World Went Wacky (book for children)

Notes

Lesson 27

Why Do We Look Different? part 1

Scripture

Selected verses

Memory Verse

Genesis 9:18–19

Visuals & Materials

From CDs: Illustrations 27-00–27-10, Memory Verse graphic, *We're One Blood* (song)

Lesson Truths

- The differences that separate the so-called "races" are just skin deep, the result of slight genetic differences
- Both the Bible and science confirm that we are all one human race, descendants of Adam and Eve, and more recently of Noah's sons and daughters-in-law
- As descendants of Adam, we are all in need of a Savior—Jesus Christ

Preparation

1. Read "Are There Really Different Races?" at the online Teacher's Resource Page (www. AnswersInGenesis.org/go/AnswersForKids)
2. Study the Scripture passage for this week
3. Review the lesson before class so that you are familiar with the content
4. Pray that your students will reject all forms of racism and will recognize their need for a Savior

Lesson 27

Lesson Overview

Racism is a hot topic in our society. Are there really different races of people? Should we be divided because of the shade of our skin or the color of our eyes? According to the Bible, there is only one race of people: the human race. No matter what we look like, we are all children of Adam and Eve (and, more recently, Noah's sons and daughters-in-law). In this lesson, children will learn how to biblically and scientifically explain that we are all related, and that we're really all the same—we're all sinners in need of a Savior.

Lesson Time

Welcome and Review

Welcome students to class, open in prayer, etc. Review the memory verse from last week.

In this series of lessons, we're learning how to answer some of the questions that people ask about Christianity and the Bible. In the last lesson, we learned why snakes are scary. They were not created that way, but as a result of Adam's sin and God's curse on creation, animals have changed, and now hunt and kill one another. But remember, one day God will restore creation so that it be like before the Fall, and animals once again will not hurt one another.

Why So Different?

Illustration 27-00. Note: You may not want to show the title slide at the beginning of class, since it is introduced after the first illustration. **Today, we're going to learn the answer to another question. First, let me ask you a question. How many of you have ever sung the song, "Jesus Loves the Little Children"?** Allow children to discuss and sing the song briefly. **This song says that all the children of the world are "red and yellow, black and white" (or "red, brown, yellow, black, and white").**

Illustration 27-01. **If we were all created in God's image, then why are there so many different skin colors? Some of us have tan skin. Others have darker skin. Some have blue eyes. Others have brown eyes. Some have dark-colored hair. Others have light-colored hair.**

We're going to find out how to answer the question: Why do we look different? This week we are going to look at the scientific answer to this question, and next week we'll look at it from a biblical perspective.

Function of Skin

Illustration 27-02. Let's begin by thinking about our skin. Our skin is our largest organ. It has many important functions. It works as a barrier between the outside world and our insides. It helps us to keep our bodies at a constant temperature. And it helps us to sense the world around us.

Illustration 27-03. While it might not seem like our skin does much except keep us covered, this covering limits water loss from our bodies. We would only survive a matter of hours without it! In fact, if we were to examine a section of our skin, we would find a lot going on. For example, we would find glands that produce sweat and oil, vessels that carry our blood, nerve endings that help us touch and feel, and places where our hair grows!

Melanocytes and Melanin

Illustration 27-04. We would also find thousands of cells, called "melanocytes," that produce a pigment called "melanin." Melanin is the pigment that helps give your skin some color. There are two forms of melanin. One is dark brownish, the other is reddish. These pigments produce our particular shade of skin color.

Scientists have found that, no matter what we look like, we all have the same amount of melanocytes in our bodies.

Illustration 27-05. Inside each melanocyte is a set of "instructions," called DNA (deoxyribonucleic acid) that tells the melanocyte, among other things, how much melanin to produce.

Illustration 27-06. If the DNA in your body tells your melanocytes to make a lot of melanin, and your skin keeps a lot of the melanin that is made, then your skin will be very dark brown. If your instructions say "make a little melanin," and your skin looses some of the melanin that is made, then your skin will be very light brown. And there are many combinations in between, as we can see from this picture.

[Technical note: Differences in the shade of skin may be based in part on how much pigment is produced, and in part on how much pigment is preserved in the skin after it is produced. Special "transport vehicles" called melanosomes carry the melanin from the melanocytes to other cells that are capable of dividing (stem cells), primarily in the lowest layer of the epidermis. In these cells, the pigment serves its function as it forms a little dark umbrella over each nucleus. This protects the epidermal cells from being damaged by sunlight. In people with lighter shades of skin, much of the pigment covering the stem cells is lost after these cells divide and their daughter cells move up in the epidermis to form the surface dead layer—the stratum corneum.]

The sun can cause our melanocytes to produce more melanin, but only to a certain point. For example, the melanocytes of the fair-skinned girl on the end will never be able to produce as much melanin as those of the darker-skinned girl on the bottom row, no matter how long she stays out in the sun.

No one really has "red" or "yellow" or "black" skin. We all have the same basic color, just different shades of it. We all share the same pigment—our bodies just have more or less of it!

Eye and Hair Color

<u>Illustration 27-07.</u> Melanin also determines the color of your eyes. If you have a lot of it in the iris of your eyes, they will be brown. If you have a little melanin, your eyes will be blue. (The blue color in blue eyes is the result of the light scattering off the thin layer of brown-colored melanin.)

<u>Illustration 27-08.</u> **What hair colors do you think result from a lot of melanin in our hair shafts?** Brown and black hair. **What hair color results from less melanin?** Blond hair. **Those with red hair lack the ability to produce much of the brownish form of melanin, so the reddish form is more evident.**

<u>Illustration 27-09.</u> Our DNA also controls the basic shape of our eyes.

<u>Illustration 27-10.</u> Some people groups tend to have dark, curly hair with dark eyes and dark skin, while others have black, straight hair, dark almond-shaped eyes, and lighter skin, while still others have light hair, blue eyes, and very fair skin. But we are all related! We all go back to Noah's sons—Shem, Ham, and Japheth. Let's read Genesis 9:18–19. Read the verse together. **This is our memory verse for this week. You see, even though we all look different, we are all related.**

Review and Prayer

Isn't it amazing that God created each of us as special, unique individuals? We can praise Him because we are fearfully and wonderfully made!

Next week we'll look at what the Bible teaches about what happened in the past that helps to explain why there are so many different people groups.

Review the memory verse for this week: Genesis 9:18–19. Pray with your students.

Discussion Questions

1. Does the DNA that you have received from your parents tell your melanocytes to produce a lot of melanin, or a little melanin, or somewhere in between? What about the DNA in your eyes? What does the DNA of your brothers and sisters tell their melanocytes to do?

   Answer: Allow for various responses. Continue to reinforce the idea that, no matter what our skin shade or eye color, we are all relatives, descendants of Adam and Eve, and all in the same boat—sinners in need of a Savior. You may want to use the science experiments in *Science and the Bible* on loving others (volume 1, number 17), or the importance of each member of the body of Christ (volume 2, number 22) to demonstrate these truths.

Activity Ideas

1. Read through today's handout together and have students complete the maze.

Extension Activities

History

Throughout history, some people have thought that those with certain skin shades are better than other people with a different skin shade or appearance. Find out about how the Australian Aborigines have been wrongly treated in centuries past. What is "apartheid"? Which people groups have been affected by apartheid? Why is apartheid wrong? See the "Get Answers: Racism" section of the AiG website. A link can be found at the online Teacher's Resource Page.

Science

Our DNA carries much more information about us than merely our skin shade or eye color. It also carries the information for how tall we can grow, what our noses will look like, how long our arms will be, how our ears will be shaped, etc. Find out more about the information-storage capacity of DNA. If you were to write the information stored on one strand of our DNA, how many books would you fill? If you unraveled a strand of DNA in just one cell of your body, how long would it be? If you unraveled all the DNA in your body, how long would it be? What else can you find out about the marvelous DNA molecule? For more information, read "Brave Warriors with Words" and "Creation in a Basket," and watch the "DNA" video. Links to these resources can be found at the online Teacher's Resource Page.

Recommended Resources

All God's Children (book for children)

Darwin's Plantation (book for teens and adults)

The Tower of Babel: Pop-up & Read (book for children)

The Not So Super Skysraper (book for children)

Lesson 28

Why Do We look Different? part 2

Scripture

Selected passages

Memory Verse

Romans 10:12–13

Visuals & Materials

From CDs: Illustrations 28-00–28-09, L28a, Memory Verse graphic, *We're One Blood* (song)

Lesson Truths

- The differences that separate the so-called "races" are just skin deep, the result of slight genetic differences
- Both the Bible and science confirm that we are all one human race, descendants of Adam and Eve, and more recently of Noah's sons and daughters-in-law
- As descendants of Adam, we are all in need of a Savior—Jesus Christ

Preparation

1. Read "Interracial Marriage: Is It Biblical?" at the online Teacher's Resource Page (www.AnswersInGenesis.org/go/AnswersForKids)
2. Study the Scripture passage for this week
3. Review the lesson before class so that you are familiar with the content
4. Pray that your students will reject all forms of racism and will recognize their need for a Savior

Lesson 28

Lesson Overview

Racism is a hot topic in our society. Are there really different races of people? Should we be divided because of the shade of our skin or the color of our eyes? According to the Bible, there is only one race of people: the human race. No matter what we look like, we are all children of Adam and Eve (and, more recently, Noah's sons and daughters-in-law). In this lesson, children will learn how to biblically and scientifically explain that we are all related, and that we're really all the same—we're all sinners in need of a Savior.

Lesson Time

Welcome and Review

Welcome students to class, open in prayer, etc. Review the memory verse from last week.

Illustration 28-00. **Last week we started looking at the answer to the question, "why do we look different?" Can someone tell me what we discussed; do you remember?** We discussed that the differences between people and people groups are due to genetic differences in our DNA, such as the effect the activity of melanin production has on skin, eye, and hair color.

But where did our DNA come from in the first place, and why do people groups look so different?

Illustration 28-01. **The Bible is the history book of the universe, so let's look and see what the Bible has to say about our past.**

Pre-Flood History

Illustration 28-02. **In the beginning, God created Adam. From the Bible, we learn that Adam was the very first man.** Read Genesis 2:7, and 1 Corinthians 15:45. **We also learn that Adam was alone—there was no one else like him.** Read Genesis 2:18–22 together.

Illustration 28-03. **Adam was alone until God created Eve from Adam's side. Eve was the very first woman—the Bible tells us that she was the mother of everyone.** Read Genesis 3:20. **God gave these first two people the best combination of DNA possible. Their skin was probably a "middle brown" shade.**

Illustration 28-04. **After they sinned and were sent from the Garden of Eden, Adam and Eve had many children. Some historians have suggested that they may have had over 50 children! Their children grew up, married each other, and had children of their own. The number of people (all children, grandchildren, great grandchildren . . . of Adam and Eve) in the world continued to increase as time went on.**

[Note: This may bring up the question: If Adam and Eve were the only people in the world, who did their son Cain marry (Genesis 4:17)? The simple answer is that in the beginning, brothers and sisters married each other! For more information, read "Cain's Wife—Who Was She?" at the online Teachers Resource Page (www.AnswersInGenesis.org/go/AnswersForKids).]

The Flood

Illustration 28-05. **When God judged the wickedness of mankind with a globe-covering flood, He saved only Noah, his wife, his three sons, and their wives on the Ark. Everyone else died in the watery catastrophe—all of Noah's aunts, uncles, cousins, nephews, nieces, grandparents, etc. When the Flood was over, and the Ark had settled in the mountains of Ararat, Noah and his family were the only humans left on the whole entire earth. The Bible tells us that Noah's three sons were the fathers of all the people groups in the world.** Read Genesis 9:18–19.

Tower of Babel

Illustration 28-06. **Noah's descendants decided to build a tall tower with which they could worship the heavens. Why is this wrong?** Allow students to respond. The Creator is the only One who is worthy to receive worship; giving worship to anything other than the Lord God is a sin. Discuss some ways that people worship the heavens today (e.g., those who believe that life originated in outer space, those who look to the stars and planets for guidance). **To encourage them to obey His command to fill the earth, God caused them to begin speaking different languages.** Read Genesis 11: 5–9.

Illustration 28-07. **Because the family groups spoke different languages, they were unable to understand each other. They couldn't work together any more. They stopped working on the tower, and many family groups packed up their belongings and left the area.**

Illustration 28-08. **They began to move to different parts of the world. Some of Ham's grandchildren started toward Africa, while others started moving toward Asia, eventually reaching the Americas. The families in Japheth's clan went toward Europe and India. And many in Shem's clan stayed in the areas of the Middle East.** For more information on this, see the "Table of Nations." A link to this can be found at the online Teacher's Resource Page.

Origin of People Groups

As they went, each of these groups took with it its own special set of characteristics (for instance, lighter skin and eye color, or darker skin and eye color). These characteristics were passed through the people's DNA to their children, and so on. Because the groups no longer freely mixed with other groups, the characteristics of each group became more and more prominent as new generations of children were born.

If we were to travel back in time to Babel and mix up the people into completely different family groups, people groups with completely different characteristics might result. For instance, we might find a fair-skinned group with tight, curly dark hair that has blue, almond-shaped eyes, or a group with very dark skin, blue eyes, and straight, brown hair! [Technical note: this is given as a general illustration that assumes each characteristic is independently inherited, although in some cases this may not be the case.]

<u>Illustration 28-09.</u> Although we may hear about many different "races" of people, there is really only one race—the human race. Even though we may look very different and speak very different languages, we are actually all part of the same family. Noah was the great, great, great, great, great, great, great, great, etc., grandfather of us all!

In fact, because they are all descendants of Noah, most people groups have stories that are similar to the true accounts given in the Bible about creation, the great Flood, and the Tower of Babel.

Choctaw Legend

You may want to summarize the following legend, depending on the time you have available.

We've already discussed a few flood legends in a lesson several weeks ago. The Choctaw Indians of North America also have a legend about a flood that has been passed down through the years:

In ancient times after men had lived a long period upon the earth, they became very corrupt and wicked. They deluged the earth with so much blood and carnage that the Great Spirit finally decided to utterly destroy them. He, therefore, sent a prophet among them, who went from tribe to tribe and from village to village proclaiming the fearful tidings that the race was soon to be destroyed. No one paid any attention to him, however, and people went on in their wickedness as carelessly as ever. But one year, with the coming of autumn, mists and clouds gathered over the earth, so that there was no sun shining by day nor did the moon and stars light up the gloom of night.

One day, very suddenly, there came a crash of thunder much louder than had ever been heard before. The whole earth seemed to shake and tremble with the reverberation. Then, as people looked toward the north, they seemed to see a light—the first they had seen for many a long dark day. But whatever hope may have been aroused in their breasts was dissipated. For what they saw was not the return of the long lost sun, but it was the gleam of a great mountain of water, advancing in great billows from the north, covering the entire earth, and destroying everything in its path. With the cry, "Oka Falamah, Oka Falamah" (the returning waters, the returning waters), the doomed people turned away in one last vain effort to escape. But there was no escape. The whole earth was soon covered even to the tops of the mountains by the vast flood, and men and animals alike perished, leaving only a desolate wilderness of waters.

Of all mankind, only one remained, and that was the mysterious prophet who had so faithfully, yet vainly, proclaimed the warnings of the Great Spirit. This prophet had been directed by the Great Spirit to build a raft of sassafras logs, upon which he floated safely above the destroying flood, while he gazed sadly upon the dead bodies of men and beasts as they floated past him in the dark waters.

The prophet floated aimlessly about for many weeks, until at last one day he saw a large black bird circling over his raft. He cried to it for help, but the bird only uttered a few harsh croaks and flew away to be seen no more. Some days later the prophet saw a smaller bird, bluish in color, with red beak and eyes, hovering over the raft. Again he asked this bird if there was a spot of dry land to be found anywhere in the waste of waters. It hovered over him for a few moments, as if trying in its soft mournful voice to give the desired information, and then flew off toward the west where the new sun was again setting in splendor. Almost at once a strong wind arose which carried the raft in the direction in which the bird had gone. All night, it floated on under the moon and stars which shone again with renewed brightness.

When the sun rose the next morning, the prophet saw in the distance an island toward which his raft seemed to be drifting. Before the sun went down again, the raft had moved along until it touched the island, and the tired prophet landed. Glad to be on the earth once more, he lay down and slept until the sun rose the next day. Much refreshed, he then began to look about the island, where to his surprise, he found every variety of animal formerly found on the earth (except the mammoth), and all the birds and fowl also.

The prophet lived on this island for many days, until finally the waters passed away. The earth once more took its former appearance, with hills, valleys, and grassy prairies. But the Indian people never again became so rashly disobedient to the Great Spirit and never forgot the lesson of Oka Falamah, the "Returning Waters."

(This legend, which pre-dated the coming of missionaries to the Choctaw, was recorded by W. B. Morrison. You can read it online at "Ancient Choctaw Legend of the Great Flood." The link is at the online Teacher's Resource Page.)

Briefly discuss some of the similarities and differences between this legend and the true account in Genesis: the reason for the flood, the prophet, how the prophet was saved, the role of birds, the activity of the winds, etc.

There are over 500 different accounts like this from people groups around the world. This shows us that as the grandchildren of Noah moved away they took with them the accounts of creation and the Flood that had been told to them by their fathers—Shem, Ham, and Japheth. Over time, the stories have changed, but God has given us His Word so that we can know the truth.

Lesson 28

Review and Prayer

As we've seen, the differences between us aren't all that great! We are actually all part of one big family. And because we are all descendants of Adam, we have all inherited his sinful nature. All of us, no matter what skin shade or eye shape, are sinners (Romans 3:23). We all need to be saved from our sin so that we can spend eternity with our Creator. Jesus Christ paid the penalty for sin by dying on a cross and rising again three days later (1 Corinthians 15:1–4). Everyone who believes this, no matter where he lives, what people group he belongs to, or what he looks like, receives the free gift of eternal life.

Read Romans 10:12–13 together. **This is our memory verse for this week.** Pray with your students.

Discussion Questions

1. Imagine if the children in your class suddenly spoke a different language, and the only people you could understand were those in your family (brothers, sisters, parents). How would you feel? What would you do?

   Answer: Allow for various responses.

2. Even though we may look very different from each other, we all have one thing in common. Every person has sinned, and is in need of hearing about salvation through Jesus Christ. Every tribe and nation needs to hear the good news of salvation. What are some ways that we can help to spread the good news?

   Answer: Allow for various responses: pray for missionaries, monetarily (or in other ways) support missionaries, go on missions trips (when older), share the good news with friends and neighbors, etc.

Activity Ideas

1. Print one copy of L28a for each child. Look through a crayon box to find a "middle brown." Use this to color Adam and Eve. Use other shades of brown to color their children to illustrate the variety within humans. What other colors represent colors within the human race? What colors are *not* shades of the human race?

2. Read through today's handout together.

Extension Activities

Language Arts

Research the flood and creation myths and legends of other cultures. Write a summary of each legend. Compile the summaries in a three-ring binder, under "Creation Legends" or "Flood Legends." Use colored markers to highlight similarities between the legends (e.g., use yellow to highlight the reason for the flood, pink to highlight descriptions of the boat). For information, see "Flood Legends" at the online Teacher's Resource Page.

Bible

What does the Bible teach about "interracial" marriage?

Read Genesis 2:19–24 and Matthew 19:1–6. What do these passages teach about the nature and origin of the doctrine of marriage?

(Marriage is to be between one man and one woman for life. Eve was made to be Adam's helper and companion for the rest of their lives. This is why we get married today—and why we stay married. This is also why men are not to marry other men [or many women]and women are not to marry other women [or many men].)

When you get older, it may be that the Lord will lead you to be married. What do the following passages teach about the type of person you are to marry? Genesis 2:19–24 (we are to marry a member of the opposite gender); 2 Corinthians 6:14 (we are not to be joined with an unbeliever but are to marry a Christian).

Because we are all members of the same race (the human race), is there any such thing as "interracial" marriage? No. In fact, the Bible mentions those who have married others from a different people group. For example, Ruth was a Moabitess who had trusted in the true God of the Israelites. She married the Israelite Boaz and is listed in the lineage from Adam to Christ (Matthew 1:5).

The only "interracial marriage" that God says we should not enter into occurs when a child of the last Adam (one who is a new creation in Christ—a Christian) marries an unregenerate child of the first Adam (one who is dead in trespasses and sin—a non-Christian). Examples of such "mixed marriages" and their negative consequences can be seen in Nehemiah 9 and 10, and Numbers 25. See "Family Foundations" at the online Teacher's Resource Page.

Lesson 28

Recommended Resources

All God's Children (book for children)

Darwin's Plantation (book for teens and adults)

The Tower of Babel: Pop-up & Read (book for children)

The Not So Super Skyscraper (book for children)

Lesson 29

Was There an Ice Age?

Scripture

Job 37:7–10; 38:22–23, 29–30

Memory Verse

Job 38:29–30

Visuals & Materials

For evaporation experiment: Thermos with hot water (please be careful with hot water—it can scald); Thermos with cold water; two empty 2-liter soda bottles with caps
From CDs: Illustrations 29-00–29-21, Memory Verse graphic, *The Seven C's of History* (song)

Lesson Truths

• The Genesis Flood caused warm oceans and cool land temperatures, leading to an Ice Age

• The Ice Age lasted about 700 years; Job probably lived during the Ice Age

• We can trust the Bible's history to be true

Preparation

1. Read "Setting the Stage for an Ice Age" at the online Teacher's Resource Page (www. AnswersInGenesis.org/go/AnswersForKids)

2. Study the Scripture passage for this week

3. Review the lesson before class so that you are familiar with the content

4. Pray that this lesson will help your students see how the Bible relates to real history and real science

Lesson 29

Lesson Overview

Was there ever a time in earth's history when it was partly covered in ice? Has there been more than one ice age? Will the earth ever experience another ice age? The secular story is that the earth has experienced at least five major ice-age periods over the past several billion years. The most recent ice age is alleged to have begun around two million years ago and ended around 10,000 years ago.

However, a proper perspective on the Ice Age comes from the pages of the Bible. The trigger for *one* Ice Age was the Flood of Noah's day and its after-effects. The Ice Age is believed to have reached its peak around 500 years after the floodwaters receded (the ice covered around 30% of the earth's surface).

Lesson Time

Welcome and Review

Welcome students to class, open in prayer, etc. Review the memory verse from last week.

<u>Illustration 29-00.</u> Note: You may not want to show the title slide at the beginning of class, so that students can guess the topic of today's lesson. **During this lesson series, we are learning how to answer some of the questions that Christians are asked.** Briefly review the main points of the previous lessons (why snakes are scary, why we look different, etc.).

<u>Illustration 29-01.</u> **Today we're going to learn about a topic discussed in movies such as *Ice Age* and *The Day After Tomorrow*. Who can tell me what that topic is?** Allow students to respond: the Ice Age.

Encourage students to discuss what they have learned about the Ice Age from these movies, books, or their teachers (e.g., that there were several ice ages over many thousands of years, that early man was "primitive"). You may want to watch these movies yourself before class, in order to gain some ideas for talking points.

As with many other movies and books, most of what they teach us is not true. Today we are going to learn the truth about the Ice Age—when it happened, what caused it, and how long it lasted.

Prehistoric?

To begin, let's think about a word that we often hear when we learn about the Ice Age. The word is *prehistoric*. What do you think *prehistoric* means? Allow students to respond: it refers to a time before history was recorded or written down. Allow students to discuss

what comes to mind when they hear the word "prehistoric" (e.g., saber-tooth tigers, woolly mammoths, dinosaurs, cave men).

Illustration 29-02. **When we hear about prehistoric beasts, we need to remember that God has given us a record of the history of the universe. The first words of the Bible are,"In the beginning." God created all things during those first six days. So, there really is no such thing as "pre-history." We have a record of history from the very beginning!**

Illustration 29-03. **In fact, the Bible gives us some clues that have helped scientists figure out that only one Ice Age occurred after the Flood, a few thousand years ago. There were not many ice ages over multiple millions of years, as you may have heard.**

The Flood's Effects

Illustration 29-04. **We'll start with an event that we're already familiar with—the Flood of Noah's day. What happened at the beginning of the Flood?** Allow students to respond: the fountains of the great deep broke open. It began to rain. **For many months, the fountains of the great deep shot hot water from deep inside the earth into the floodwaters. Volcanoes around the world erupted, dumping hot lava into the waters. What do you think happened to the oceans?** Allow students to respond: the ocean waters heated up.

Let's take a look at what happens to warm or hot water.

Conduct this experiment, which shows that warm water evaporates more quickly than cold water. Before class, pour hot water into a thermos and cold water into another thermos. During class, carefully pour hot water into one empty soda bottle and replace the cap. Pour cold water into another empty soda bottle and replace the cap. Watch as the hot water quickly evaporates and condenses on the inside surface of the bottle, while relatively little evaporation takes place in the cold-water bottle.

Post-Flood Climate

Illustration 29-05. **After the Flood much evaporation took place because the ocean waters were so warm.**

Illustration 29-06. **What happens when water evaporates?** Allow students to respond: when it cools, the water vapor condenses, forming clouds. Point out the condensation on the interior of the warm-water soda bottle.

Illustration 29-07. **Eventually, the condensation falls back to earth as precipitation. After the Flood, all the dust and debris in the air from the volcanoes kept some sunlight from reaching the surface of the earth. The air stayed cool year round. Because the**

weather stayed cooler, there wasn't much of a summer. What type of precipitation falls in cold air? Allow students to respond: snow, sleet, ice.

Illustration 29-08. **For many years after the Flood, volcanoes around the world continued to erupt. The dust and debris that the volcanoes released into the air kept the temperatures cool during the whole year in many parts of the world. This means that the snow didn't have a chance to melt. It continued to build up, until great sheets of ice, many hundreds of feet thick, covered much of the land.**

Illustration 29-09. **In some areas, large walls of ice, like the wall pictured here, formed.**

What do you think life would have been like for those living near the great sheets of ice during the Ice Age? Allow students to respond.

Cavemen

Illustration 29-10. **Many people during that time made their homes in caves, like the family in this illustration. Let's take a look around their cave. What do you notice about it?** Allow students to respond. Discuss the following: the fire at the entrance to the cave (used to keep warm, cook, and keep unwanted animals from entering the cave); the hands "painted" on the wall (a way of signing one's name to a picture); their clothing (made from animal skins); the spears leaning against the side of the cave (used for hunting and protection); woven basket holding berries (the cave people knew how to weave baskets and also which plants were edible and non-toxic); jewelry (we'll show a few pieces in more detail later—but the point is that they were skilled at making jewelry from objects that they found or carved); the tents in the cave (used to keep warm in the chilly dampness of the cave—more on this in the next illustration). [For more information on humans during the Ice Age, see "Where Was Man During the Ice Age?" at the online Teacher's Resource Page.]

Illustration 29-11. **Caves tend to stay around 50 degrees Fahrenheit (10 degrees Celsius) year round. This is a bit chilly when it is already cold outside (as it was during the Ice Age—year round). So, many of those who lived in caves built tents for themselves. This helped them to stay warm while they were sleeping, and to have some privacy. This picture shows how they built their tents. They used branches to make a frame. Then they covered the frame with skins. They used rocks to hold down the edges of their tent, which kept breezes from blowing through.**

Illustration 29-12. **How many of you like jewelry? Many of the people groups living during the Ice Age also enjoyed making and wearing jewelry like these necklaces. The top necklace was made with fox teeth and shells. The bottom necklace was made from carved mammoth tusks. If you were to make jewelry out of items that you found near your home, what would your jewelry be made of?** Allow students to respond. Spend a few

minutes discussing how they would make jewelry. Use these ideas to make jewelry during the activity time.

Illustration 29-13. **Some of the people groups that lived during the Ice Age used stones to make tools. The tool at the top is called a** *perforator*. **What do you think they used this tool for?** Allow students to respond: perforators were used to punch holes in leather (then needles with sinew were threaded through the holes and used to sew clothing and other items). Perforators were also used as drills, to drill holes in wood, bone, and antler.

The bottom tool is called a *burin*. **What do you think this tool was used for?** Allow students to respond: a burin was a razor-sharp tool made from flint. It was used as a knife and could cut any material that was softer than it was: antlers, ivory, animal bones. It was used to make sewing needles, harpoons, spear throwers, and jewelry.

Illustration 29-14. **These people also knew how to make and use musical instruments, such as this flute made from hollowed out bird bone. How many of you would know how to make such an instrument?** Allow students to respond. Discuss which instruments they might be able to make (recorder, guitar, drum, etc.)

Illustration 29-15. **These people also knew how to draw magnificent pieces of artwork on the cave walls. They made their own paint by crushing natural materials (ochre, ash from the remains of their fires, etc.) and mixing them with juices from plants, fruits, and vegetables, and with egg whites, blood, and animal fat. In this illustration, the artist is painting a picture of a woolly mammoth. He is leaving a record of a successful mammoth hunt that he and his family members went on. What kinds of things would you have drawn on the walls of your cave?**

We can see that people who lived during the Ice Age were quite intelligent, can't we? They were not primitive or prehistoric. Instead, they were fully human, just as we are! In fact, one of the humans that lived during the time of the Ice Age may have left us some references to it. Read Job 37:7–10, 38:22–23, 29–30. Note that most biblical scholars believe that Job lived sometime between the Tower of Babel (c. 2242 BC) and Abraham (c. 2000 BC)— during the middle years of the Ice Age, which peaked around 500 years (c. 1800 BC) after the Flood (c. 2348 BC) and ended around 200 years later (c. 1600 BC).

End of the Ice Age

After awhile, the volcanic activity began to die down. The dust in the atmosphere began to clear, and sunlight began reaching more parts of the earth again. This helped melt the great ice sheets. Also, the oceans had cooled down. So there wasn't as much evaporation. With less evaporation, precipitation decreased. Rain and snow didn't fall as much. The ice sheets continued to melt.

Evidence for the Ice Age

<u>Illustration 29-16.</u> **Scientists who have studied glaciers and ice movement can tell where the ice sheets were during the Ice Age. This picture shows how much of the earth was covered with ice during the Ice Age.** Point out your area on the map—was your area covered with ice at one time?

<u>Illustration 29-17.</u> **As the ice melted, it left behind some clues that tell us where it was. For example, the gigantic glaciers changed V-shaped valleys into U-shaped valleys, like the ones pictured here. During the Ice Age, these valleys were filled with ice, which has since melted.**

<u>Illustration 29-18.</u> **Icebergs carried large rocks for many miles. When the ice melted, the rocks were dropped. This is why we sometimes see large boulders (such as the ones in this picture) in the middle of flat plains. These are called "glacial erratics."**

<u>Illustration 29-19.</u> **When the ice sheets moved, they pushed dirt and rocks into mounds along the sides and ends of the glaciers. These mounds are called "moraines." The debris is called "till." In this picture, the ice is now gone, and a beautiful lake has filled the area carved out by the glaciers.**

<u>Illustration 29-20.</u> **The ice also scraped the rock underneath it, leaving scratch marks, like the ones pictured here.**

Review and Prayer

<u>Illustration 29-21.</u> **The Bible helps us to understand the world around us. It also helps us figure out that there was one Ice Age that occurred just a few thousand years ago, after the Flood of Noah's day, not many ice ages over countless millions of years as some have suggested.**

Review today's memory verses: Job 38:29–30. Pray with your students.

Discussion Questions

1. Do you think there will ever be another ice age? Why or why not?

   Answer: Since the Flood provided the right conditions for the Ice Age to commence, and since God has promised that He will never again flood the entire earth, we can be pretty sure that there will not be another ice age.

2. When you see an exhibit on the ice age in a museum, how can you decide which parts of the exhibit are based on reality and which are simply stories about the past?

   Answer: Allow for individual responses. We need to carefully evaluate what we see in light of what the Bible teaches and not simply accept everything at face value. For example, we know that statements that mention "millions of years" or pre-history are not true. We also need to be careful of human reconstructions—sometimes they may be portrayed as prehistoric brutes who were less intelligent than we are.

Activity Ideas

1. Make Ice Age jewelry. Cut string into 18-inch segments. Allow children to design their own necklace using various types of pasta (rigatoni, macaroni, elbow, etc.) in various colors and sizes.

2. Paint an Ice Age picture. Use what you can find around you to paint a picture (non-toxic berries, crushed leaves, ash, etc. mixed with water for paint; feathers, animal hair, twigs, moss, plant leaves as brushes). What story does your picture tell?

3. Make Ice Age instruments. Use objects found around you to make your own instruments, just as those who lived during the Ice Age made instruments from bird bones and other objects. See "Make Your Own Instruments" and "Musical Craft Projects" for help. Links to these resources can be found at the online Teacher's Resource Page.

Lesson 29

Extension Activities

History

A common claim made by those who reject the biblical account of history is that early man was "primitive." Read Genesis 1–7, and make a list of the accomplishments of the earliest men (e.g., they knew how to make and play musical instruments, how to work with metals, how to build a large wooden ship, how to speak, how to build cities).

Even after the Flood, when mankind was once again populating the earth, technology was still advanced. Find out more about our early ancestors with the resources at the online Teacher's Resource Page (www.AnswersInGenesis.org/go/AnswersForKids).

Language Arts

Read *Life in the Great Ice Age*. Write a short story about what you think life may have been like during the Ice Age. What would you have seen? What was the weather like? What types of stories would you have heard from the elders in your clan? What would a typical day have been like?

Science

The Ice Age played a part in forming the massive desert areas found around the world today. How? Find out by reading "The Snowblitz" and "The Mystery of the Ice Age." Links to these articles can be found at the online Teacher's Resource Page.

Bible

The Bible describes many different instruments. Read Genesis 4:21, and skim through the Psalms. Make a list of the different types of instruments the Bible talks about. Sometimes Scripture gives a description of the various instruments. Include this description in your list when possible.

Recommended Resources

Life in the Great Ice Age (book for children)

The Puzzle of Ancient Man (book for teens and adults)

Frozen in Time (book for teens and adults)

Answers BIBLE CURRICULUM for Kids

Lesson 30

What About Aliens?

Scripture

Psalm 8

Memory Verse

Psalm 19:1

Visuals & Materials

From CDs: Illustrations 30-00–30-14, Memory Verse graphic, *I Don't Believe in Evolution* (song)

Lesson Truths

- The media, NASA, and others tell us that alien life must exist
- The Bible indicates that man is the focus of God's creation and Christ's redemption
- Science indicates that Earth is unique and only here has life been found
- It is very doubtful that aliens exist; instead of searching for aliens, people should seek the Creator, Jesus Christ

Preparation

1. Read "Are ETs and UFOs Real?" at the online Teacher's Resource page (www.AnswersInGenesis.org/go/AnswersForKids)
2. Study the Scripture passage for this week
3. Review the lesson before class so that you are familiar with the content
4. Pray that your students will understand the importance of the gospel message for them and seek their Creator for salvation

Lesson 30

Lesson Overview

Some of the highest-grossing movies of the past few decades are those that feature alien life forms. Even movies and television programs geared toward children are spotlighting beings from outer space (e.g., *Lilo and Stitch*). Is there really a possibility that intelligent life may exist in outer space? Should we be waiting anxiously for messages from other worlds? Are programs such as SETI (Search for Extra-Terrestrial Intelligence) and the millions of its dedicated followers on the right track?

Although the Bible does not explicitly say, "There are no intelligent life forms in other places besides earth," it *does* provide some principles that we can use to guide our thinking in this area. In this lesson, we will explore those principles, as well as the scientific evidence (or lack thereof). We will develop a biblical perspective on the topic of alien life and come to the conclusion that a galactic battle as featured in the Star Wars saga is very unlikely.

Lesson Time

Welcome and Review

Welcome students to class, open in prayer, etc. Review the memory verse from last week.

During this lesson series, we are learning how to answer some of the questions that Christians are asked. Do you remember what we learned about last week? The Ice Age. Who can tell me what we think caused it and how long it lasted? Warm oceans and cool weather after the Flood caused evaporation and snowfall that built up great ice sheets. The Ice Age lasted about 700 years.

Illustration 30-00. **This week we are looking at the topic of UFOs and ETs. Do aliens really exist?**

Illustration 30-01. **Movies such as *Star Trek*, *Star Wars*, *Lilo and Stitch*, *Men in Black*, *E.T.*, *Superman*, *Signs*, *Chicken Little*, and *War of the Worlds* teach us that aliens live on other planets in outer space. Some people even believe that life began in outer space.**

How many of you think there may be some type of alien life out there? Allow students to discuss briefly their thoughts about aliens.

Some people say that there must be life out there since the universe is *so* humungous. However, the size of the universe has nothing to do with whether or not intelligent life might exist on other worlds. This isn't a good argument to use to suggest that space aliens exist.

The Size of the Universe

Let's take a quick look at how big the universe is. It might be a bit difficult to really understand how big the universe is, but we'll try.

Remember, God created all the stars and galaxies that we're going to see in just *one* day, 6,000 years ago. He simply spoke them into existence on Day 4. Read Genesis 1:14–15.

Illustrations 30-02. This illustration shows our planet earth, its position in the solar system, its position in our galaxy, and its position in the universe.

Amazing, isn't it? Let's see what else the Bible says about the heavens. Read and discuss Psalm 19:1 (the heavens declare the glory of God) and Psalm 147:4 (God knows the number and names of the stars).

Even though the universe is so large, God cares for His children on the one small planet we call Earth. He deserves our worship. Read and discuss Psalm 8 together.

What Does the Bible Say?

Illustration 30-03. Let's take a look at what we can learn from the Bible about aliens in space, and see if it's possible that Superman might actually visit us someday.

Illustration 30-04. God created the universe and everything in it in six days around 6,000 years ago. So if there *are* aliens out there, they are part of God's creation and not the products of millions of years of evolution, as some people suggest.

Illustration 30-05. However, the Bible does *not* mention space alien life forms. If extra-terrestrials *did* exist, we might expect the Bible to reveal *something* about them or tell us to expect a visit from them someday, don't you think?

Illustration 30-06. Remember, God placed a curse on the entire universe after Adam sinned. Read Romans 8:22. So if there *were* other beings out there, they would also be suffering from the effects of *our* sin. Does that seem fair to you? Allow students to respond. Additionally, when Jesus came to earth, He came as a man, didn't He? Jesus didn't become an alien. And He remains forever the God-man Jesus Christ.

Illustration 30-07. God created the sun, moon, stars, and other planets with special purposes. Read Genesis 1:14–15 again. Discuss the purposes of the sun, moon, and other heavenly bodies. The sun gives the earth light during the day, and the moon gives the earth light during the night by reflecting the sun's light. The stars and other heavenly bodies mark off the seasons and years and provide special signs for those on earth (remember the special star that led the wisemen to Jesus?). God designed the heavenly bodies to support life on earth. The earth has a very special place in the universe.

What is the primary message of the Bible? Allow students to respond. **The whole of the Bible is centered on how God has dealt with humans since the beginning. Jesus became a man and came to earth to die for the sin of mankind (1 Corinthians 15:1–4), not for a race of alien beings. He is preparing a place in heaven for His children, not a race of extraterrestrials.**

What Does Science Say?

In addition, after 40 years of searching the skies for signs of life, not one real, live alien has been found, despite what you may have heard. Scientists have also found that there are many features that set the earth apart from other planets, and help us know that God created it to be inhabited (Isaiah 45:18). Let's look as some examples of these features.

Illustration 30-08. **God created the sun to give us light during the day. The earth is the right distance from the sun. If it were any closer, we would burn up. If it were farther away, we would freeze.**

Illustration 30-09. **Because the earth is the right distance from the sun, we have liquid water. So far, earth is the only planet known to have liquid water. Over 70% of the earth's surface is covered with water! We need liquid water to live. Our bodies are made of 65% water. It helps to keep our bodies free from poisons. It helps dissolve and carry vitamins and minerals through our bodies. When we sweat, the water that evaporates from our bodies helps keep us cool when it's hot outside.**

Illustration 30-10. **Some have claimed that they have discovered evidence of water on Mars. To date, scientists have not discovered liquid water on Mars or any other planet. However, water in the form of ice is found throughout the solar system. In fact, some creation scientists have suggested that water in some form should be found throughout the universe, since the creation began with water (Genesis 1:1–8).**

Illustration 30-11. **God created our moon to give us light at night. The phases of the moon have helped people groups mark off the months and keep track of the seasons. The force of gravity between the earth and moon helps keep our oceans clean by causing high and low tides.**

Illustration 30-12. **Although some scientists have found other planets outside of our solar system, none of them is exactly like our planet earth.**

Review and Prayer

Illustration 30-13. **So, according to what the Bible and science teach us, do you think it's possible that Lilo would ever find a creature like Stitch? Or that we will be attacked by a race of alien beings?** Allow students to respond. **It seems very unlikely, based on what the Bible *does* tell us. And those who are studying the universe seem to have confirmed what the Bible says.**

Instead of believing in beings who probably don't exist, we need to trust in the One who made the heavens and the earth. Who is that? Allow students to respond: The Creator God.

Illustration 30-14. **Instead of waiting to hear a message from an intelligent life in space, we need to accept the message that our Creator has already given us in His Word. The *real* message from outer space is the message that God has given us in the Bible. Jesus Christ the Creator came to earth as a human to live a perfect life. He died and rose again so that all those who believe in Him will have eternal life.**

Review today's memory verse: Psalm 19:1. Pray with your students, thanking God for His Word, which tells us of His wonderful plan of salvation.

Discussion Questions

1. The next time you see a movie about aliens, what are some biblical principles you can think about to help you know the truth?

   Answer: The universe was created by God. It did not evolve from a big bang. The universe was cursed by God after Adam sinned. Jesus Christ came to earth to redeem mankind from the curse of sin. Jesus died and rose again on behalf of humans, not an alien race.

2. Our verse for today says the heavens declare the glory of God. In what ways can you use the heavens to tell others about our Creator?

   Answer: Allow children to respond. The size of the universe reflects the infinite nature of God. God has positioned earth the right distance from the sun and moon.

Lesson 30

Activity Ideas

1. Make a galaxy montage using coffee filters, water-based markers, and black construction paper. Directions are available from NASA at the link on the online Teacher's Resource Page. Across the top of the montage, write "The Heavens Declare the Glory of God."

2. Several space-oriented activities with food are featured at NASA as well. Make a gingerbread robot, shuttle dog, pop rockets, or cook with the sun. Links to these activites can be found at the online Teacher's Resource Page.

3. There are many ways to make a scale model of the solar system. Several examples are listed below. Links to these activities can be found at the online Teacher's Resource Page.

   • "Build a Solar System"—Make a scale model of the solar system depending on the size of your sun (note, if the sun is .85 inches in diameter, you can fit the solar system into a football field).

   • "How Big is the Solar System?"—Go on a thousand-yard "planet walk" (sun is eight inches in diameter, earth is the size of a peppercorn).

   • "The Toilet Paper Solay System"—Make a toilet-paper model of the solar system.

4. *Science and the Bible* volume 3 features an experiment that demonstrates how the planets obey God's laws of motion.

5. Read through the student handout.

Extension Activities

History

H.G. Wells played an important part in developing the science-fiction genre. One of his most famous works is *War of the Worlds*. Write a short biographical sketch on Wells. Find out how evolutionary ideas influenced him, and how he, in turn, used evolutionary ideas to influence others. For help, see the links at the online Teacher's Resource Page.

Language Arts

Learn more about the science fiction genre. Who were some of its major contributors (besides H.G. Wells)? What did they believe about God? How has science fiction changed society? Choose a sci-fi work to read and analyze. Write a report summarizing your findings.

Science

1. Several Bible-believing scientists were pioneers in the field of astronomy. Choose one of the following scientists and commemorate his life on a postage stamp. On the front of the stamp, sketch important scenes from his life. On the back of the stamp, record a timeline of his life, his beliefs about God and the heavens, and his contributions to science. For help, see "Creation Scientists and Other Biographies of Interest" at the online Teacher's Resource Page. Links to postage stamp outlines that you can print, can be also be found at the online Teacher's Resource Page.

2. The online NASA Kids' Club features many space-oriented games. The link to this site can be found at the online Teacher's Resource Page.

3. Some have claimed that life originated on other planets. Is this true? Find out more at the "Get Answers: Astronomy" section of the AiG website. A link to this can be found at the online Teacher's Resource Page.

Bible

1. Look up the following passages. What does the Bible say about the heavens?

    *   Genesis 1:1; Genesis 1:14–18; Genesis 15:1–6; Exodus 20:11; Deuteronomy 4:19; Deuteronomy 10:14; 1 Chronicles 29:10–12; Nehemiah 9:5–6; Psalm 33:1–8; Psalm 102:24–27; Psalm 115:15–16; Psalm 121:2; Psalm 148:1–6; Isaiah 40:21–22; Isaiah 47:13–14; Isaiah 55:8–9; Jeremiah 8:1–2; Jeremiah 32:16–17; Colossians 1:13–17; Hebrews 1:10–12; 2 Peter 3:7–13; Revelation 21:1–4

2. Some have claimed that the "sons of God" and/or "nephilim" mentioned in Genesis 6:2–4 are aliens. Is this true? Find out more by reading "Who Were the Nephilim?" at the online Teacher's Resource Page.

Recommended Resources

Taking Back Astronomy (book for teens and adults)

Creation Astronomy: Viewing the Universe through Biblical Glasses (DVD for teens and adults)

The Astronomy Book (book for teens and adults)

God's Design for Heaven and Earth: Our Universe (textbook for children)

Destination: Moon—the Spiritual and Scientific Voyage of the Eighth Man to Walk on the Moon (book for children)

Notes

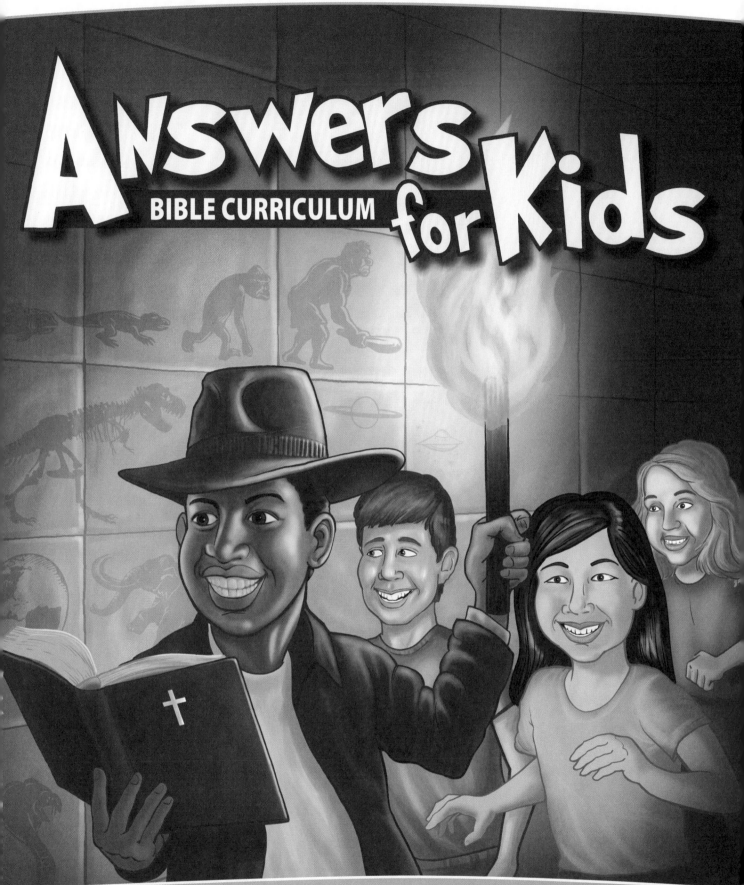

Helping kids answer questions about their faith

Answers for Kids
BIBLE CURRICULUM

STUDENT HANDOUTS

by Stacia McKeever & illustrated by Dan Lietha

"The Seven C's of History" (Creation, Corruption, Catastrophe, Confusion, Christ, Cross, Consummation) help us remember the big events which have affected —— and will affect —— the history of the universe.

"In the beginning God created the heavens and the earth" (Genesis 1:1).

The first "C" is the Creation of all things. In the book of Genesis (which means "beginnings"), God tells us He created everything in six days.

Let's take a quick look at what happened on each of those six days.

DAY 1 — EARTH, SPACE, TIME & LIGHT

Day 1—God says, "Let there be light" and there is! He separates the light from the darkness and calls the light "Day" and the darkness "Night." This light comes from a source other than the sun—the sun isn't created until Day 4.

DAY 2 — ATMOSPHERE

Day 2—God makes an expanse (something "stretched out," like a space) and separates the waters above the expanse from the waters below.

DAY 3 — DRY LAND & PLANTS

Day 3—God causes the waters under the expanse to come together, so that dry ground appears. Then He tells the land to bring forth plants and trees.

DAY 4 — SUN, MOON & STARS

Day 4—God makes the sun, the moon, and the stars. These are to serve as signs to mark seasons, days, and years. The sun and moon will rule the day and night, which cycle began on Day 1.

DAY 5 — SEA & FLYING CREATURES

Day 5 God creates the animals which live in water and those which fly in the air.

DAY 6 — LAND ANIMALS & MAN

Day 6 God creates the land animals, including the dinosaurs, and—His most special creation—humanity. Adam and Eve are the first people— the great, great, great . . . grandparents of us all! God gave them—and the animals—plants to eat.

When God had completely finished creating, He labeled all He had done as "very good." What would a "very good" creation be like? Imagine a place with no death, no violence, no disease, no sickness, no fear. Sounds like a great place to live!

Day 7—God "rests"—or stops—His work of creation. Now He keeps up-holding His creation (Colossians 1:17).

God created all things in six days and rested on the seventh. This became the first "week." Today, we follow this example by working for six days and resting for one!

The first six days are history!

There are those who say the first few chapters in Genesis are merely fairy tales with some truth. However, since God is "all knowing" and since He wrote the original book of Genesis, He should know how and when He created. He says "six days," so it must be "six days"!

"You are worthy, O Lord, to receive glory and honor and power; for You created all things, and by Your will they exist and were created" (Revelation 4:11).

What is the difference
between the two piles of wood below?

Of course, one pile of wood has been built into a tree house, while nothing has been done to the second pile of wood. Now, we all know that the first pile didn't organize itself. Rather, someone used the information from a drawing to build the wood into something you can play in!

Just as a blueprint was used to plan the assembly of the wood into a tree house, so a "blueprint" is used in our bodies to plan the many complex systems that make us who we are. Our blueprint is called deoxyribonucleic acid (or DNA for short!). DNA stores the information needed to build our cells.

Science has shown that information can come only from intelligence. In the story above, the blueprints containing the information needed to build the tree house were drawn from the ideas of the designers. Where, then, did the information found in our cells come from?

In the beginning, matter . . .

There are those who say all things (living and non-living) came from an explosion of matter (stuff that we're made of) billions of years ago. Over time, this matter supposedly organized itself into the many complex living creatures we see today—such as a blue jay or a daisy. However, we've seen that science has shown the matter cannot rearrange into high-information structures by itself.

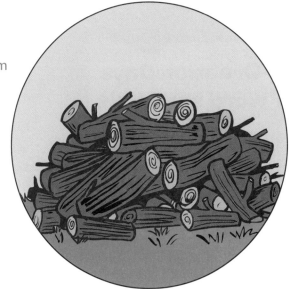

Since the information in our DNA (which is far more complex than the information on the tree-house blueprint) can only come from a source of greater information (or intelligence), there must have been something other than matter in the beginning.

In the beginning, God!

This "other source" must have no limit to its intelligence—in fact, it must be an ultimate source of intelligence from which all things have come. The Bible tells us there is such a source—God. Since God has no beginning and no end and knows all (Psalm 147:5), it makes sense that God is the source of the information we see all around us! This fits with real science, just as we would expect.

Which of the following creatures have been on the earth the longest?

A
B
C
D

DO YOU KNOW YOUR BIBLE?

Which of the Ten Commandments tells us God created the heavens and the earth in six days?

LET THERE BE FUN!

Creation Days word scramble

These numbers stand for the six days of creation. Each of the scrambled words relates to the creation day it is found in. See if you can unscramble each word!

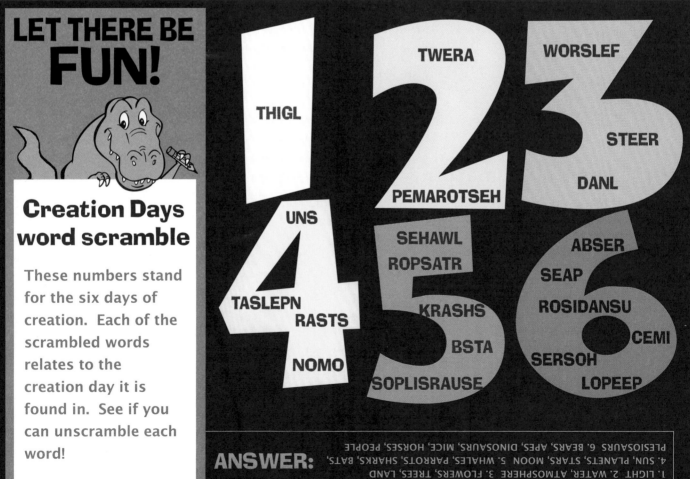

1
THIGL

2
TWERA
PEMAROTSEH

3
WORSLEF
STEER
DANL

4
UNS
TASLEPN
RASTS
NOMO

5
SEHAWL
ROPSATR
KRASHS
BSTA
SOPLISRAUSE

6
ABSER
SEAP
ROSIDANSU
CEMI
SERSOH
LOPEEP

"The Seven C's of History" (Creation, Corruption, Catastrophe, Confusion, Christ, Cross, Consummation) help us remember the big events which have affected——and will affect——the history of the universe.

". . . but of the tree of knowledge of good and evil you shall not eat, for in the day that you eat of it you shall surely die" (Genesis 2:17).

We've seen that in the beginning God created the heavens and the earth and everything was very good (Genesis 1–2). The next "C," Corruption, found in Genesis 3, is sad.

From perfection ...

For a while, things were perfect in the Garden of Eden. Adam and Eve lived in a beautiful garden (planted especially for them by God) and could eat of any tree in Eden, except one. This first couple had a perfect relationship with their Creator, a perfect marriage and a perfect place to live. The animals, which Adam ruled over, got along perfectly. Something has obviously corrupted this "very good" world into the world we see today, which is full of sickness and death.

To imperfection ...

Adam and Eve both knew they could eat from any tree in the Garden of Eden except the one known as the Tree of the Knowledge of Good and Evil. God had forbidden them to eat of it, telling them that they would surely begin to die (the Hebrew in Genesis actually says, "dying, you shall die") the very day they ate of it.

The devil, who took the form of a serpent, knew what God had said, but he caused Eve to question God's words by asking, "Did God say you weren't to eat of any tree of the garden?" and then lying, "You won't really die." Eve believed the serpent, rather than God, and ate the forbidden fruit. Then she gave some to Adam, who hadn't been deceived by the serpent but ate it willingly (1 Tim. 2:14). This caused them both to immediately die spiritually (be separated from God) and to begin to die physically.

Because of his disobedience (sin), all of his descendants (this includes you and me!) are born with sin in our nature. Because of Adam's sin, our bodies will die. Because of Adam's sin, God cursed His precious creation. The world we see today, while reflecting God's original creation, has been corrupted by sin.

To perfection ...

The good news of this sad tale is that God did not abandon His creation after Adam's sin! He promised that one day He would send a Savior, the "seed of a woman" to bruise the head of the serpent (Genesis 3:15). This Savior, Jesus Christ, was indeed born of a woman without a human father, about 4,000 years later. He died on the Cross, and rose again to save His people from their sins, so indeed dealing a death-blow to (bruising the head of) the devil (serpent).

Good enough isn't good enough!

Because God is holy, His standard is perfection (Matthew 5:48). Because we sin, we are unable to work our way to Heaven (Romans 3:23). Eternal life is a gift offered by God (Ephesians 2:8-9) to those who realize they are sinners and are in need of a Savior, who is Jesus Christ (Romans 6:23). Jesus Christ died on the Cross and rose from the grave to pay for sin and to purchase a place in Heaven for those who turn from their sin and believe on Him (Isaiah 53 & John 3:16).

"For we know that the whole creation groans and labors with birth pangs together until now" (Romans 8:22).

We need to remember that what we see in the world today is only a dim reflection of God's perfect creation. The corruption that came through Adam's disobedience in the Garden of Eden changed God's handiwork completely. The effects of the Curse that God placed on His creation can be seen in various ways throughout our lives.

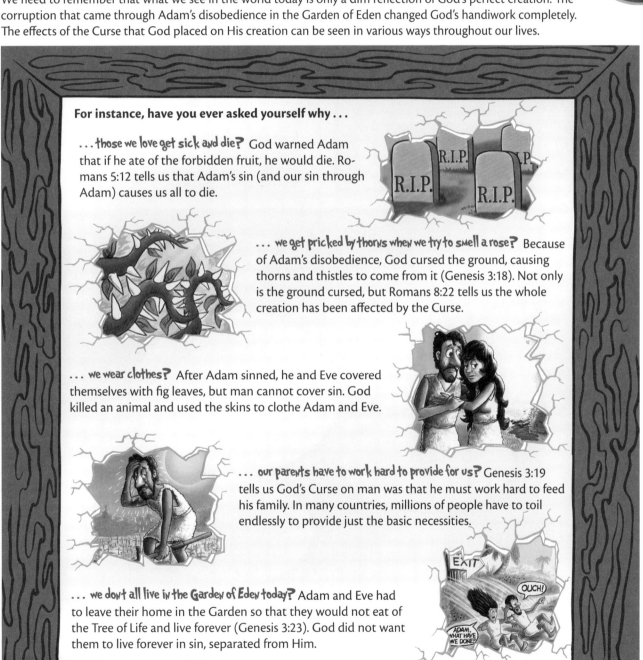

For instance, have you ever asked yourself why . . .

. . . those we love get sick and die? God warned Adam that if he ate of the forbidden fruit, he would die. Romans 5:12 tells us that Adam's sin (and our sin through Adam) causes us all to die.

. . . we get pricked by thorns when we try to smell a rose? Because of Adam's disobedience, God cursed the ground, causing thorns and thistles to come from it (Genesis 3:18). Not only is the ground cursed, but Romans 8:22 tells us the whole creation has been affected by the Curse.

. . . we wear clothes? After Adam sinned, he and Eve covered themselves with fig leaves, but man cannot cover sin. God killed an animal and used the skins to clothe Adam and Eve.

. . . our parents have to work hard to provide for us? Genesis 3:19 tells us God's Curse on man was that he must work hard to feed his family. In many countries, millions of people have to toil endlessly to provide just the basic necessities.

. . . we don't all live in the Garden of Eden today? Adam and Eve had to leave their home in the Garden so that they would not eat of the Tree of Life and live forever (Genesis 3:23). God did not want them to live forever in sin, separated from Him.

As terrible as things like pain, sickness, and death are, they are not permanent parts of God's creation. We look forward to the last "C" of history—Consummation—when the Curse will be no more (Revelation 22:3) and those whose names have been written in the Lamb's Book of Life will spend eternity in a perfect place.

DID YOU KNOW...

Fossilized thorns have been found?

Psilophyton crenulatum

Many claim these fossils are millions of years old. Does this fit with what we find in the Bible? Since fossils don't come with age-tags attached, it's impossible to know precisely how old they are. Since the Bible tells us thorns entered the world after God cursed the ground because of Adam's disobedience, these plants were fossilized after Adam sinned—not millions of years before.

DO YOU KNOW YOUR BIBLE?

Does the Bible say the forbidden fruit was an apple?

Answer: No. The forbidden fruit is only referred to as a "fruit." The Bible doesn't tell us what kind of fruit it was.

LET THERE BE FUN!

Who said it?

Below are seven quotes found in Genesis 1-11. See if you can match the quotes with who said them!

GOD (A)

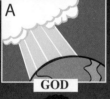
ADAM (B)

THE SERPENT (C)

EVE (D)

E

CAIN

F

NOAH

G

PEOPLE AT BABEL

1 "I do not know. Am I my brother's keeper?"

2 "Blessed be the LORD God of Shem, and Canaan shall be his servant ..."

3 "This is now bone of my bones and flesh of my flesh."

4 "Let us make man in our image, after our likeness."

5 "But of the fruit of the tree which is in the middle of the garden, God has said, You shall not eat of it, neither shall you touch it, lest you die."

6 "Come, let us build us a city and a tower, and its top in the heavens."

7 "You shall not surely die, for God knows that in the day you eat of it, then your eyes shall be opened ..."

ANSWERS:
A-4, B-3, C-7, D-5, E-1, F-2, G-6

"The Seven C's of History" (Creation, Corruption, Catastrophe, Confusion, Christ, Cross, Consummation) help us remember the big events which have affected——and will affect——the history of the universe.

"So He destroyed all living things which were on the face of the ground: both man and cattle, creeping thing and bird of the air. . . . Only Noah and those who were with him in the ark remained alive" (Genesis 7:23).

God created a perfect world in six normal-length days (Genesis 1–2), but Adam disobeyed God's command not to eat the forbidden fruit and brought corruption and death into the world (Romans 5:12). Adam's sin passed to his children, his children's children, and so on. This brings us to the third "C" of history found in Genesis 6–9 . . .

As time went by, people began to invent new machines, explore new places, try new ideas.

Because their hearts were wicked, though, they did things that displeased their Creator. They didn't listen to their ancestor Adam as he told them what had happened in the Garden of Eden and how they needed to obey and worship only the Lord. This grieved God so much that He determined to destroy everything with the breath of life in it. Only one man, Noah, found favor in His eyes. God told Noah that He would send a great flood to judge the entire globe by covering it with water.

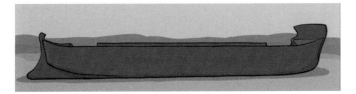

Lions and tigers and . . . dinosaurs?

Because the Creator knew Noah was a righteous man, God provided a way for him, his wife, his three sons, their wives, the land animals and birds (the fish and other sea creatures could survive in the water) to survive this catastrophe by building

an ark. Noah and his family worked on the Ark for many years, probably warning those around them about God's judgment that was coming. Nobody but his family believed. When they finished building, God brought two of every animal (including dinosaurs!), and seven of some, to the Ark.

And the rains came down . . .

After all were on board, the "windows of heaven" opened and the "fountains of the great deep" broke up. These provided the water that would cover every spot on the whole earth.

We've all seen the damage a local flood can do—ripping up trees, depositing layers of mud, destroying everything in its path. Now imagine the damage done by a flood covering the entire planet!
Nothing would be the same after the waters had left and the earth had dried. How strange everything must have looked to Noah and his family as they came off the Ark!

After leaving the Ark, Noah built an altar to the Lord, sacrificing one of each of the clean animals. The Lord saw the sacrifice and promised to never flood the entire earth again. The sign of this promise is the rainbow.

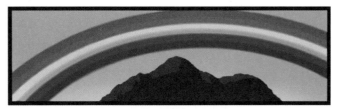

That's not the Ark . . . THIS is the ARK!

Do the differences between these two drawings of Noah's Ark really matter?

1 Look at what the Bible says about the shape of the Ark.

CUTE ARK PLANS

> ... the length of the ark shall be three hundred cubits, the breadth of it fifty cubits, and the height of it thirty cubits.
> Genesis 6:15

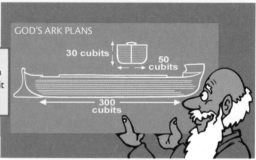

GOD'S ARK PLANS

30 cubits • 50 cubits • 300 cubits

2 The Ark must float.

AAAAAAAAAAA AI!!!

This type of boat will tip over easily in rough water.

God designed the Ark to stay upright in the violent storms and huge waves of a global flood.

3 It must be BIG!

Ham, move over!

OUCH! That hurt!

Shem, get off my foot!

Most "arks" look tiny and over-crowded.

The real Ark had the same capacity as 522 railroad stock cars! It had lots of room.

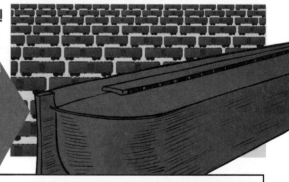

You believe in that? HA HA HA!

Why make Bible story pictures look like fairy tales? Too many people already think the Bible is impossible to believe.

2 Peter 3:5–6

Yes, Noah's Ark WAS real. In fact . . .

WOW!

The next time you see one of these  just remember what the Bible says!

"**Thus I establish My covenant with you: never again shall all flesh be cut off by the waters of the flood; never again shall there be a flood to destroy the earth**" (Genesis 9:11).

Thinkin' about fossils!

Some scientists spend their whole lives studying the petrified remains of dead things (fossils) to try to understand what life was like in the past. This can be a fascinating job as these "paleontologists" seek to determine when the animals (or plants, etc.) died, what they looked like while they were alive, how they moved, what they ate, etc. Each paleontologist looks at a fossil with certain ideas about what the past was like. In fact, we all do!

For instance, take a look at the fossil at the right. Now take a moment and write down five things you know about that fossil.

Perhaps you said "it's millions of years old," or "it took a long time to form." Now think about what you've written for a moment—do you really know these things or are they just your ideas about the fossil? How do you know how old the fossil is or how long it took for the animal to be fossilized?

It's important, as Christians, that our ideas about the past are based on what the Bible tells us has happened. Using the Bible's true record of history to help us understand, we might say the following things about the fossil:

1. This animal died. Animal death was not a part of God's original creation, so the animal must have died after the world was corrupted through Adam's sin.

2. The fossil can't be "millions of years" old, since adding up the years in the Bible shows us the world is only about 6,000 years old.

3. An animal that is buried quickly is more likely to be preserved than to decay and fall apart. The worldwide Flood in Noah's day provided great conditions for quickly burying lots of animals and plants, so the animal may have died at this time.

These are just a few things we can learn from the Bible about this fossil.

Studying the fossils you find (maybe even in your own backyard!) can be exciting, but it's important to distinguish between what we actually find and what others may say about our findings. Since God's Word gives us the true history of the world, we need to apply this to fossils as well.

DID YOU KNOW?

Water covers 70% of the earth's surface? Yet many deny the earth was completely covered in water at one time. Did you also know . . . no (liquid) water has been found on Mars? Yet many believe water shaped the surface of the Red Planet (Mars) in the past. Why would people deny a huge flood on Earth and promote one on Mars?

2 Peter 3:5–6 reminds us, "For this they willfully forget: that . . . the world that then existed perished, being flooded with water."

DO YOU KNOW YOUR BIBLE?
Who closed the door to the Ark?

Answer: Genesis 7:16 "And they that entered, went in male and female of all flesh, as God had commanded him: and the LORD shut him in."

LET THERE BE FUN!

All aboard Noah's Ark?

God told Noah to have at least two of certain kinds of animals (seven of some) on board the Ark (Genesis 6:19–7:3). The animals shown here in pairs were on the Ark. There are fifteen pairs for you to match. These animals *were* on the Ark. Ten of the animals shown here were not on the Ark because they could survive outside of it. These animals do not have a pair. Circle the animals that were not on the Ark!

Animals on the Ark: *Apatosaurus*, bat, bird (flying), dodo bird, giraffe, horse, kangaroo, mammoth, mouse, monkey, rabbit, rhinoceros, skunk, snake, *Tyrannosaurus rex*
Animals not on the Ark: dolphin, eel, fish (gold), *Kronosaurus*, plesiosaur, octopus, sea horse, shark, starfish, whale

"The Seven C's of History" (Creation, Corruption, Catastrophe, Confusion, Christ, Cross, Consummation) help us remember the big events which have affected——and will affect——the history of the universe.

"'Come, let Us go down and there confuse their language . . . .' So the LORD scattered them abroad from there over the face of all the earth, and they ceased building the city" (Genesis 11:7–8).

In the beginning

God's perfect creation was corrupted by Adam's sin. During the days of Noah, God judged the wickedness of man with a great catastrophe, covering the entire planet with water.

After Noah and his family came off the Ark, God commanded them to spread out and fill the earth (now very different from before the Flood). But the descendants of Noah disobeyed God.

Tower plans

They decided to stay in one place, building a tall tower, they hoped would help keep them all together.

When the Lord saw their disobedience, He was displeased—as He is with all disobedience—and He confused the language of the people so they couldn't understand each other (until this time, they all spoke one language).

In this way, the Creator scattered them over all the earth.

The several different languages created suddenly at Babel (Genesis 10–11) could each subsequently give rise to many more. Language gradually changes, so when a group of people breaks into several groups which no longer interact, after a few centuries they may each speak a different (but related) language. Today,

we have thousands of languages but fewer than 20 language "families."

Back up a minute

Adam and Eve were the first humans. Then all humans died except Noah, his wife and their three sons and daughters-in-law during the Flood of Noah. If we're all descended from the same two people, then why do we look so different from each other?

Creative differences

Actually, this "C" has a lot to do with answering this question!

God created Adam and Eve with the ability to produce children with a variety of different characteristics. This ability was passed on through Noah and his family.

As the people scattered, they took with them different amounts of the information for certain characteristics—e.g., height, the amount of pigment for hair and skin color (we all have the same pigment, just more or less of it), etc.

From this one event, the tribes and nations of the world have resulted. Because we all came from Noah's family a few thousand years ago, we're all related!

The Land of Shinar 4,000 years ago

A story based on Genesis 11:1–9

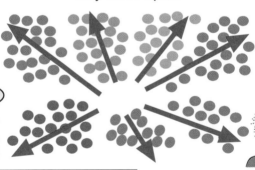

"And He has made from one blood every nation of men to dwell on all the face of the earth . . ." (Acts 17:26).

Where'd they come from?

"Cavemen" supposedly lived thousands of years before "modern man" came on the scene. But God, in His Word, tells us the true history of these people. In Genesis, He tells us that Adam and Eve were the first two people on earth. Later, only Noah and his family were left on earth after God judged man's disobedience with a worldwide Flood.

Then, after God *confused* the languages at Babel because of man's disobedience, various groups split up, taking with them their individual knowledge of technology. Some knew more about farming, some knew more about building great structures, and some knew how to use metal to make tools. Those groups which didn't know how to do any of these things would be forced to "begin again"—learning these skills on their own. Those who did have these skills were able to use them once they found a suitable place to settle—building great pyramids or magnificent gardens.

Where'd they live?

Many families who weren't expert builders would have found caves a good place to quickly make new homes. Today, the people who lived in these caves are called "cavemen." There was nothing "primitive" about them, however—they used musical instruments, drew fascinating pictures on cave walls, knew how to make stone tools, could sew their own clothes, and hunted their food with great skill. When their bones are found, they are similar to our bones, showing they really were people like us!

Where do you live?

"In the brick house down the street on the right" may be the answer you give to that question. Others may say they live in a house made of wood, or in a flat, or on a houseboat, or even underground. Are those who live in brick houses more intelligent than those who live underground? Absolutely not! These families simply live in different places, just as happened after Babel.

In fact, in Coober Pedy (in Australia), living above ground is very hot, so many people build their homes underground—real live "cavemen" with television sets!

Who were they?

Evolutionists believe the evidence they find of those who lived in caves points toward us having less-than-human ancestors. However, seeing these things through "biblical glasses" helps us rightly understand that these people were descendants of Noah and were, in fact, our relatives!

DID YOU KNOW ...

hundreds of "flood legends" have been found throughout the world? In fact, most of today's people groups tell stories that sound very similar to what we read in Genesis. Why? It makes sense that, as the people split up after Babel, they took with them the tales their ancestors had passed on to them about the great catastrophe of Noah's day.

The true account was preserved by God and written down by Moses so that all would remember what had happened and would learn to obey Him.

DO YOU KNOW YOUR BIBLE?

Does the Bible call the tower in Genesis 11:1-9 the "Tower of Babel"?

Answer: No. Genesis 11:1-9 only refers to it as "a tower." However, it is called the Tower of Babel today because the city where the tower was built was called Babel.

LET THERE BE FUN!

Babel word scramble

Read Genesis 11:1-9, and then unscramble the words below to find out what they say.

1. EHLOW

2. RAHTE

3. PESKO

4. MEAS

5. NULEGAGA

6. SRODW

Babel word find

The thirteen words listed below are hidden in the tower-shaped puzzle. Look forward, backward, up and down. See if you can find them all.

Shinar, people, sin, build, tower, bricks, city, God, language, confusion, Babel, scatter, Genesis

```
          SHINARN
          ODALNAD
         TEFTREWOT
        EDLBINMBABEL
      CAFVATYHUJIDASKEM
      SSCONFUSIONANIHFE
    OSKERFGOTMARCIANDUJIM
    AKCTHIUFGOBHRETTACSUN
  AJEFGIJKLAERATGHGHBUILDNNG
  AWLEDRFTIGENESISYGEBAICATS
  YTICZBUJIEHOPEOPLEUNJIMGOD
```

"The Seven C's of History" (Creation, Corruption, Catastrophe, Confusion, Christ, Cross, Consummation) help us remember the big events which have affected——and will affect——the history of the universe.

"So all this was done that it might be fulfilled which was spoken by the Lord through the prophet, saying: 'Behold, the virgin shall be with child, and bear a Son, and they shall call His name Immanuel,' which is translated, 'God with us.'" (Matthew 1:22–23).

God's perfect creation was corrupted by Adam when he disobeyed God. This disobedience brought sin and death into the world. Because of Adam's disobedience, and because we have all sinned personally anyway, we are all deserving of the death penalty and need a Savior (Romans 5:12).

God did not leave His precious—but corrupted—creation without hope. He promised to send Someone one day who would take away the penalty for sin, which is death (Genesis 3:15; Ezekiel 18:4; Romans 6:23).

God slew an animal in the Garden (a lamb/sheep?) because of the sin of Adam, so Adam's descendants sacrificed animals. Such sacrifices could only *cover* sin—they looked forward to the time when the ultimate sacrifice would be made by the One whom God would send (Hebrews 9).

When God gave Moses the Law, people began to see that they could never measure up to God's standard of perfection (Romans 3:20)—if they broke any part of the Law, the result was the same as breaking the whole lot (James 2:10)!

They needed Someone to take away their imperfection and present them faultless before God's throne (Romans 5:9; 1 Peter 3:18).

God's gift to us

Just as God has a purpose and plan for everything and everyone, so He sent His promised Savior at just the right time (Galatians 4:4). There was a problem, however. All humans are descended from Adam, and therefore all humans are born with sin. God's chosen One must be perfect, as well as infinite, to take away the infinite penalty for sin.

God solved this "problem" by sending His Son Jesus Christ—completely human and completely God. Think of it—the Creator of the universe (John 1:1-3, 14) became part of His creation so that He might save His people from their sins!

Jesus was born to a virgin over 2,000 years ago in a town called Bethlehem, as the prophets Isaiah (7:14) and Micah (5:2) had foretold 700 years previously. His parents took Him to Egypt to escape the anger of King Herod, and the family later settled in Nazareth.

Jesus fulfilled more than 50 prophecies made about Him centuries before, showing He was the One promised over 4,000 years before by His Father. While He spent over 30 years on Earth, He never once

sinned—He did nothing wrong. He healed many people, fed huge crowds and taught thousands of listeners about their Creator God and how to be reconciled to Him. He even used the book of Genesis to explain that marriage is between one man and one woman (Matthew 19:3-6, quoting Genesis 1:27 and 2:24).

Jesus Christ came to earth so that we might have eternal life with Him!

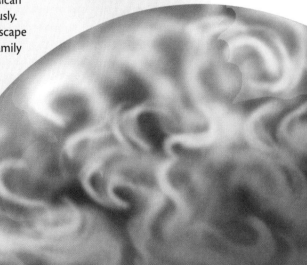

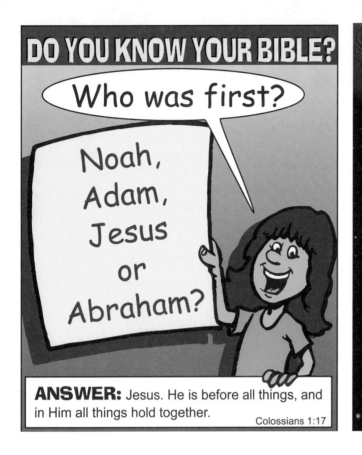

Who was first?

Noah, Adam, Jesus or Abraham?

ANSWER: Jesus. He is before all things, and in Him all things hold together.

Colossians 1:17

What was Jesus's first miraculous act?

Many would answer "turning water into wine" (John 2). However, the Apostle John says this is just the first sign that Jesus performed in His earthly ministry. The Bible actually records a miracle of Jesus that occurred over 4,000 years before He was even born. John began his gospel by saying that Jesus, the Word, "was God" and "all things came into being through Him, and without Him not even one thing came into being that has come into being" (John 1:3). Paul tells us, "For all things were created by Him ..." (Colossians 1:16).

The first miracle Jesus performed that the Bible tells about is that of creation!

Jesus the Christ

The list of people from Adam to Christ (on the *From Creation to Christ!* chart) shows that Jesus was a human—a descendant of the first man, Adam. In fact, Jesus referred to Himself many times as the "Son of Man" (e.g., Matthew 9:6; 12:40). The Bible also tells us that Jesus was God. John says, "... the Word [Jesus] was God" (John 1:1, 14). Paul calls Jesus "our great God and Savior" (Titus 2:13), and Thomas refers to Him as "my Lord and my God" (John 20:28). Many addressed Him as the "Son of God" (John 11:27, etc.)—a name which Jesus also used about Himself (John 10:36). Matthew gives Him the title Emmanuel, which means "God with us" (Matthew 1:23).

In addition, just as God did in the Old Testament, Jesus raised the dead (John 5:21; 1 Samuel 2:6), forgave sins (Matthew 9:2, 6; Jeremiah 31:34), and healed the sick (Luke 8:47; Exodus 15:26). As God, Jesus deserves our worship for who He is and what He has done for us (John 5:23).

LET THERE BE FUN!

Each of the people in the answers is shown on the *From Creation to Christ!* chart.

1 Jude 14 tells about a man who was the "seventh from Adam."

2 He had 12 children who became the leaders of the 12 tribes of Israel.

3 This man led the captive Jews back to Palestine in 536 BC under the permission of Cyrus, King of Persia.

A This man lived the longest— 969 years!

B This king reigned the longest of any king of Judah— 55 years.

C This king was struck with leprosy because of his disobedience toward God at the end of his reign.

Answers: A. Enoch B. Methuselah C. Jacob D. Manasseh E. Zerubbabel F. Uzziah

"The Seven C's of History" (Creation, Corruption, Catastrophe, Confusion, Christ, Cross, Consummation) help us remember the big events which have affected——and will affect——the history of the universe.

"For I delivered to you first of all that which I also received: that Christ died for our sins according to the Scriptures, and that He was buried, and that He rose again the third day according to the Scriptures" (1 Corinthians 15:3–4).

The First Adam

Our first "parent," Adam, did not lead the perfect life he should have. He disobeyed his Creator's command not to eat from the Tree of the Knowledge of Good and Evil. Because of God's judgment on this one act of rebellion, the entire creation, which was originally perfect (Genesis 1:31), became subject to death and corruption. Because of Adam's sin, and because we sin personally, we all die (Romans 5:12–19).

The Last Adam

Around 4,000 years after Adam disobeyed, God sent the perfect sacrifice, in the form of His Son, Jesus Christ, to take away the sin of the world, fulfilling the promise God made in Genesis 3:15. Jesus is called the "Last Adam" in 1 Corinthians 15:45, and He came to restore the fellowship with the Creator that was broken by Adam's sin.

Adam disobeyed God's command not to eat the forbidden fruit; Jesus fulfilled the Creator's purpose that He die for the sin of the world.

The First Adam brought death into the world through his disobedience; the Last Adam (Jesus Christ) brought eternal life with God through His obedience (1 Corinthians 15:21–22).

Because God is perfectly holy, He must punish sin—either the sinner himself, or a substitute to bear His wrath.

God Himself made the first sacrifice for sin by killing an animal (this was the first death in God's creation) after Adam disobeyed (Genesis 3:21). But we should not offer animal sacrifices for sin any more. This is because the Lamb of God (John 1:29; Revelation 5:12) was sacrificed once for all (Hebrews 7:27). Jesus bore God's wrath on our sin by dying in our place (Isaiah 53:6). So all those who believe in Him will be saved from the ultimate penalty for sin (eternal separation from God), and will live with Him forever.

But Jesus Christ, the Creator of all things (John 1:1–3; Colossians 1:15–16), was not defeated by death. He rose three days after He was crucified, showing that He has power over all things, including death, the "last enemy" (1 Corinthians 15:26)!

This is why the Apostle Paul says, "O death, where is your sting? O grave, where is your victory? . . . But thanks be to God who gives us the victory through our Lord Jesus Christ" (1 Corinthians 15:55, 57).

When we believe in the Lord Jesus Christ and understand what He has done for us, we are passed from death into life (John 5:24). The names of those who receive Him are written in the Lamb's Book of Life (Revelation 13:8; 17:8)—when they die, they will go to be with Him forever (John 3:16)!

DO YOU KNOW YOUR BIBLE?

In Genesis, God cursed the earth with something His Son, Jesus, later wore on the Cross. What is it?

ANSWER: Thorns
The Curse: Genesis 3:17-18
The Crown: John 19:2-6

LET THERE BE FUN!

See if you can find the 12 hidden words in the Cross word find. Look up, down, forward and backward.

ADAM
DISOBEY

JESUS
CROSS
NAILS

SIN
FORGIVEN
DEAD
TOMB

RAISED
ALIVE
HEAVEN

```
        J E B B J B A D A M H
        K V N H E V V F D V A
        J I H J S G V B I N R
H C I M G L H J U K K T S E A S L L I
E X T V N A I L S E R T O V U I O M B
L F O V B N E V A E H B B I D X C F V
E S M X F C V C G S I N E G N M M M J
F V B B T H A N Y D X D Y R B D E A D
        E J U H Y G R F R O E
        B D I S O B A U V F F
        L C D S R E I N A E D
        E J H O U Y S N D D L
        H K J R H B E A C V A
        C A R C I N D R A R U
```

Up from the grave He arose!

There are those who do not believe the historical accounts that Jesus really died and rose again. They have made up many stories to try to explain why the tomb where Jesus was buried is now empty.

- Some say Jesus just fainted while on the Cross, later revived in the cool tomb and then left. But . . . Jesus would have had to unwrap Himself from the grave clothes, push aside the stone (which was too heavy to be moved by a single man) across the entrance to the tomb, and then walk past the soldiers outside. He would have been too weak to do this, and the guards would have stopped Him. Further, the Roman soldier pierced Him with a spear while He was still on the Cross, and the blood and water that flowed from this wound showed that He was truly dead.

- Others believe the disciples stole Jesus' body and then lied, saying He arose. But . . . the disciples would not have made it past the tomb guards without the guards noticing them. Most of the disciples later died for their belief that Jesus arose—they would not have died for something they knew to be a lie.

- Some suggest the Romans or Jews removed Jesus' body from the tomb. But . . . these two groups of people had no reason to do so—in fact, they would have wanted a body in the tomb to stop any stories that Jesus had risen. And when the followers of Christ began saying that they had seen Him alive, the Jews or Romans had only to produce the body showing the Christians' claims to be false—yet they didn't.

Still others say the story that Jesus rose from the dead is just a myth or legend. But . . . the gospels were written between 25 and 65 years after the crucifixion of Christ—far too little time for a myth to develop because eyewitnesses to the events were still around at that time to answer any questions. Further, many of those who saw Jesus after His Resurrection did not like Him. They would have certainly corrected the reports that claimed they had seen Him.

Answers for Kids

BIBLE CURRICULUM

for Kids Consummation

Lesson 11

"The Seven C's of History" (Creation, Corruption, Catastrophe, Confusion, Christ, Cross, Consummation) help us remember the big events which have affected——and will affect——the history of the universe.

"Now I saw a new heaven and a new earth, for the first heaven and the first earth had passed away . . ." (Revelation 21:1).

In the beginning, God created a perfect world. It was a beautiful place—full of life, without death, disease, pain, or suffering. Adam's disobedience changed all that. When he ate the fruit God had told him not to eat, sin and death entered the world (Romans 5:12). This corruption changed the world so much that what we see today is only a dim reflection of the world that was. Adam's sin led to the catastrophe of Noah's day, the confusion at Babel, and the death of Christ on the Cross.

Is there an end in sight?

Death has been around almost as long as humans have. Sometimes it might seem as if it is a permanent part of God's creation. Romans 8 tells us the whole of creation is suffering because of Adam's sin. It might seem as if there is no end to the suffering brought about by this act of disobedience. Of course, none of us can say that we have not also disobeyed God in our own lives (Romans 3:23; 1 John 1:10), so all of us in a sense share in the blame for what we see around us.

However, God, in His great mercy, has promised not to leave His creation in its sinful state. He has promised to do away with the corruption Adam brought into the world. He offers us this salvation through His Son. Also, He has promised to remove, in the future, the Curse He placed on His creation (Revelation 22:3)!

He will make a new heavens and a new earth one day—one which we can't even begin to imagine (2 Peter 3:13). In this new place there will be no death, no crying, no pain (Revelation 21:4). Nobody will be sad.

As those who have repented and believed in what Jesus did for us on the Cross, we can look forward to this new heaven and earth, knowing we will enjoy God forever in a wonderful place. The corruption that was introduced in the Garden of Eden will be taken away by God, giving us, once again, a perfect place to live.

Back to Very Good

The Bible tells us God originally created the world "very good."

It was perfect!

But Romans 8:22 says, "For we know that the whole creation groans and travails in pain together until now."

Something has changed this world. Now we see bad and good. The "good" things are just remnants of that original "very good" creation, while the bad things were a later intrusion, not part of what God originally created.

In today's world we have...

Beauty & **Ugliness** | Pleasure & **Pain** | Health & **Sickness** | Happiness & **Sorrow** | Life & **Death**

Some people blame God for the bad THINGS in our world.

God, why did you do this?

But it's not God's fault!

The bad we see in this world is man's fault. Man's sin brought the curse of death and corrupted the whole creation.

However, God knew all this would happen, and He had a plan to rescue his children from this cursed world.

We think of this present world as home, but it is only temporary. God has new heavens and a new Earth in store for those who believe in His Son's death and Resurrection.

Those who don't believe in Jesus' death and Resurrection will have a different eternal home.
2 Thessalonians 1:8–10
Revelation 20:12–15

Once again, God's children will enjoy a perfect creation. This new home will last forever. All the bad things will be no more. How great it will be when God restores His creation, back to "VERY GOOD"!

Make sure this new world will be your future home, too! John 3:16; Romans 10:8–10

Answers for Kids

BIBLE CURRICULUM

Is There Really a God?

LESSON 12

"Before the mountains were brought forth, or ever You had formed the earth and the world, even from everlasting to everlasting, You are God" (Psalm 90:2).

God is *infinite*—He has no beginning (He was never born), and He has no end (He can never die). He is the eternal Creator of all things—space, matter and even time itself.

Some people don't believe what the Bible says about God—they even deny He exists! The Bible tells us that these people deliberately reject the Creator (2 Peter 3:5). As a result, they are blinded to the evidence around us that is consistent with God's existence. For example . . .

1. Unlike the "Energizer Bunny," which just keeps going and going on its own power (or so the ad would have you believe), the universe is running out of available energy and is becoming more chaotic, or disorderly, as time goes on. Eventually, there will be no more energy available throughout the universe to accomplish any work. So where did all the original available energy come from? How was it "wound up" initially? Someone outside of the universe had to have created it orderly in the beginning—that Someone was God.

YOU ARE HERE

UNIVERSE ENERGY

E F

2. Our bodies are made up of trillions of cells. Just one of those cells contains enough information about who we are to fill 500,000 close-typed pages! Scientists who study DNA (or *deoxyribonucleic acid*—a special large molecule that stores all that information in our cells) have not observed huge amounts of new information

originating by chance as it is passed from parent to child. The information stored in our DNA is only rearranged or decreased. So where did the information in all living things come from in the first place? Current scientific observations show that information can only come from a source of intelligence, ultimately. Since God is *infinitely* intelligent, it makes sense that He is the Author of all the information.

3. Those who believe that molecules have evolved into man (contrary to modern scientific observation which shows it just isn't possible) must also believe that the universe is billions of years old. Yet there is **much** evidence that is consistent with the Bible's teaching that the universe has not been around for billions of years, but was created by God around 6,000 years ago.

WOW! ALL THESE DATING METHODS POINT TO A YOUNG EARTH!

YOUNG EARTH EVIDENCES

4. Many tribes and nations share stories or legends similar to the original, unchanged accounts of creation, Noah's Flood and the break-up of the people at Babel found in the Bible. Why is this so? The Bible explains it! As Noah's descendants spread around the earth after the Flood, they took the knowledge of creation and the Flood with them, but the stories have gradually changed over the years. Also, scientists are finding that there is no significant difference between the various so-called "races" of people. This is consistent with the Bible's teaching that there is only one "race"—all humans are descendants of Adam.

The Bible says those who deny God are without excuse, since the creation makes it plain that there is an all-powerful God, as shown by the above examples (Romans 1:20).

Decipher the Code

WOL-LA-CHEE ...... ANT
NA-HASH-CHID ..... BADGER
MOASI .... CAT
BE .... DEER
AH-JAH .... EAR
CHUO ....FIR
AH-TAD .... GIRL
TSE-GAH .... HAIR
TKIN .... ICE
AH-YA-TSINNE ...... JAW
JAD-HO-LONI ...... KETTLE
AH-JAD .... LEG
BE-TAS-TNI .... MIRROR
TSAH .... NEEDLE
A-KHA .... OIL
NE-ZHONI .... PRETTY
CA-YEILTH .... QUIVER
GAH .... RABBIT
DIBEH .... SHEEP
D-AH .... TEA
SHI-DA .... UNCLE
A-KEH-DI-GLINI .... VICTOR
GLOE-IH .... WEASEL
AL-NA-AS-DZOH .... CROSS (X)
TSAH-AH-DZOH ..... YUCCA
BESH-DO-TLIZ ..... ZINC

Imagine you're a Navajo code talker who needs to know what your fellow soldiers are telling you. Use the code key to the left to decode the message on the right. Place the first letter of the English word in the blank beside the Navajo word.

A real Navajo code talker could do this in 20 seconds—how long will it take you?

CHUO.............................. ____
GAH .... ____
A-KHA .... ____
BE-TAS-TNI .... ____

AH-JAH........................... ____
A-KEH-DI-GLINI .... ____
AH-JAH........................... ____
GAH .... ____
AH-JAD........................... ____
WOL-LA-CHEE .... ____
DIBEH .... ____
D-AH.............................. ____
TKIN .... ____
TSAH.............................. ____
AH-TAD .... ____

D-AH.............................. ____
A-KHA............................ ____

AH-JAH........................... ____
A-KEH-DI-GLINI .... ____
AH-JAH........................... ____
GAH .... ____
AH-JAD........................... ____
WOL-LA-CHEE .... ____
DIBEH .... ____
D-AH.............................. ____
TKIN .... ____
TSAH.............................. ____
AH-TAD .... ____

TSAH-AH-DZOH............... ____
A-KHA............................ ____
SHI-DA .... ____

WOL-LA-CHEE .... ____
GAH .... ____
AH-JAH........................... ____

AH-TAD .... ____
A-KHA............................ ____
BE .... ____

ANSWER: FROM EVERLASTING TO EVERLASTING, YOU ARE GOD PSALM 90:2B

Of course I exist!

God's Word assumes He exists. In fact, the very names God uses in dealing with His creation tell us more about His eternal existence.

When Moses asked who it was that was sending him to deliver Israel from the Egyptians, God said, "Tell them, I AM has sent me unto you" (Exodus 3:14). About 1,500 years later, Jesus again used this name with the Jews, showing He is the eternal God (John 8:58). These names also show God exists forever:

I AM!

Elohim

(translated "God")
Eternal Creator and Judge of the universe

YHWH

(translated "LORD")
The personal name of God; reflects His eternal, living, personal nature

El Olam

(translated "The Everlasting God")
Shows that He is eternal, and not bound by time

"All Scripture is given by inspiration of God, and is profitable for doctrine, for reproof, for correction, for instruction in righteousness . . ." (2 Timothy 3:16).

The universe and all in it screams, "There is a God!" (Romans 1:18–21), but the universe cannot tell us how it was made, its history, how we should live our lives, or about when its Creator came to earth.

For that, God has given us His Word, the Bible. Because of the Word of God, we know that God created all things in six normal-length days, that it was originally a "very good" place, and that the first man, Adam, disobeyed the Creator, thus corrupting the entire creation (Genesis 1–3; Romans 8:20–22). We know that Jesus Christ (the Creator) came to earth to save His people from their sins, died, was buried, and rose again on the third day, according to the Scriptures (1 Corinthians 15:3–4).

Where did the Bible come from?

What we today call "the Bible" is actually a collection of 66 books, written by about 40 different authors from all walks of life (kings, fishermen, a tax collector, tent maker, etc.) over a period of 1,600 years. Each book was considered God-breathed and was received as part of the *canon* of Scripture, since it came from a recognized speaker of God (normally a prophet or apostle, or someone under their supervision), and contained no historical, factual, or doctrinal mistakes.

The various authors wrote their books under the *inspiration* of the Holy Spirit (2 Timothy 3:16, literally "All Scripture is God-breathed"). This means that God the Holy Spirit guided the writers so that all of the very words they recorded in their own distinctive styles on the original scrolls were without error (2 Peter 1:21). The men who penned the books listed in what we call the "Old Testament" (OT) wrote mainly in the Hebrew language (a few parts were written in Aramaic). The writers of the "New Testament" (NT) books (written after Jesus returned to Heaven) wrote mainly in the common language of their time—Greek.

Since the Bible *is* the complete Word of God, who cannot lie, we can trust it to tell us the truth about the things we need to know. Because it is the Word of the Creator, we accept it as our final authority in every area it touches on. When we take the Bible as the writer intended, and in the way his original audience would have understood it, we have a basis for understanding and explaining what we observe in the world.

All scripture is given by inspiration of God, and is profitable for doctrine, for reproof, for correction, for instruction in righteousness . . . 2 Timothy 3:16

Meaning Match

2 Timothy 3:16 is an important verse that tells us about God's Word.
In the puzzle below, match the words from the verse with the correct definition.

1. Scripture

2. Inspiration

3. Profitable

4. Doctrine

5. Reproof

6. Correction

7. Instruction

8. Righteousness

A an act of expressing disapproval

B a lesson

C without sin

D the sacred writings of the Bible

E a belief (or system of beliefs) accepted as authoritative by some group or school

F the act of removing errors from something

G helpful

H divine guidance of the mind & soul of men

Answers: 1D, 2H, 3G, 4E, 5A, 6F, 7B, 8C

Answers for Kids
BIBLE CURRICULUM

How Did We Get the Bible? Part 2

Lesson 14

". . . no prophecy of Scripture is of any private interpretation, for prophecy never came by the will of man, but holy men of God spoke as they were moved by the Holy Spirit" (2 Peter 1:20–21).

Bible

Four hundred years after Jesus Christ returned to Heaven, people began to use the Greek word *biblia* (meaning "books") to describe the collection of the sacred writings. Our word "Bible" comes from *biblia*.

Canon

Canon originally referred to a "reed," which was used as a measuring rod, much as we use a yardstick or meter rule today for measuring. The complete list of biblical books is called the canon, meaning the "measuring rod," or the "authority," for truth.

Scripture

This word was used by the NT authors to refer to the sacred books of the OT (Mark 12:10; 2 Timothy 3:15) and also to other books of the NT (2 Peter 3:15–16; 1 Timothy 5:18; 2 Timothy 3:16). Christ Himself cited the Bible as the final authority many times and said, "Scripture cannot be broken" (John 10:35).

Word of God

The Bible claims to be the "Word of God" over 3,000 times (John 10:35; Hebrews 4:12). The authors of NT books often begin a quote taken from the OT with the phrase, "God said" (Matthew 15:4–6). And direct quotes of God speaking in the OT are often begun with "Scripture says" in the NT (Romans 11:2; 1 Timothy 5:18). So the NT authors believed the "Word of God" and "Scripture" were the same.

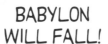

BABYLON WILL FALL!

Prophet

A prophet was a special spokesman for God—he spoke, by God's power, the actual words God gave him.

Apostle

An apostle, as used here, was a man who had seen Christ after His Resurrection (Acts 1:21–22), and who was called by Jesus to be His "messenger."

GENESIS

Did you know?

Some people claim the Bible was merely written by men. But in many places, the Bible claims to be the very Word of God (2 Timothy 3:16). The following points are consistent with the truth that the Bible was not written only by men, but was inspired by the all-knowing Creator God.

• More than 40 men wrote the 66 books of the Bible over a period of 1,600 years, yet the Bible has the same message from beginning to end. Some claim the Bible contains many unresolvable contradictions, but all these claims have been shown to be false.

• Throughout history, many have tried to destroy the Bible—one Roman emperor even attempted to burn all known copies of it! Yet it remains the most-read book of all time.

• Archaeological finds continue to confirm what the Bible says about historical events.

• The Bible makes many specific predictions that have since come to pass; and when it touches on scientific things, it is totally accurate.

• The Bible's message of the Creator who became our Savior has transformed countless lives. It is completely honest about the sinfulness of man (including those seen as "heroes of the faith") and gives all honor and glory to the holy and faithful Creator God.

• The Bible's teachings have been the foundation for many great nations.

"The grass withers, the flower fades, but the word of our God stands forever" (Isaiah 40:8).

How old is the earth? 6,000 years? 10,000 years? 4.5 billion years? These figures (and others) have been tossed around as the "real" age of the earth. So, since they can't all be true, how can we know how old the earth really is?

Since none of us has been around since the beginning of time, we can only guess at what happened and when—unless, of course, there was a record written down for us by someone who *was* there at the beginning. Then we could study that record and figure out how long ago "the beginning" was.

Actually, we *do* have such a record (the 66 books of the Bible), which was given to us by someone who *was* there in the beginning—God. Now, the Bible doesn't say, "God created the earth . . . years ago." But it does give us some important clues. To figure out the age of the earth, you'll need your Bible, a sheet of paper, and a pencil.

Make three columns on your paper, labeled "Verse," "Event," and "Age of Earth" (years), and complete the chart which was started for you from the geneaologies in Genesis 5. Now do the same for the list beginning in Genesis 11:10. (Hint: Noah was 502 when Shem was born.)

This final destruction of Jerusalem by Nebuchadnezzar occurred around 584 BC. Our current calendar assumes that Jesus was born in AD 1—about 2,010 years ago (although He was probably born about 6 BC). And since the calendar system has no year zero, we can add the numbers to get the rough date of creation: 2,010 + 584 + 3,419 = 6,013 (give or take a few years). Since the stars, our solar system, and all the other galaxies were created a few days after the earth, they're around 6,013 years old, too!

Since God always tells the truth, we can trust His account of history (in His Word, the Bible)!

Genesis 5 gives a list of men. From this, fill in your paper, adding to the earth's age as you go:		
Verse	**Event**	**Age of Earth (years)**
Genesis 1:1–2:4a	Creation (in six days)	0
Genesis 5:3	Adam 130, Seth born	130
Genesis 5:6	Seth 105, Enos born	235 [=130 + 105]
Genesis 11:10	Noah 502, Shem born	1,558
This list finishes with Abraham, but be a bit careful here:		
Genesis 11:26, 32; 12:4	Terah 130 (=205-75; _not_ 70), Abraham born	2,008
The next event is when Abraham leaves Haran, and journeys to Canaan:		
Genesis 12:4	Abraham leaves Haran (age 75)	2,083
Abraham's descendants (the Israelites) stayed in Canaan and Egypt until they were delivered from the Pharaoh by Moses:		
Genesis 12:10	Israelites live in Egypt for 430 years	2,513
Exodus 12:40		
Galatians 3:17		
The Israelites return to the Promised Land with Moses. They continued to live there, under the rule of Joshua, then the judges, then the kings. From the time they left Egypt until Solomon began to build the temple was 479 full years:		
1 Kings 6:1	Solomon builds the Temple after reigning 3 full years	2,992
King Solomon ruled for another 37 (40–3) years, and then the kingdom was divided between Jeroboam and Rehoboam:		
1 Kings 11:42	Solomon dies	3,029
The time from the kingdom's division to the destruction of Jerusalem by the Babylonians was 390 years:		
Ezekiel 4:4-6	Ruled by kings	3,419
	Jerusalem destroyed	

What Happened Here?

Even if you did scientific tests and detected elephant blood in the wreckage, for example, you would be very unlikely to work out the correct explanation. In the same way, we can't know for sure from scientific tests what happened in the earth's past, since we weren't there.

For example, the fossils we find of dinosaurs or other animals do not come with tags attached saying how old they are. We can try to make up stories about what we **think** happened to them and when, but unless we have an eyewitness account to rely on, it will be impossible for us to know **exactly** what happened.

LOOK AT THE PICTURE ABOVE. Can you guess what happened to this village?

Perhaps you thought an elephant just came and rampaged through the village. Well, actually, there's a lot more to this story. And since you weren't there, it is hard for you to know exactly what happened. The only way you could know for sure is if someone who witnessed the event told you how it all came about.

What happened was this: a man in India owned an elephant named Madhubala, and kept her chained to a tree. A bull elephant wandered by one day and spotted her. It was love at first sight for the elephants. The bull elephant refused to leave Madhubala until the villagers began tossing firecrackers and flaming sticks at it. Later, he snuck back to Madhubala and broke her chains, and they both ran away. The owner tracked her down and brought her back to the village. But the bull elephant soon showed up to claim his true love. He roared through the village in a rage, ramming through huts, tearing down anything in his way, and causing the people to run into the jungle. He freed Madhubala again, and the two ran off, never to return.

Many people make statements about the beginning of the universe, claiming they know exactly when and how it all began. However, since they weren't there, these statements are only stories of their beliefs about the past.

There is only One alive today who was there in the beginning—God. He tells us how He created and what has happened since then in His written Word, the Bible.

Since we know God's Word is true, we can trust God when He says He created everything in six normal days. And many scientists today agree.

"For in six days the LORD made the heavens and the earth, the sea, and all that is in them, and rested the seventh day . . ." (Exodus 20:11).

Exodus 20:11 says, "For in six days the LORD made the heavens and the earth, the sea and all that is in them, and rested the seventh day . . . ." From this verse, it seems clear that God created all things in just six normal-length days, doesn't it? And yet, there are many who say that God created over millions of years or that He used the process of evolution to bring about the universe we see today.

So, why do we believe that, according to Genesis 1, God created in six normal-length days? To understand the answer to this, we need to learn some Hebrew. That's the language Moses used to compile the book we call "Genesis," under the guidance of the Holy Spirit. It is important that we understand what Moses originally wrote because those are the words God inspired!

The Hebrew word for "day" is יוֹם (pronounced "yom"). *Yom* can have many meanings—a period of daylight, time, a specific point in time, a year, or a period of 24 hours (actually, much like the word "day" in English). *Yom* is the word used in Genesis 1 when God describes what He created on each day.

So, how do we know which definition of *yom* Moses meant in Genesis 1? The meaning depends on the *context*—the words surrounding *yom*. Throughout the Old Testament, when the phrase "evening and morning" or a number is used with *yom*, it refers to a "period of 24 hours"—a normal-

length day, not "time" in general or a "year" or "millions of years."

Both "evening and morning" *and* a number are used with *yom* in Genesis 1 (look up verses 5, 8, 13, 19, 23, 31), so we know it refers to a day of regular length. It is as if God wanted to remove any doubt, so He defined the word *yom* all six times He used it.

Because of the words of Scripture, we can be confident that God didn't take millions of years or use evolution. He created the universe in six real days, and rested on the seventh!

Think about it!

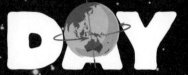

DAY — The earth's rotation on its axis is responsible for our "day" (it takes about 24 hours for one rotation).

MONTH — The moon's cycle of shadow is the basis for our "month" (it takes about 30 days to go through the cycle of phases, e.g., full moon to full moon).

YEAR — The earth's trip around the sun is the basis for our "year" (it takes about 365 days for the earth to journey around the sun).

WEEK — But the only basis for our seven-day week is the account in Genesis of God creating in six days and resting for one!

LET THERE BE FUN!

Genesis 1 has some very important words that tell us God created in six regular days and not in millions of years. These words are found in the wordfind game below. See if you can find them all. Look for these words forwards, backwards, up, and down.

BEGINNING
DAY
NIGHT
FIRST
SECOND
THIRD
FOURTH
FIFTH
SIXTH
EVENING
MORNING
YEARS
SEASONS
DAYS

```
        U I K N V B G F C D
      L I Y B F E J O M Y T H I R D
    S E A G N I N E V E R D E H W F I N
    E E R S G U I S J O K J P T O O E F G
    D C U R Y A D C R Y A E E L F J U H O S
    O O N V E D R I A O O N H U I E R A W Y D
    F N Y I A A E R E G T K I B F D T Z O A U
    F D U R R H S O Y S H I R D K A H R C D O
    F S N O S A E S D N G I C R A T S R I F
    E C O N D G I N N I C O N S I X T H
      M O B E G I N N I N G T H A E
        S E M O R N I N G T S
```

"By the word of the LORD the heavens were made, and all the host of them by the breath of His mouth" (Psalm 33:6).

How many times have you heard something like, "This animal lived 50,000 years ago" or "This person died 20,000 years ago"? Have you ever wondered how the scientists come up with the age of the bone? After all, the scientists haven't been around that long, have they?

There are a number of different ways to figure out how old an object is.

Of course, the best method is to check the account of a reliable eyewitness, if one is available. The Bible is such a record. Since it is the Word of God, we can trust it to tell us the truth about the past. Carefully studying what the Bible says, we find that the universe has an age of around 6,000 years, and that a world-changing, global Flood occurred about 4,300 years ago.

Those who don't accept the biblical account of history look for other ways to figure out the age of things. One of these methods is based on a substance found in all living things—it's called carbon.

How Carbon Dating Works

There are two basic forms of carbon: one that occurs naturally, called carbon-12 (^{12}C), and one that forms from processes acting on nitrogen in the atmosphere, called carbon-14 (^{14}C). Both of these combine with oxygen to form carbon dioxide (CO_2), which we breathe out and plants "breathe" in. When a cow eats grass, its body absorbs the carbon (both ^{12}C and ^{14}C) in the plant.

When the cow dies, it stops taking in carbon (for obvious reasons). The amount of ^{12}C in the cow's body stays the same after death, but the amount of ^{14}C changes because it returns to nitrogen.

^{14}N ^{14}N
^{14}C formed ^{14}N
^{14}C
^{14}C
^{14}C
^{14}C
^{14}C
^{14}C
^{14}C
^{14}C taken in by plants

^{14}C taken in by plant eaters

^{14}C taken in by eaters of the plant eaters

At death, intake stops.

As time goes on, the amount of ^{14}C continues to decrease until nothing is left, which is supposedly about 50,000 years later.

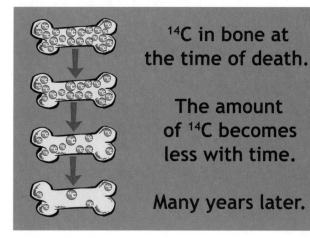

^{14}C in bone at the time of death.

The amount of ^{14}C becomes less with time.

Many years later.

measure the amount of ^{14}C and ^{12}C it contains. Based on how much ^{14}C is left, she can supposedly calculate when the animal (or plant) died.

Sounds like a good idea, doesn't it? But there's a problem (see below).

When a paleontologist (a scientist who studies bones) finds a bone (or a piece of wood), she can

The problem is

There are many things that affect how much ^{14}C an animal (or a person or plant) has in it when it dies. This changes how long ago the animal appears to have died.

For instance, plants don't take in as much ^{14}C as scientists expect. So, after they die, there is less ^{14}C in the plants to change back to nitrogen. This makes the plant appear to have died many more years ago than it actually did (for example, the plant might appear to be, say, 3,000 years old, rather than 2,000).

Also, the amounts of ^{14}C and ^{12}C in the atmosphere haven't been constant throughout history (for instance, Noah's Flood lowered the total amount of available carbon by burying lots of animals and plants, while the atmosphere continued to produce ^{14}C). So something that lived (and died) when the proportion of ^{14}C was

less than normal would appear to have died more years ago than it actually did (for example, it might give an age of 3,000 years before the present, rather than its true age of 2,000 years).

Even many archaeologists don't think "carbon dating" is completely accurate all the time.

When these (and other) problems are taken into account, a scientist can interpret the result of the carbon dating within a biblical time frame, but even so, these results can not be used to *prove* the age of once-living things.

KidsAnswers.org

". . . by the word of God the heavens were of old, and the earth standing out of water and in the water, by which the world that then existed perished, being flooded with water" (2 Peter 3:5–6).

Most people think that scientists can actually measure the ages of rocks, using a method called "radiometric" or "radioisotope" dating. More often, rocks are "dated" by the fossils they contain, based on a belief in evolution. But even radiometric dating does not directly measure the age of something (there is no substance called "age"). It measures the amounts of certain radioactive substances. This information then has to be *interpreted*, based on certain beliefs.

In fact, most fossils do not even contain radioactive minerals. So if scientists wanted to measure the age of a fossil using this method, they would look for a nearby layer of igneous rock (e.g., rock that forms from lava from a volcanic eruption)—perhaps in the rock layers above where the fossil was found or in the layers below. When they find one, they gather a sample of the hardened lava and send it off to a laboratory to test it for radioactive elements.

The idea behind radiometric dating goes like this (hang on—this gets a bit technical, but we're sure you'll get it!):

When a volcano erupts, hot, molten rock (called "lava") from deep inside the earth is released. This lava is made of various elements. Elements are the "building-blocks" of the universe (for example, water is made from the elements hydrogen and oxygen).

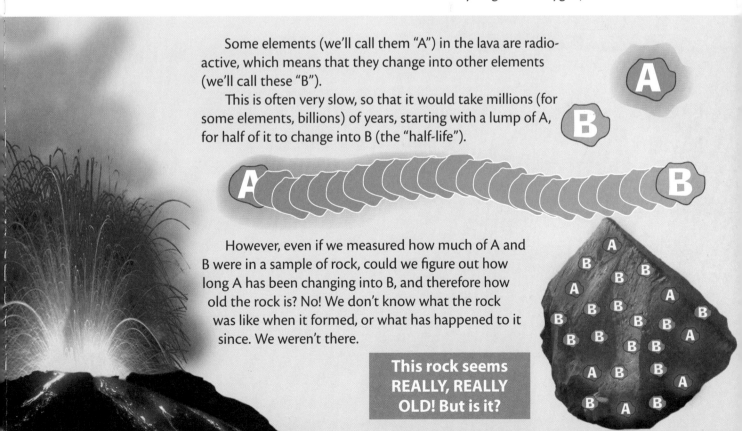

Some elements (we'll call them "A") in the lava are radio-active, which means that they change into other elements (we'll call these "B").

This is often very slow, so that it would take millions (for some elements, billions) of years, starting with a lump of A, for half of it to change into B (the "half-life").

However, even if we measured how much of A and B were in a sample of rock, could we figure out how long A has been changing into B, and therefore how old the rock is? No! We don't know what the rock was like when it formed, or what has happened to it since. We weren't there.

This rock seems REALLY, REALLY OLD! But is it?

To test the radiometric dating method, some scientists gathered samples from hardened lava at Mount St. Helens, which erupted most recently in the early 1980s. The samples, which came from rocks that formed between 1980 and 1986, were sent to a lab and were "dated" using the potassium-argon (K-Ar) method. The test results ranged from between 340,000 to 2.8 million years old!

Other scientists collected samples from cooled lava flows from Mt. Ngauruhoe in New Zealand. These rocks are known to be less than 50 years old because people observed the volcano erupting in 1949, 1954, and 1975. But the lab results indicated that the rocks were up to 3.5 million years old!

But is it a good date?

The scientists who interpret these amounts of A and B to conclude that millions of years have passed must first *assume* three main things about the rock:

1. How much A and B was in the rock when it hardened.
2. A has decayed into B at the same rate over the years.
3. The amount of A or B has not increased or decreased in any other way.

But because we haven't been able to study all the rocks everywhere all the time, it's impossible for us to know:

1. if B was in the rock before it hardened.
2. if A has always decayed at the same rate.
3. if water, for instance, has removed some A or carried some B into the rock from elsewhere.

All of these factors will affect how "old" the rock appears—in practice, usually making it appear a lot older than it really is.

Known age: 50 years

Tested age results: 1,350,000 years.

WRONG!

Age: Unknown

Tested age results: 2,750,000 years.

RIGHT?

The bottom line

If radiometric dating doesn't work on rocks for which we know the ages, how can we trust it to work on rocks of unknown age?

After examining the assumptions behind this "dating method" and doing scientific experiments to see if this method works on rocks of an already known age, we find that "radiometric dating" isn't all it's cracked up to be. (Actually, *any* process used to find ages for things is based on assumptions, and so is not reliable.)

It's important that we allow God's written record of history, the Bible, to guide our thinking about the past—this includes our understanding of the age of the earth/universe *and* the age of fossils.

KidsAnswers.org

Compromise

(kŏm′prə-mīz′)

"And do not be conformed to this world, but be transformed by the renewing of your mind, that you may prove what is that good and acceptable and perfect will of God" (Romans 12:2).

A compromise is a "settlement of differences in which each side gives something up." Sometimes compromise is necessary and good, but not when it involves giving up truth.

Those who *compromise* by believing that the earth is many millions of years old, and claim that this fits what the Bible teaches, fall into three main groups.

Gap Theory: This is the idea that there was a long, long time between what happened in Genesis 1:1 and what happened in Genesis 1:2. During this time, the "fossil record" was supposed to have formed, and millions of years of earth history supposedly passed.

Progressive Creation: This is the idea that God created various creatures to replace other creatures that died out over millions of years.

Theistic Evolution: This is the idea that God used the process of evolution over millions of years (involving struggle and death) to bring about what we see today.

A *compromise* between a belief in "billions of years" of history and an acceptance of the biblical account of history destroys the authority and message of the Bible. All these ideas put death and bloodshed *before* sin. These compromising views aren't necessary and, in fact, are harmful to the teachings of God's Word. Instead of compromising, we need to accept what God has plainly revealed to us through His Word—the world is about 6,000 years—not billions of years—old. And true science supports this conclusion!

Do you know when compromise began?

Today, many people choose to reject the Word of God in favor of their own opinions. This isn't an original idea, however. Our first parents, Adam and Eve, were the very first compromisers. They chose to believe the words of someone other than God. When Adam ate from the Tree of Knowledge of Good and Evil, he deliberately chose to disobey God's word to him. In that case, his compromise resulted in death—for us all (Romans 5:12).

When we're tempted to doubt the plain teaching of Scripture because of someone else's opinion, keep in mind that God's Word is perfect (Psalm 119:140). He expects us to follow His commands (2 Timothy 3:16–17) and trust what He says—without compromise (Psalm 119:128).

"I will praise You, for I am fearfully and wonderfully made; marvelous are Your works, and that my soul knows very well" (Psalm 139:14).

Every so often, we'll read in the newspaper, or hear on TV something like, "Skull find proves man and apes share a common ancestor." But is this really true?

Some background

There are two main (and very different) ideas about the history of our universe.

The first idea comes from the collection of 66 books we call the Bible. From it, we can learn that God created all things in six normal-length days only a few thousand years ago. He explains in Genesis that He created the first man and woman on the sixth day of that first week, along with the various kinds of land animals. (He made the air and water creatures on Day 5. The various kinds of plants were made on Day 3.) Those who accept this view use the Bible to help them make sense of the world around them.

The second belief is based on the idea that the universe came into being on its own. Countless millions of years ago,

Man's Opinion

a single-celled creature appeared on earth. This was supposedly our first ancestor, which we share with all living things. Over the years, this creature's descendants gradually changed into the wide variety of animals and plants that we see today. This view is known as "evolution."

Those who accept this view use evolutionary ideas to help them make sense of the world around them.

Which is right?

Is it possible to know for certain which view of the past is correct? After all, none of us were around "in the beginning!" It's impossible for us to know firsthand what happened, and when.

However, because the Bible is the written record of One who has always existed and who always tells the truth, we can trust it to be an accurate account of history.

What's the truth?

So, do headlines, like the one quoted on the previous page, tell the truth? No. The first man was created from the dust of the ground (Genesis 2:7). God created the first woman from his rib (Genesis 2:21–24). Both were made in the image of God (Genesis 1:27). We don't share a common ancestor with apes!

It's important to carefully check what was actually found when we hear claims like the one on the previous page. Many times, the supposed "proof" of evolution is based on only a few bone fragments. Or it turns out to be a type of monkey or ape, or even a true human. But it is never a "transition" between an ape and humans.

The "evidence" (bones, for example) doesn't prove evolution is true. Neither does it "prove" the Bible is true. Rather, we interpret the evidence based on our belief in either evolution or the Bible. When we come across claims that a fossil discovery "proves" evolution, we should look more closely at what was really found.

"Know that the LORD, He is God; it is He who has made us, and not we ourselves; we are His people and the sheep of His pasture" (Psalm 100:3).

Looking a Little Closer

Evolutionists claim that humans and apes share a common ancestor that lived millions of years ago.

They say they have uncovered the fossils of supposed "ape-men." But the first apeman was described and drawn long before any bones were found. The drawing was based purely on the belief that things made themselves without God (evolution).

If evolution were true, there should be thousands of fossils showing the transition from apelike creatures to humans. However, the "missing links" turn out to be nothing more than bones of humans, or bones of some type of extinct ape. Even evolutionists themselves don't always agree on how the bones should be interpreted!

We can't go wrong if we trust in the Word of God, which never changes and never needs to be updated. It tells us that humans are not evolved animals, but were created in the image of God.

Let's take a look at some of the more famous ape-men fossils, and find out what they really are.

Neanderthal man—Neanderthal is German for Neander Valley. This is where bones of this supposed "missing link" were first found about 150 years ago. Scientists now realize that Neanderthals were humans. They were our relatives—descendants of Adam and Eve (through Noah).

Java man—He was first found in East Java over 100 years ago. Now that we have more of the bones, it is clear that his body was similar to ours. He walked just like we do. The same is true for Peking man, who was discovered in China during the 1920s and '30s. Both

are now called *Homo erectus*, or "upright man." Recent evidence shows that modern-looking early humans had children by both Neanderthals and *Homo erectus*, showing that they are all fully human people groups.

"Lucy"—"Lucy" is among the more famous "missing links." Careful research on the skull, inner ear, and other bones shows that Lucy is very similar to a pygmy chimpanzee. She did not walk upright like humans. Instead, she used her knuckles, like gorillas and chimps.

THE EVIDENCE

Thy word is true from the beginning: and every one
of thy righteous judgments endureth for ever.
Psalm 119:160

"And God made the beast of the earth according to its kind, cattle according to its kind, and everything that creeps on the earth according to its kind. And God saw that it was good" (Genesis 1:25).

Have you ever heard that a long time ago, fish developed arms, legs, and lungs and eventually turned into amphibians, or that birds have evolved from dinosaurs?

Some people believe that life began a long time ago in a sea of chemicals which organized themselves. Evolution is the idea that over millions of years, one kind of animal turned into another kind. Eventually, the abundant variety of life we have today came about. But is this really a true story? Can one kind of animal really turn into a completely different kind?

What does the Bible say?

The Bible teaches us that God is the Creator (Genesis 1:1). In the beginning (about 6,000 years ago—not millions!), He created plants and animals after their "kinds" (Genesis 1:11–12, 21, 24–25). This means that each kind of plant would produce plants like themselves. And the many different animal kinds would produce animals like themselves. For example, the dog kind would produce more dogs, a cat kind would produce cats, an elephant kind would produce elephants, a bear kind would

produce bears, and so on. In fact, this is what we observe happening today!

From studying the Bible, we also learn that two of every kind of air-breathing land animal and bird (seven of some) survived the worldwide Flood on the Ark. Many of the sea creatures were able to survive in the water. These animals refilled the earth after the Flood.

We know that God created animals and plants to produce others like themselves. But the Bible does not teach that one kind can turn into a completely different kind. For example, a fish can't turn into a frog. In fact, today we observe animals and plants reproducing according to their kinds, don't we?

REAL ANIMALS?

Circle the real animals. Remember that one animal KIND cannot be mixed with another KIND. Example: A gorilla and a dolphin could never produce a "gorphin," but a dolphin and a small whale can produce a "wolphin."

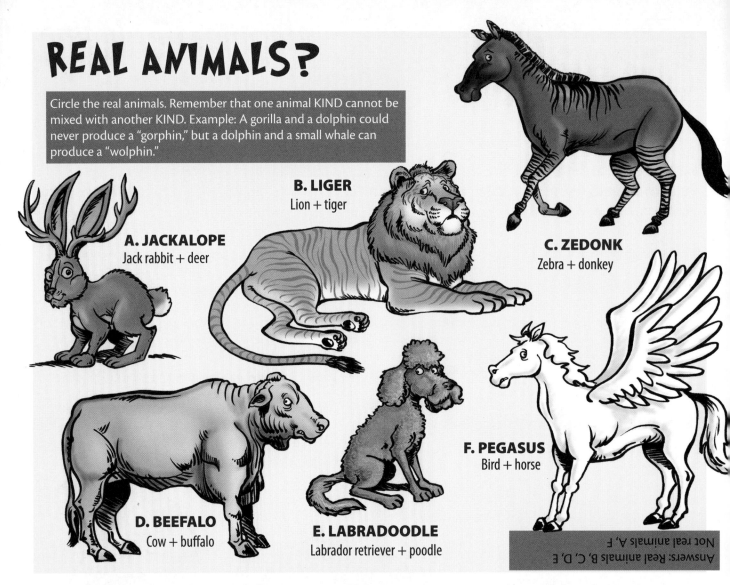

A. JACKALOPE
Jack rabbit + deer

B. LIGER
Lion + tiger

C. ZEDONK
Zebra + donkey

F. PEGASUS
Bird + horse

D. BEEFALO
Cow + buffalo

E. LABRADOODLE
Labrador retriever + poodle

Answers: Real animals B, C, D, E.
Not real animals A, F.

MIX ANIMAL NAMES

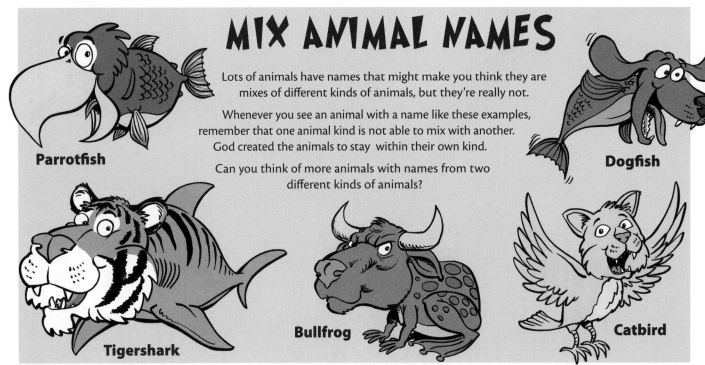

Lots of animals have names that might make you think they are mixes of different kinds of animals, but they're really not.

Whenever you see an animal with a name like these examples, remember that one animal kind is not able to mix with another. God created the animals to stay within their own kind.

Can you think of more animals with names from two different kinds of animals?

Parrotfish

Dogfish

Tigershark

Bullfrog

Catbird

KidsAnswers.org

"O LORD, how manifold are Your works! In wisdom You have made them all. The earth is full of Your possessions" (Psalm 104:24).

What does science say?

Scientists have found that inside plants and all living things is a special chemical called DNA (which stands for "deoxyribonucleic acid"). DNA carries the recipe that tells each plant and living thing what to look like, how to grow, and so on. Parents pass a combination of their DNA on to their children.

To understand what this means, let's use the dog kind as an example. Scientists have found that all dogs are descended from a wolf-type dog. (This is probably the type of dog that was on the Ark with Noah.)

As the DNA has been combined and passed down over the years, the recipe from the original dogs has produced a wide variety of dogs:

- dogs with short legs and small bodies (chihuahuas)
- dogs with short legs and long bodies (dachshund)
- dogs with longer legs and large bodies (mastiffs)
- dogs with longer legs and thin bodies (greyhounds)
- dogs with thicker fur (collies)
- dogs with longer fur (cocker spaniels)

Even though they may look very different, they are all still obviously dogs, and examples of the dog kind. Many of the different varieties are able to mate with other varieties. However, there is a limit to what the DNA recipe within the dog kind can produce. Dogs cannot grow fins or gills like a fish, or wings and feathers like a bird because dog DNA doesn't carry the recipe for these features. Scientists have found that there is no known way that new recipes can be added by natural processes, for example, to the dog kind DNA.

This is true for the other kinds of animals and plants, too. On its own, a fish could never develop the DNA recipe for lungs, legs, and arms and turn into an amphibian. A dinosaur could never turn into a bird. And a cow could never turn into a whale. Each kind will simply continue to reproduce more of its kind.

In the beginning, God created each kind with the right mix of DNA to produce much variety within the kind. Those animals and birds that survived the Flood on the Ark were the ancestors of today's variety. Scientists have confirmed that animals reproduce according to their kinds, just as the Bible teaches!

Hunting for "Missing Links"

LET'S GO ON A HUNT FOR SOME VERY UNIQUE ANIMALS! ANIMALS ON THEIR WAY TO BECOMING OTHER KINDS OF ANIMALS!

YOU SAY THEY DON'T EXIST? I FIND THEM ALL THE TIME ...

... IN BOOKS WITH EVOLUTIONARY IMAGES OF "PREHISTORIC" ANIMALS.

ACCORDING TO THE EVOLUTION STORY, THESE CREATURES WOULDN'T BE ALIVE TODAY SO IMAGES OF THEM ARE CREATED BY ARTISTS.

LOOK FOR PICTURES OF ANIMALS THAT LOOK LIKE THEY ARE IN THE MIDDLE OF CHANGING FROM ONE KIND OF ANIMAL INTO ANOTHER.

PAKICETUS

PRORASTOMUS

HMMM, I WONDER ...

SOME ANIMALS HAVE HAD MORE "CREATIVE LICENSE" APPLIED TO THEM THAN OTHERS. HOW CAN YOU TELL HOW CREATIVE THE ARTIST HAS BEEN? LOOK IN THE TEXT ABOUT THE ANIMAL TO SEE HOW MANY OF THE ANIMAL'S BONES HAVE BEEN FOUND.

"Only part of its skull has been found"

"Only its skull and parts of its backbone and ribs have been found so far"

IT'S IMPORTANT NOT TO BE FOOLED BY IMAGES OF ANIMALS THAT ARE THE PRODUCT OF A NEED FOR THESE ANIMALS TO EXIST SO EVOLUTION CAN BE "TRUE".

GOD'S WORD TELLS US ANIMALS WERE CREATED IN KINDS. THEY DON'T EVOLVE ONE KIND INTO ANOTHER. SO HAPPY HUNTING; FIND THOSE IMAGINARY ANIMALS AND KNOW THE TRUTH ABOUT THEM.

KidsAnswers.org

"Look now at the behemoth, which I made along with you; he eats grass like an ox . . . He moves his tail like a cedar; the sinews of his thighs are tightly knit" (Job 40:15, 17).

The Bible doesn't use the actual *word* dinosaur (which was first invented in 1841). But it uses some very interesting phrases to describe creatures that sound like they could be dinosaurs! For instance, God describes a beast that is the largest of His creation. It eats grass, has strong legs and bones, and a "tail like a cedar." Of course, cedar trees are huge. They can grow up to 40 feet in diameter! So this beast was no small animal. Many people believe God may have been referring to some type of sauropod dinosaur here—perhaps a *Brachiosaurus* or *Apatosuarus*!

The Bible presents a different picture from what we usually hear, doesn't it? But since it is the written word of the Creator God, we can trust it to provide us with a true and accurate picture of history that helps us understand the world we live in.

WHAT'S ON THE MENU?

Circle the items that *T. rex* would have eaten in God's original "very good" creation.

TYRANOSAURUS REX
has teeth up to six inches long!

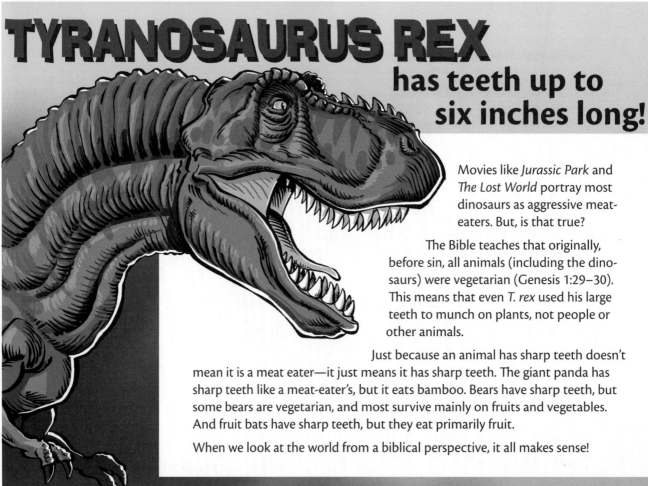

Movies like *Jurassic Park* and *The Lost World* portray most dinosaurs as aggressive meat-eaters. But, is that true?

The Bible teaches that originally, before sin, all animals (including the dinosaurs) were vegetarian (Genesis 1:29–30). This means that even *T. rex* used his large teeth to munch on plants, not people or other animals.

Just because an animal has sharp teeth doesn't mean it is a meat eater—it just means it has sharp teeth. The giant panda has sharp teeth like a meat-eater's, but it eats bamboo. Bears have sharp teeth, but some bears are vegetarian, and most survive mainly on fruits and vegetables. And fruit bats have sharp teeth, but they eat primarily fruit.

When we look at the world from a biblical perspective, it all makes sense!

KidsAnswers.org

"Can you draw out Leviathan with a hook, or snare his tongue with a line which you lower? Can you put a reed through his nose, or pierce his jaw with a hook?" (Job 41:1–2).

Tyrannosaurs, triceratops, stegosaurs, iguanodons, velociraptors . . . Dinosaurs are fascinating creatures, aren't they? But how much of what we think we know about them is actually true?

For instance, when did dinosaurs live? You might answer "millions of years ago!" Did dinosaurs ever live with people? "No!" you might shout. If asked what dinosaurs ate originally? "Meat!" you'd probably say. Are dinosaurs mentioned in the Bible? "Of course not!" you might think. Did dinosaurs turn into birds? "Yes!" you might reply. But actually, all of those answers are wrong.

Let's rethink the answers to these questions, using the Bible (which tells us the true history of the universe) as the foundation for our thoughts, rather than just relying on what we've always heard or been taught.

God reveals to us through His Word that He spoke the whole of creation into existence in six actual days just a few thousand years ago. So did dinosaurs live on earth millions of years ago if the earth is only thousands of years old? No. They must have come into existence sometime during those first six days.

Can you figure out when?

God created air and sea creatures on the fifth day of that first week. This includes the dinosaur-type flying creatures like *Pteranodon*, *Quetzalcoatlus*, and *Rhamphorhynchus*, and the dinosaur-like swimming creatures like *Plesiosaurus*, *Kronosaurus*, and *Liopleurodon*.

On the next day, Day 6, God created all the kinds of land-dwelling creatures—cats, dogs, giraffes, horses, bears, koalas, kangaroos—and all the kinds of dinosaurs we know and love.

Did dinosaurs ever live with people?

Yes! God also fashioned the first man, Adam, on that sixth day. *Adam* was actually the first human to discover dinosaurs! This also means that dinosaurs didn't turn into birds. Birds were formed the day before dinosaurs!

What did dinosaurs eat originally?

Genesis 1 teaches that at the end of the sixth day, God declared His completed creation "very good." He instructed Adam, Eve, and all the animals to eat from the plants and trees. So, all dinosaurs (including the mighty *T. rex*!) munched on fruits and veggies in the very beginning.

Where did they go?

What really happened to the dinosaurs? It's a question with multiple answers. See if you can find these words in the puzzle.

Formed
Fearless
Fallen
Flood
Faded

Found
Fiction
Behemoth
Leviathan
Dragon

Dinosaur
Meteor
Fossils
Extinct

```
F L S S E L R A E F
B E H E M O T H A O
E V D Z E O S A U R
X I R W T E X I D M
T A A F E A R E D E
I T F L O O D Y I D
N H P D R A G O N R
C I V K F O S S O A
T A F O S S I L S E
M N U B E H E I A T
E N E L L A F O U E
D F I C T I O N R M
```

LET THERE BE FUN!

Where should you go first to find out the truth about dinosaurs?

65,000,000 YEARS AGO

6 NEWS

"So the LORD God said to the serpent: 'Because you have done this, you are cursed more than all cattle, and more than every beast of the field; on your belly you shall go, and you shall eat dust all the days of your life'" (Genesis 3:14).

Consider the lion . . . its powerful jaws are well equipped for biting into its prey. Its stomach readily welcomes the fresh meat. But wait . . . the Bible says that God gave plants to all the animals to eat in the very beginning (Genesis 1:29–30). He declared His finished creation "very good" (Genesis 1:31). So, why does the lion appear to be so well designed to catch and digest a diet of meat? Why are snakes programmed to attack and kill animals? Why do some frogs have bright colors to warn attackers to stay away from their poison glands?

If God created everything "very good," then why do so many animals appear designed to attack other animals, or to defend themselves from attacks?

Creation corrupted

God's perfect universe changed when Adam disobeyed God. Adam ate the fruit from the Tree of the Knowledge of Good and Evil. This sin affected the entire creation (Romans 8:22)—including the animals.

Some Christians believe that the harmful structures (such as sharp teeth or claws) had a different function before Adam disobeyed. For example, giant pandas use their sharp teeth and claws to eat mainly bamboo. Maybe cats originally used their teeth to chomp on vegetables. Or, perhaps, the original "very good" structures have been changed by mutations over time.

Others believe that many of the plants and animals were "redesigned" after the Fall. For example, the serpent changed with the Curse God placed on it (Genesis 3:14). Thorns and thistles began to grow; so perhaps God also changed some of the features in other animals as well. Perhaps, because He foreknew the Fall, God programmed the genes with information for these structures.

So, how did the animals change? The Bible simply doesn't give us enough information to say for sure. It may be that some of the above ideas apply for some animals, but not for others. Scripture is clear, however, that the bad things we see in today's world didn't have a place in God's original, perfect creation. They won't have a place in the future, restored world either (Acts 3:21, Isaiah 11:6–9; 65:25).

God didn't make things bad

It's important to remember that the bad things are not something we should blame God for. They are the result of sin—Adam's and ours (because we are descendants of Adam, and each of us sins as well). In fact, God provided a way for us to be free from the penalty of sin (eternal separation from Him). He sent Jesus Christ to die in the place of all those who receive His free gift of eternal life. And God will create a new heaven and earth for His children. There will be no more death, suffering, or other bad things.

Did you know?

Even though we are living in a world that is groaning under the weight of the curse of sin, we are still able to catch glimpses of what life may have been like before Adam disobeyed—when everything was perfect and God completely upheld His creation. For example:

- When the Israelites wandered in the desert for 40 years, their feet did not swell; and their shoes did not wear out (Deuteronomy 8:4).

- When Shadrach, Meshach, and Abednego came out of the furnace, they didn't even have the smell of smoke on their clothes. They hadn't been hurt at all (Daniel 3:27).

- Some types of orb-weaving spiders are able to survive for short periods of time on pollen caught in their webs, instead of on other insects.

- One lioness, Little Tyke, refused to eat any type of meat or bones throughout her lifetime. Instead she ate only mixtures of grain, milk, and eggs!

I ♥ VEGGIES!

"Now the sons of Noah who went out of the ark were Shem, Ham, and Japheth . . . and from these the whole earth was populated" (Genesis 9:18–19).

Jesus loves the little children—all the children of the world. Red and yellow, black and white, they are precious in His sight . . .

We've probably all sung this song at one time or another. But is it really true? Are there really red, yellow, black, and white children? The answer, believe it or not, is, "Not really."

Let's find out why

If you were to look through a microscope at a piece of your skin, you would find lots of interesting cells. Some help repair your skin when you cut it. Others help to continually make new skin to replace that which wears off at the surface. Still others (called "melanocytes") make a pigment (called "melanin") that helps to give your skin some color. The more melanin that these melanocytes produce, the darker the skin will be.

Scientists have found that we all have the same amount of melanocytes in our bodies.

Inside each melanocyte is a set of "instructions" (called DNA). The DNA tells the melanocyte how much melanin to produce, among other things. If the instructions in your body tell your melanocytes to make a lot of melanin, and your skin keeps a lot of the melanin that is made, then your skin will be very dark brown. If your instructions say "make a little melanin," then your skin will be very light brown. And there are all combinations in between.

So, no one really has "red" or "yellow" or "black" skin. We all share the same brownish pigment; our bodies just have more or less of it!

The very same pigment, melanin, also determines the color of your eyes. If you have a lot of it in the iris of your eyes, they will be brown. If you have a little melanin, your eyes will be blue. Brown and black hair results from a lot of melanin in the hair shafts, blond hair from less melanin.

Melanin consists of two forms, normally produced together. One is dark brownish, the other reddish.

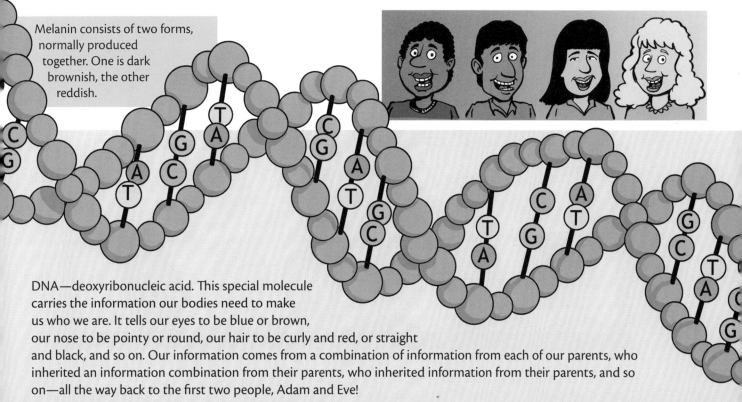

DNA—deoxyribonucleic acid. This special molecule carries the information our bodies need to make us who we are. It tells our eyes to be blue or brown, our nose to be pointy or round, our hair to be curly and red, or straight and black, and so on. Our information comes from a combination of information from each of our parents, who inherited an information combination from their parents, who inherited information from their parents, and so on—all the way back to the first two people, Adam and Eve!

"For there is no distinction between Jew and Greek, for the same Lord over all is rich to all who call upon Him. For 'whoever calls on the name of the LORD shall be saved'" (Romans 10:12–13).

Some people groups tend to have dark, curly hair with dark eyes, and dark skin. Other groups have black, straight hair, dark almond-shaped eyes, and lighter skin. Still others have light hair, blue eyes, and very fair skin.

Why? Well, it started around 4,200 years ago—at a place called Babel (probably corresponding to the later name Babylon). Noah's descendants had decided to disobey the Creator's command to spread out and fill the earth after the great Flood. They wanted to stay together; so they built a tall tower (Genesis 11:4). So, God gave to each family group a different language. This made it impossible for the groups to understand each other. So they split apart. Each extended family went its own way and found a different place to live.

As they went, each of these groups took with it its own special set of characteristics (for instance, for lighter skin and eye color, or for darker skin and eye color). These people's characteristics were passed through their DNA to their children, and so on. Because the groups no longer freely mixed with other groups, the characteristics of each became more and more prominent as new generations of children were born.

If we were to travel back in time to Babel, and mix up the people into completely different family groups, then people groups with completely different characteristics might result. For instance, we might find a fair-skinned group with tight, curly dark hair that has blue, almond-shaped eyes, or a group with very dark skin, blue eyes, and straight brown hair!

Even though we may speak very different languages, we are actually all part of the same family. Noah was the great, great, great, great, great, great, great, great, etc., grandfather of us all!

We're all different

Sometimes people use the differences between us (hair color, skin color, etc.) as an excuse to do terrible things to other people: tease them, call them names, fight with them—even hurt or kill them.

Wars have been fought because of the idea that some people groups are better than others, perhaps because their bodies aren't as hairy or their arms aren't as long. (Japanese biologists taught this in the years leading up to World War II.) One time, a man was put on display in a zoo's monkey house simply because he was a pygmy from Africa. He was thought to be "less evolved" than the zookeepers!

These terrible crimes were committed because people chose not to regard the biblical teaching that we're really all the same.

We're all the same

We all have the same skin-coloring pigment (just more or less of it); we all have eyes, noses, mouths, and hair (well, most of us do). And the Bible teaches that we all come from the same two people (Adam and Eve—Acts 17:26). We all have the same Creator God (Acts 17:24–25).

The Bible also tells us that we all have the same problem—sin—that separates each of us from God (Romans 3:23). We therefore all have the same need for a Savior (1 Corinthians 15:3–4). The real reason we don't get along with everyone all the time is not because of our differences, but because we're all sinners.

With the parable of the Good Samaritan, Jesus taught us that we are to love our neighbors—no matter what people group they are part of (Luke 10:25–37).

We all have the same choice

No matter what color our skin, where we live, or how we talk, we are all faced with the same choice: where we will spend eternity.

The Creator God offers the gift of spending eternity with Him to those who believe that Jesus Christ paid the penalty for their sin by dying on a cross and rising again three days later (John 3:18).

Those who refuse this gift will spend forever in a place of darkness and torment.
What will you choose?

"From whose womb comes the ice? And the frost of heaven, who gives it birth? The waters harden like stone, and the surface of the deep is frozen" (Job 38:29–30).

Antarctica today is almost completely covered in ice. So is much of Greenland. But did you know that great sheets of ice used to be in many other places, like the Alps, Tasmania (Australia), and even Ohio (USA)? Where did that ice come from, and where has it gone?

Ice, ice, and more ice

Around 4,300 years ago, God judged the sin of mankind with a globe-covering watery catastrophe (Genesis 6–9). Many scientists who believe the Bible explain that this Flood provided just the right conditions for great sheets of ice to form afterwards.

At the beginning of the Flood, the "fountains of the great deep" broke open. Hot water from inside the earth gushed into the oceans. Eventually, the land was completely covered with water.

At the end of the Flood, the waters drained off the land into the oceans. The oceans were warmer than they are today from all the volcanic activity caused by the "fountains" breaking open and the land masses moving around.

Being warmer, the water in the oceans evaporated faster than it does today. Clouds formed, like we see on the weather reports today. But these clouds were bigger. They carried more water than today's clouds, because there was more evaporation from the oceans. So, there was much more snow and rain in the years after the Flood.

Also, the snow fell over a much larger area—in places that do not have snow today. That is because the volcanoes had blasted so much fine dust high into the air that the sun's warmth was blocked from the earth. So places which are warm today were much cooler then.

The volcanic dust and clouds kept the land cool. The snow on the ground didn't melt during the summer.

Instead, it turned to ice. Gradually thick ice sheets built up. They eventually covered about one-third of the land on earth!

After many years, the oceans cooled down. With less evaporation, there was less snowfall. Also, the volcanoes weren't as active, and the dust cleared away. The sun's warmth was able to melt the snow and ice each summer. Eventually, the "Ice Age" was over.

Scientists believe that the Ice Age lasted around 700 years—500 years to build up, and 200 years to melt back.

COOLER OCEAN

How do we know where the great ice sheets were?

Some parts of the world are still covered with ice, especially on and near the snow-capped mountains. Often the ice moves slowly down the steep slopes of the mountains. These glaciers, as they are called, grind up the rock they creep over. They carve U-shaped valleys, leave groove marks behind, and also carry heaps of broken rock long distances.

That's why we know that there must have once been much bigger ice sheets than we have today. We see the tell-tale U-shaped valleys, groove marks, and heaps of crushed rocks and boulders in many places around the world.

Although some people claim there have been many "ice ages" over millions of years, the truth is that there really was only one. It was caused by the results of the Flood. Its effects can still be seen today!

By the way

The Bible tells about one of the descendants of Noah (a man named Job), who possibly experienced the effects of the Ice Age. God asked Job, "From whose womb comes the ice? And the frost of heaven, who gives it birth? The waters harden like stone, And the surface of the deep is frozen" (Job 38:29–30).

Mammoth Mystery SOLVED!

Some people believe mammoths lived and died out around 10,000 years ago. But is that really true?

By carefully studying the Bible, we learn that God created the original kinds of animals (such as the elephant/mammoth kind) around 6,000 years ago. Two of every kind of land animal (seven of some!) were on Noah's Ark and saved from the Flood, which happened around 4,300 years ago.

This means that mammoths could *not* have died out more than 10,000 years ago. In fact, some mammoths may still have been alive just a few hundred years ago!

"The heavens declare the glory of God; and the firmament shows His handiwork" (Psalm 19:1).

Superman came from the planet Krypton. Mr. Spock is from the planet Vulcan. Chewbacca is a Wookiee from Kashyyyk. Movies, television programs, and books tell us of worlds and life forms in far away galaxies.

But is any of it true? Could there really be aliens in outer space?

What can we learn from the Bible?

- God created the universe and everything in it in six days around 6,000 years ago. So if there *are* aliens out there, they are part of God's creation and not the products of millions of years of evolution.

However,

- The Bible does *not* mention alien life forms. If extraterrestrials *did* exist, we might expect the Bible to reveal *something* about them, or tell us to expect a visit from them someday.

- God placed a curse on the entire universe after Adam sinned (Genesis 3, Romans 8:18–22). So if there *were* other beings out there, they would also be suffering from the effects of *our* sin.

- God created the sun, moon, stars, and other planets with special purposes (Genesis 1:14). The sun gives the earth light during the day. The moon gives the earth light during the night.

The heavens declare the glory of God; And the firmament shows His handiwork. (Psalm 19:1)

Light Echo from Star V838 Monocerotis-December 17, 2002 • NASA

The stars and other heavenly bodies mark off the seasons and years, and provide special signs for those on earth. Remember the special star that led the wisemen to Jesus? The earth has a very special place in the universe. God designed the heavenly bodies to support life on earth.

- The Bible's message is about how God has dealt with humans since the beginning. Jesus became a man and came to earth to die for the sin of mankind (1 Corinthians 15:1–4)—not for a race of alien beings. He is preparing a place in heaven for His children—not for a race of extraterrestrials.

It's fascinating to learn about the heavens God created to glorify Himself and for our good. It's amazing to think that God knows the number of stars in the universe. He has given each one a name!

But, could Luke Skywalker ever bump into Yoda on Dagobah? Is there intelligent life somewhere out there on a planet far, far away? It seems very unlikely, based on what the Bible *does* tell us. And, after 100 years of searching the skies for signs of life, not one real live alien has been found!

Instead of believing in beings who probably don't exist, we need to trust in the One who made the heavens and the earth—the Creator God who offers us salvation through Jesus Christ.

AAAARRRGGGHHH!

I'M NOT SO SUPER!

AND I'M ILLOGICAL!

Alien looking?

Many times animals that are strange-looking, such as many of the creatures that live deep in the oceans, are often described as "alien looking" meaning they look like they came from outer space. Do these creatures really look like aliens from space? How do they resemble aliens and what do space aliens look like anyway? The ideas of space alien appearance come mainly from the images we see of them in fictional TV shows and movies.

These images are produced by artists' imaginations and ideas taken from creatures that live on earth. So if you think about it, even the strangest looking creatures on earth look like nothing more than earth creatures. There's nothing alien about them! Our Creator God has a wonderful and infinite imagination, and He created without using the ideas of someone else!

Longnose Chimaera

Monkfish

Robust armoured-gurnard

Life from beyond has visited earth!

Millions of dollars are spent each year looking for life in outer space. But life not from earth has already visited us. Is this biblical? Solve the code puzzle below to find out.

ANYBODY OUT THERE?

```
T _ e   wo _ _ _   _ e _ a _ e
  12        4  9     7   8   2

_ _ e _ _,   a _ _
10 1 5 12    3 9

_ i _ e   _ a _ o _ _     u _ .
1 6  9    2  3  11          5

            JO _ _ _  1:14a
               12 3
```

Code Key

1 = L		7 = B
2 = M		8 = C
3 = N		9 = D
4 = R		10 = F
5 = S		11 = G
6 = V		12 = H

ANSWER: The Word became flesh, and lived among us. John 1:14a The Bible tells us that Jesus Christ, the Creator Himself, became a human and lived on earth for a time so that He could die for our sins to provide the way of salvation! Life outside this planet has already been here!

KidsAnswers.org

The Seven C's of History!

Confusion

Christ

Cross

Consummation

Catastrophe

Corruption

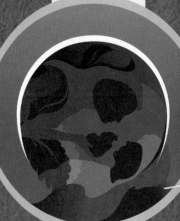

Creation

The Seven C's of History!

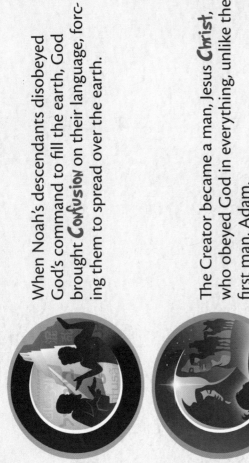

In the beginning—in six, 24-hour days—God made a perfect *Creation*.

The first man, Adam, disobeyed the Creator. His sin brought death and *Corruption* into the creation.

Adam's race became so wicked that God judged the world with a great *Catastrophe*—a global Flood—saving only those on the Ark built by Noah.

When Noah's descendants disobeyed God's command to fill the earth, God brought *Confusion* on their language, forcing them to spread over the earth.

The Creator became a man, Jesus *Christ*, who obeyed God in everything, unlike the first man, Adam.

Jesus, the Messiah, died on the *Cross* to pay the penalty for mankind's sin against God. He rose from the dead, providing life for all who trust in Him.

One day, at the *Consummation*, the Creator will remake His creation. He will cast out death and the disobedient, create a new heaven and new earth, and dwell eternally with those who trust in Him.

Answers Kids for Kids
BIBLE CURRICULUM

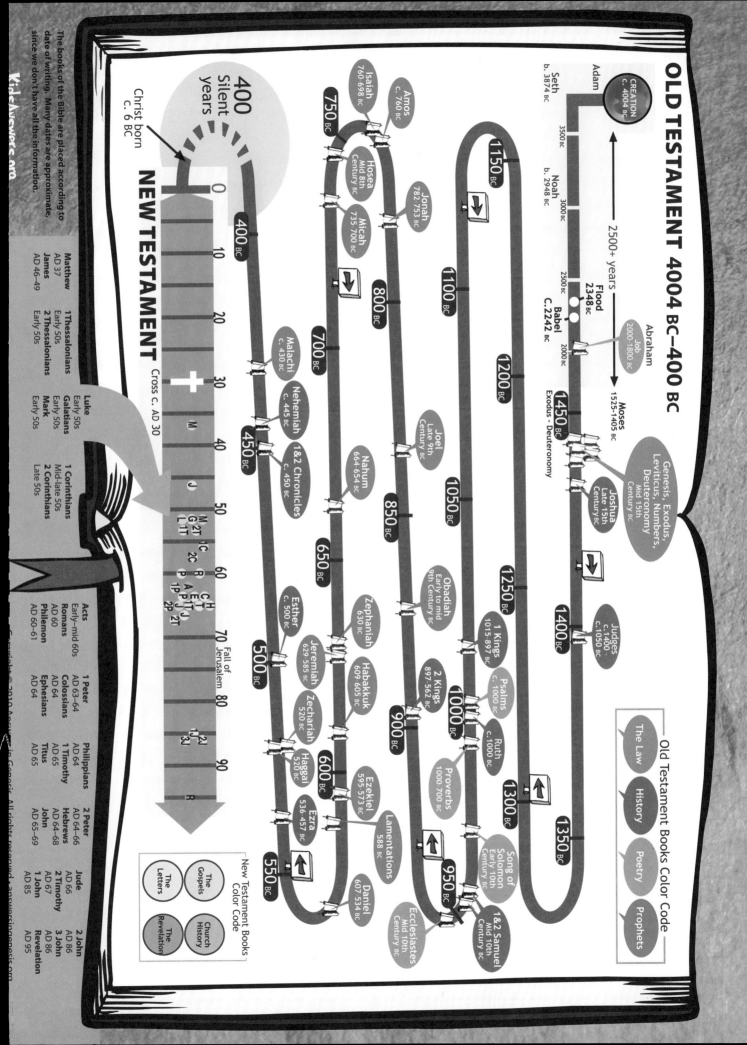

OLD TESTAMENT 4004 BC–400 BC

The books of the Bible are placed according to date of writing. Many dates are approximate, since we don't have all the information.

CREATION
c. 4004 BC

Adam

Seth
b. 3874 BC

Noah
b. 2948 BC

3500 BC
3000 BC
2500 BC

2500+ years

Flood
2348 BC

Babel
c. 2242 BC

2000 BC

Job
2000–1800 BC

Abraham
2000–1800 BC

Moses
1525–1405 BC
Exodus – Deuteronomy

Genesis, Exodus, Leviticus, Numbers, Deuteronomy
Mid 15th Century BC

Joshua
Late 15th Century BC

Judges
c. 1400 – c. 1050 BC

Isaiah
760–698 BC

Amos
c. 760 BC

Hosea
Mid 8th Century BC

Jonah
782–753 BC

Micah
735–700 BC

400 Silent years

Christ born
c. 6 BC

NEW TESTAMENT
Cross c. AD 30

0
10 BC
20
30
40 450 BC
50
60
70 Fall of Jerusalem
80
90

400 BC

750 BC

800 BC

700 BC

Malachi
c. 430 BC

Nehemiah
c. 445 BC

1&2 Chronicles
c. 450 BC

Nahum
664–654 BC

Joel
Late 9th Century BC

Obadiah
Early to mid 9th Century BC

Zephaniah
630 BC

Esther
c. 500 BC

Jeremiah
629–585 BC

Habakkuk
609–605 BC

Zechariah
520 BC

Haggai
520 BC

Ezra
536–457 BC

1150 BC

1100 BC

1200 BC

1250 BC

1050 BC

1000 BC

1300 BC

1400 BC

1350 BC

850 BC

900 BC

650 BC

600 BC

500 BC

550 BC

950 BC

1 Kings
1015–897 BC

2 Kings
897–562 BC

Psalms
c. 1000 BC

Ruth
c. 1000 BC

Proverbs
1000–700 BC

Ezekiel
595–573 BC

Lamentations
588 BC

Daniel
607–534 BC

Ecclesiastes
Mid 10th Century BC

Song of Solomon
Early 10th Century BC

1&2 Samuel
Mid 10th Century BC

Old Testament Books Color Code
- The Law
- History
- Poetry
- Prophets

New Testament Books Color Code
- The Gospels
- Church History
- The Letters
- The Revelation

Matthew AD 37	**1Thessalonians** Early 50s	
James AD 46–49	**2 Thessalonians** Early 50s	
Luke Early 50s	**1 Corinthians** Early 50s	**Philippians** AD 64	**2 Peter** AD 64–66
Galatians Early 50s	**2 Corinthians** Mid-late 50s		
Mark Early 50s	**Acts** Early–mid 60s	**1 Peter** AD 63–64	**Jude** AD 86
		Romans AD 60	**Colossians** AD 64	**1 Timothy** AD 65	**Hebrews** AD 64–68	**3 John** AD 86
		Philemon AD 60–61	**Ephesians** AD 64	**Titus** AD 65	**John** AD 65–69	**1 John** AD 85
					2 John AD 86	**2 Timothy** AD 67	**Revelation** AD 95

Books of the Bible TIMELINE

The **Old Testament** has 39 books. The Jews divided these books into three groups: the Law, the Prophets, and the Writings. Our English Bible divides the OT into four main groups:

1. The Law: These five books tell about the history of the universe from the very beginning. They also tell about God's working through the nation of Israel, and the laws given for Israel to follow.

2. History: These 12 books continue the history of Israel, cover 1,000 years, and show the results of disobedience or obedience to God.

3. Poetry: These five books express worship toward God, give advice, and address some deep issues.

4. Prophets: These 17 books proclaim God's blessings and judgments, and tell about future events. They are divided into Major and Minor prophets depending on the length of the book.

The 27 books of the **New Testament** are arranged into four divisions:

1. The Gospels: These four books record the time Jesus spent on earth, His death, and His Resurrection.

2. Church history: The book of Acts, written by Luke, records the beginning of the church, and the spread of Christianity to the time of the Apostle Paul.

3. The Letters: These 21 letters from apostles (or their close associates) were addressed to churches in such places as Rome, Galatia, Ephesus, and Colossae, or to individuals, or to Christians in general. They teach about Christianity and how to live the Christian life.

4. Revelation: This book by the Apostle John was written to encourage Christians suffering persecution. It also reveals what will happen in the future, when a new heaven and a new earth will be created for those who have received the free gift of eternal life.

AnswersKids
BIBLE CURRICULUM for Kids

From Creation to Christ!

A Genealogy from Adam to Christ

When Adam disobeyed, the perfect fellowship he had enjoyed with his Creator was destroyed. God promised that one day, Someone would be born—a descendant of Adam—who would rescue His creation from the Curse that God had placed on it (Genesis 3:15). This person was Jesus Christ—the Messiah. This chart lists all the men who were descendants of Adam and ancestors of Jesus.

Adam C. 4004 BC

Seth
Enos
Cainan
Mahalaleel
Jared
Enoch
Methuselah
Lamech

Noah C. 2348 BC

Shem
Arphaxad
Salah
Eber
Peleg C. 2242 BC
Reu
Serug
Nahor
Terah

Abraham C. 2000 BC

Isaac
Jacob
Judah
Perez
Hezron
Ram
Amminadab
Nahshon
Salmon
Boaz
Obed
Jesse

David C. 1000 BC

Solomon
Rehoboam
Abijah
Asa
Jehoshaphat
Jehoram
Ahaziah
Joash
Amaziah
Uzziah
Jotham
Ahaz
Hezekiah
Manasseh
Amon
Josiah
Jehoiakim
Jeconiah
Zerubbabel
Shealtiel

Nathan
Mattathah
Menan
Melea
Eliakim
Jonan
Joseph
Judah
Simeon
Levi
Matthat
Jorim
Eliezer
Joshua
Er
Elmodam
Cosam
Addi
Melchi
Neri
Shealtiel
Zerubbabel
Rhesa
Joannas
Judah
Joseph

Semei
Mattathiah
Maath
Naggai
Esli
Nahum
Amos
Mattathiah
Joseph
Janna
Melchi
Levi
Matthat
Heli

Abiud
Eliakim
Azor
Zadok
Achim
Eliud
Eleazar
Matthan
Jacob

Joseph C. 6 BC
Mary

Special Women

Matthew's list of people from Abraham to Christ mentions four women. Rahab was involved in a very sinful lifestyle before turning from her sins and trusting the true God, who is gracious to repentant sinners. Only one of the four (Bathsheba) was an Israelite. Nevertheless, God allowed all of them to be included in the ancestry of His Son.

Prophecies

The prophecies concerning the promised Messiah were made between 400 and 4,000 years before Jesus was born. A few of those prophecies are listed here, along with the places in Scripture indicating Jesus fulfilled these prophecies.

The Messiah would be:

- Born in Bethlehem—Micah 5:2; Matthew 2:1
- Presented with gifts—Psalm 72:10; Matthew 2:1, 11
- Called Lord (a reference to His deity)—Psalm 110:1; Luke 2:11
- Called "Almighty God" and Father of Eternity—Isaiah 9:6; John 20:28
- Born of a virgin and called Emmanuel—Isaiah 7:14; Matthew 1:23; cf. Genesis 3:15
- Riding into Jerusalem on the foal of a donkey—Zechariah 9:9; Matthew 21:5
- Pierced in His hands and feet—Psalm 22:16; compare the whole Psalm with the details of crucifixion
- Killed 483 (69x7) years after the decree to rebuild Jerusalem—Daniel 9:24-27
- Thrust through—Zechariah 12:10; John 19:34
- Called a Prophet like Moses (i.e., who would receive face-to-face revelation from God the Father)—Deuteronomy 18:18–19; Matthew 21:11
- Called Priest—Psalm 110:4; Hebrews 3:1
- Preceded by a messenger (John the Baptist)—Isaiah 40:3; Matthew 3:1–2

Problem Solved

God promised that David would always have a descendant on his throne (Jeremiah 23:15; 1 Chronicles 17:10–14). The legal right to this throne was passed through David's son, Solomon, to his descendants. Jeconiah (or Jehoiachin), a great, great ... grandson of Solomon and king of Judah, was so wicked that God punished him by declaring that none of his children would ever again sit on the throne (Jeremiah 22:17–30). This caused a "problem" since Joseph, the supposed "father" of Jesus, was a descendant of Jeconiah. If Joseph had been Jesus' *biological* father, Jesus would have had the *legal* right to the throne, but would have been unable to occupy it due to being under Jeconiah's curse. God solved this problem by using Mary: Jesus was the first-born son of Mary, a virgin (Matthew 1:23) and a descendant of David through another son, Nathan. So Jesus has the right to sit on the eternal throne of David—legally, through his adoptive father, Joseph; and physically, through His natural mother, Mary. In this way, God's promise mentioned above in Jeremiah and Chronicles was fulfilled.

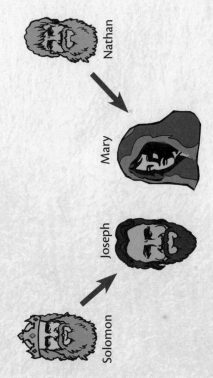

Solomon   Joseph   Mary   Nathan

The 7 Fs of Dinosaur History

Answers for Kids
BIBLE CURRICULUM

1 2 3 4 5 . 6

Formed

God brought dinosaurs into existence on the sixth day of the very first week in the history of the universe—about 6,000 years ago! On that day He also created all the other animals that make their homes on land, along with the very first people—Adam and Eve. Just one day earlier, God created the dinosaur-like swimming and flying creatures. It was a perfect place in which all living things dined on the green plants God had created for them.

Fearless

God's original creation was "very good." There was no disease, sickness or death. Animals and humans were not afraid of each other. People didn't eat animals, and animals didn't eat people—they all ate plants. Animals did not fear one another, and man did not need to be afraid of animals either. And that includes dinosaurs—even the mighty T. rex! Man and dinosaurs lived together without fear in the beautiful world God had created.

Fallen

The universe was changed when Adam disobeyed and took a bite of the fruit from the tree God had forbidden him to eat. Before that sad event, death wasn't part of God's beautiful creation. But after Adam disobeyed, he and Eve began immediately to die, and the animals began to desire other food besides the plants God had given them. Adam's disobedience brought sin, suffering, disease, and death into the world.

Flood

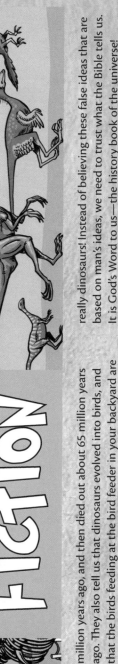

As time went on, things got so bad that God judged the wickedness He saw with an earth-covering flood. He brought two of every kind of land creature—including dinosaurs!—

on board Noah's Ark. There, they were safe from the storms and waves, volcanoes, and earthquakes. Those air-breathing animals that weren't selected to go on the Ark perished in

the great Flood. Many of these animals became fossils that have since been found around the world.

Faded

After the Flood, the dinosaurs, people, and the rest of the animals left the Ark and began to refill the earth. Some of the animals found it difficult to survive in the new world. Many animals

became extinct because of changes in the climate and their food sources. Many were probably killed by people (for food, clothing, weapons, jewelry, etc.). As they slowly died out over the years,

men began to forget that they had ever lived with the huge creatures. All that was left of the dinosaurs were their bones and stories about them. Over the years these stories turned into legends.

Found

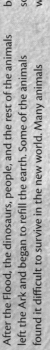

In the 1800s, these colossal creatures were "rediscovered." The actual word "dinosaur" was invented in 1841 by Sir Richard Owen who was studying bones of creatures that he thought

were "terrible lizards." Once these creatures were rediscovered, people became fascinated by what they were, how they lived, what they looked like, and how they died. Unfortunately,

instead of looking to God's Word for answers, they began choosing to believe unproven ideas from men, such as evolution and millions of years.

Fiction

65,000,000 YEARS AGO

6 NEWS

Today, secular scientists make up stories about dinosaurs, and teach these ideas through books, television programs, movies, and museums. They claim that dinosaurs evolved about 200

million years ago, and then died out about 65 million years ago. They also tell us that dinosaurs evolved into birds, and that the birds feeding at the bird feeder in your backyard are

really dinosaurs! Instead of believing these false ideas that are based on man's ideas, we need to trust what the Bible tells us. It is God's Word to us—the history book of the universe!

If you liked **Answers for Kids** then you need to try...

It All Begins With
Genesis

Building a Biblical Worldview

Ages: 11–15

In this 34-lesson inductive Bible study, you will guide students through the foundational book of the Bible—Genesis—with an up-close look at chapters 1–11. The lesson plans will help you teach your students how to defend their faith, the importance of having a biblical worldview, and to trust in the authority and accuracy of God's Word.

Available in NIV/NAS or KJV